PSYCHOLOGICAL RESPONSES TO EATING DISORDERS AND OBESITY

PSYCHOLOGICAL RESPONSES TO EATING DISORDERS AND OBESITY

Recent and Innovative Work

Edited by

Julia Buckroyd and Sharon Rother

University of Hertfordshire

John Wiley & Sons, Ltd

Other Wiley Editorial Offices

John Wiley & Sons Inc., 111 River Street, Hoboken, NJ 07030, USA

Jossey-Bass, 989 Market Street, San Francisco, CA 94103-1741, USA

Wiley-VCH Verlag GmbH, Boschstr. 12, D-69469 Weinheim, Germany

John Wiley & Sons Australia Ltd, 42 McDougall Street, Milton, Queensland 4064, Australia

John Wiley & Sons (Asia) Pte Ltd, 2 Clementi Loop #02-01, Jin Xing Distripark, Singapore 129809

John Wiley & Sons Canada Ltd, 6045 Freemont Blvd, Mississauga, ONT, L5R 4J3, Canada

Wiley also publishes its books in a variety of electronic formats. Some content that appears in print
may not be available in electronic books.

Library of Congress Cataloging-in-Publication Data

Psychological responses to eating disorders and obesity : recent and
innovative work / edited by Julia Buckroyd and Sharon Rother.
        p.   cm.
    Includes bibliographical references and index.
    ISBN 978-0-470-06163-3 (cloth) – ISBN 978-0-470-06164-0 (pbk.)
    1. Eating disorders.   2. Obesity–Psychological aspects.   3. Food habits.
I. Buckroyd, Julia.   II. Rother, Sharon.
RC552.E18P79 2008
362.196'8526–dc22

                                                            2007044835

British Library Cataloguing in Publication Data

A catalogue record for this book is available from the British Library

ISBN: 978-0-470-06163-3 (hbk)   978-470-06164-0 (pbk)

Typeset in 10/12pt Palatino by Aptara Inc, New Delhi, India
Printed and bound in Great Britain by TJ International Ltd, Padstow, Cornwall
This book is printed on acid-free paper responsibly manufactured from sustainable forestry
in which at least two trees are planted for each one used for paper production.

CONTENTS

ABOUT THE EDITORS

Julia Buckroyd is Professor of Counselling at the University of Hertfordshire and Director of the Obesity and Eating Disorders Research Unit. The Unit was established in 2005 and focuses on the development of psychological responses to disordered eating of all kinds. She trained first as a counsellor and then as a psychotherapist and has worked clinically in the field of eating disorders since 1984. Her interest in obesity grew out of her work with eating disordered young women and she has brought to it many of the psychological perspectives current in that field. She began carrying out research into the treatment of obesity in 1999 and has developed an ongoing portfolio of research projects. She has co-authored, with Sharon Rother, *Therapeutic Groups for Obese Women* (2007).

Sharon Rother is a Lecturer in Counselling at the University of Hertfordshire and Research Coordinator for the Obesity and Eating Disorders Research Unit. She completed an MA in Counselling Inquiry for which she investigated recovery in anorexics. She trained as a counsellor and currently continues a practice, specialising in working with eating disordered and obese people. She has worked in the field of obesity research with Julia Buckroyd since 2002. She has co-authored, with Julia Buckroyd, *Therapeutic Groups for Obese Women* (2007).

LIST OF CONTRIBUTORS

Sarah Barnett has practised as a Counsellor, in private practice, since 1994. She specialises in working with people who have eating disorders. Her main research interest concerns the way in which eating disorders are passed through the generations by the internalisation of dysfunctional eating behaviour. Her research for a PhD at the University of Hertfordshire developed from working with people with eating disorders and the evidence of repeating behaviour in clients and their mothers.

Verity Byrne is a Senior Dietician working at St Ann's Eating Disorder Unit, North London. She has been working in the specialist field of eating disorders for over five years, managing a workload of in-patients and out-patients with anorexia, bulimia and binge eating disorder. Within the service she is also the lead dietician in the rehabilitation unit and for student training. Her special interest in obesity led her to co-facilitate the Obesity and Binge Eating Disorder Group, which was set up in 2001.

Emma Corstorphine is a Clinical Psychologist who has worked with patients with eating disorders since qualifying from the University of East London in 2001. She is an Honorary Research Fellow at the Institute of Psychiatry, London, has published a number of papers in the field of eating disorders and has spoken at various national and international conferences on the cognitive behavioural treatment of eating disorders. She is also co-author of *Cognitive Behavioural Therapy for Eating Disorders: A Comprehensive Treatment Guide* (2007).

Patricia Goodspeed Grant is an Assistant Professor of Counseling at the State University College at Brockport, USA. She has an MS in Industrial/Organizational Psychology from Springfield College (Massachusetts) and a doctorate in counseling and human development from the University of Rochester. She is a qualitative researcher, with expertise in hermeneutic phenomenology. She has made several international presentations in her areas of research and practice, including the meaning of work, unemployment and the loss of relationships through death and divorce. Her current research interests focus on the psychological, social and cultural aspects of food, eating and morbid obesity.

Colleen Heenan is Senior Lecturer in Psychology at Bolton Institute and a psychotherapist in private practice. She was a co-founder of the Leeds (UK) Women's Counselling and Therapy Service. Her area of interest and research is gender, psychoanalysis and post-modern thinking, with particular reference to women, bodies and eating problems. She has edited a number of special features as well as contributing to other texts and journals on these subjects. She is the co-author of two books and has also co-edited a book in her areas of interest. She can be contacted at c.heenan@bolton.ac.uk

Saskia Keville is a Clinical Lecturer for the Doctorate in Clinical Psychology at the University of Hertfordshire. She is a Chartered Clinical Psychologist and has been working within eating disorder services for 10 years. Clinically, she has been facilitating therapy groups for obesity and binge eating disorder for five years, in addition to assessing and treating anorexia, bulimia and eating disorders with complex comorbid aspects. She has been involved in a number of projects and publications within this field and is particularly interested in exploring underlying psychological issues in eating disorders.

Carolina Lopez is a Clinical Psychologist and Lecturer Assistant in the Faculty of Medicine of the University of Chile. In 2005 she was awarded a MIDEPLAN-CHILE scholarship to study for a PhD in the Eating Disorder Unit at the Institute of Psychiatry (King's College London) under the supervision of Professor Janet Treasure and Kate Tchanturia.

Gerry McCarron is a Senior Cognitive Behavioural Therapist, Supervisor and Trainer working for Barnet, Enfield and Haringey Mental Health Trust and Goldsmiths College, London. His clinical work largely focuses on more complex presentations and is informed by the recent developments stressing acceptance and mindfulness principles.

Jane Ogden is currently Professor in Health Psychology at the University of Surrey. She is involved in research exploring a number of aspects of health including obesity and eating behaviour. In particular, she explores the mechanisms involved in under- and overeating, the predictors of weight concern, the psychological consequences of the medical and surgical management of obesity and the many uses of food. She is author of four books including a textbook in health psychology and *The Psychology of Eating: From Healthy to Disordered Behaviour* and has published over 100 refereed articles.

Marion Roberts completed her undergraduate and graduate psychology studies at Victoria University of Wellington, New Zealand. She taught in the psychology department at Victoria University for a year, before moving to London to study for her PhD under Professor Treasure at the Eating Disorder Unit, King's College London. On completion of her PhD she hopes to stay in the eating disorder field as both a clinician and researcher.

Deborah Seamoore is a Nurse Therapist working within a Community Mental Health Team. She has been a Nurse Therapist since 1982, initially working in adolescent psychiatry and in adult mental health since 1987. Currently she is a PhD student at the Eating Disorders and Obesity Research Unit, University of Hertfordshire, researching the correlation between psychological factors and obesity and the implications for treatment.

Ana Sepulveda has been a Post Doctoral Fellow at the Institute of Psychiatry since October 2004. She is the coordinator of the Collaborative Carers Project at the Eating Disorder Unit which looks at developing ways to deliver skills for families. She completed her PhD with an epidemiological study at both the Public Health Institute and the Autonoma University of Madrid, Spain. She has been a visiting teacher for the Clinical MSc and the PhD courses at the School of Psychology at the same university since 2003. In parallel, she is working with adolescents and children from a prevention perspective together with the Carers Association.

David Stott has worked since 2002 as a Statistician in Applied Medical Research at the East of England RDSU Hertfordshire (HRDSU) based at the University of Hertfordshire. For the preceding 35 years he lectured in Geography and subsequently Health Statistics and Epidemiology at what became the University of Luton/Bedfordshire. At HRDSU he has advised on a wide range of projects.

Madeleine Tatham is a Chartered Clinical Psychologist currently working with the Hertfordshire Community Eating Disorders Service. Since completing her clinical training at the University of Hertfordshire in 2004, she has pursued and developed her interest in this field with the local NHS service, providing assessment and treatment interventions for anorexia nervosa, bulimia nervosa and binge eating disorder on an out patient basis. Academic and research interests include attachment, emotional regulation and coping. Her doctoral research study investigated differences in attachment styles between sisters discordant for eating disorder pathology.

Janet Treasure is a Psychiatrist based at the Eating Disorder Unit at the South London Maudsley Hospital NHS Trust, a leading centre in clinical management of eating disorders and training. Professor Treasure has specialised in the treatment of eating disorders for over 24 years. She was chairman of the Physical Treatment section of the UK NICE guidelines committee. She is the Chief Medical Advisor for b-eat formerly the Eating Disorders Association and is the patron of the Sheffield Eating Disorders Association. She is on the Academy of Eating Disorders Accreditation Committee. She is the Medical Advisor for the Capio Nightingale Hospital. In 2004 she was awarded the Academy for Eating Disorders (AED) Leadership Award in Research.

Glenn Waller is Consultant Clinical Psychologist with the Vincent Square Eating Disorders Service, Central and North West London NHS Foundation Trust. He is also Visiting Professor of Psychology with the Eating Disorder Unit, Institute of Psychiatry, King's College, London. He has published widely in the field of the eating disorders and is lead author of a recent book on the application of cognitive behavioural therapy to the eating disorders. He is a Fellow of the Academy of Eating Disorders and frequently presents to national and international clinical and research meetings.

Karen Windle is Senior Research Fellow for Health Care Policy and programme lead for the policy programme at the Centre for Research in Primary and Community Care (CRIPACC) at the University of Hertfordshire. She works on research projects exploring the policy/practice research cycle including leading the National Evaluation of the Partnerships for Older People's Projects. She lectures on the taught doctoral Programme in Health Research and supervises PhD students. She has also worked at the National Children's Bureau and the University of Bath, undertaking numerous projects with health and social services.

PART I

OVERVIEW

INTRODUCTION

PSYCHOLOGICAL RESPONSES TO EATING DISORDERS AND OBESITY: AN OVERVIEW

JULIA BUCKROYD AND SHARON ROTHER, *University of Hertfordshire, UK*

In this volume we have gathered together a range of contributions from clinicians working with the whole spectrum of disordered eating, all of whom are involved in current thinking on how psychological issues are relevant to the treatment of these conditions. The physical consequences of disordered eating in its more serious manifestations are so alarming that attention has very often focused solely on attempts to modify eating behaviour. Yet, as these chapters repeatedly emphasise, simple injunctions to change food use are rarely effective and although necessary, need to be supplemented with a far more sophisticated understanding of the context of the individual's emotional and cognitive history. We are pleased to present a volume which offers innovative and sometimes radical strategies to address the psychological needs of patients.

There has been huge debate in the last few years about the limitations of systems of diagnosis of eating disorders (see Waller, this volume). This book deals with the whole spectrum of disordered eating. Although the book is divided into sections on anorexia nervosa (AN) bulimia nervosa (BN) and obesity and binge eating, we consider that the implications of the work and ideas described for each one may well have application to the others. They are also relevant to subclinical versions of those conditions and the other forms of disordered eating described within Eating Disorders Not Otherwise Specified (EDNOS). Our focus is not so much on the highly specific details of diagnosis but on new understanding of disordered eating in its various forms and innovative approaches to their treatment.

One of the constant themes in the chapters that follow is that disordered eating, in its more serious and chronic forms, is extremely difficult to cure. In recent years much hope has been invested in cognitive behavioural therapy

Psychological Responses to Eating Disorders and Obesity: Recent and Innovative Work.
Edited by J. Buckroyd and S. Rother. © 2008 John Wiley & Sons, Ltd

(CBT) which is without doubt the best researched modality for the treatment of disordered eating. However, as the contributors to this volume acknowledge, despite the benefits, many patients still fail to profit from this or any of the other existing treatments that are on offer. This volume is remarkable for the way in which clinicians have thought again about the evidence and have explored new approaches or modified those that are more familiar. We have been struck by how many of the chapters describe what we would call an integrated treatment where attention to cognitive and behavioural features is combined with attention to the patient's emotional and psychosocial history.

These developments are of particular interest to us because we have been impressed by the research which has repeatedly shown that the therapeutic modality does not account for a substantial part of the therapeutic benefit. The evidence suggests that generic features such as the capacity of the therapist to form an empathic relationship; the patient's readiness for change; and their joint capacity to agree on the goals of treatment are the most significant indicators of therapeutic success (see O'Brien & Houston, 2007, for an overview). We look forward to the developing rapport between modalities and an end to the antagonisms, which have stood in the way of patient benefit.

In focusing on psychological responses to disordered eating we by no means discount other related factors which have themselves been the subject of a great deal of research. Genetic, physiological, nutritional, social, cultural, class and gender issues are undoubtedly relevant. However, we are surprised by the relative lack of attention to underlying psychological factors especially where binge eating and obesity are concerned. We have repeatedly been made aware of responses to disordered eating from health professionals, which ignore or take little notice of emotional issues. We hope that this book will raise awareness of them and provide a range of ideas about more appropriate responses.

In our own clinical work, and in reading the chapters which make up this volume, we have been made aware many times of the symbolic nature of disordered eating. It seems to us that we are most likely to meet the needs of our patients when we understand the eating behaviour as a voice and a communication. The difficulty for all of these patients in eating 'normally' and in finding their innate desire for a 'normal' amount of food, is evidence for us of their difficulty in managing desires and needs of many kinds. We hope that this book will enable clinicians to listen more carefully to their patients' hidden voices and help them better identify their unacknowledged needs.

We begin the book with Jane Ogden's chapter, 'The Many Meanings of Food and their Impact on Eating Behaviour'. This chapter is remarkable for showing the complexities of all eating behaviour and for reminding us all that finding our way to a regular and ordinary way of eating is far from simple. We have included it as a reminder that psychological issues affect everyone's eating and need to be taken into account if any change is likely to occur.

Ogden first of all outlines the conventional ways in which psychology has accounted for eating behaviour. She describes biological models of eating which suggest that we have little conscious control over our eating behaviour but rather are influenced by innate preferences and the influence of hunger and satiety. She continues by outlining the best-known psychological theories of eating behaviour including the theory of planned behaviour (TBA) and the theory of reasoned action (TRA). These two theories can both help predict eating behaviour. She goes on to describe developmental theories of food preferences in terms of exposure, social learning or associative learning. Together these theories suggest that our eating preferences are learned from our experience as we grow up, especially the influence of parents and peers. Finally eating behaviour is described in terms of restraint theory, which has been explored extensively by feminist writers and suggests that the more we try to restrict our intake, the more obsessed with food we become and the more likely to overeat and gain weight.

Ogden then continues by addressing the meanings of food, which are often implicit in the theories described, but rarely addressed. Fundamentally, she asserts that the complex and diverse meanings ascribed to food have a great deal to tell us about eating behaviour and that the emotional power of these meanings is important in understanding it. Drawing on her recent research on how people describe their relationship with food, she categorises these meanings into four themes: emotional roles, conflict, social roles and health.

Emotional eating is universal; food, Ogden reminds us, is used for every conceivable purpose including celebration, indulgence, comfort, pleasure, boredom, upset and relief. Here she is describing a normal population, not a population whose eating is disordered. However, meaning is more complex even than this. Women particularly have internalised the conflicting messages about food offered to them in the media, which suggest that food is both desirable and forbidden and induces both pleasure and guilt. As those providing food, women are often torn between their wish to provide pleasure by giving their families what they like to eat rather than what they know is healthy. A further familiar conflict is experienced between control and lack of control – well-known issues for those with disordered eating.

Food, as Ogden goes on to describe, also has social meanings. Mealtimes are used for communication; food is used to show love and has strong sexual connotations. The preferential distribution of food, where men are often privileged above women and children, echoes power relationships within families. Food rituals are common in religious practice. Food is used to indicate social power – those with the most power are offered the best food. In contrast food refusal, as every anorexic knows, also conveys both personal and political power.

Finally Ogden discusses the relationship between food and health. She points out that fashions for what is healthy or not have changed over time; what is seen as healthy now, is vastly different from what was seen as healthy

200 years ago. Whatever the fashion, food that is preferred or disdained is then invested with meanings. When food scares take place, the food in question becomes a source of danger – eggs with salmonella or beef with BSE – and leads to significant changes in eating behaviour.

Ogden concludes her paper with a discussion of how the concept of the meaning of food can inform our understanding of disordered eating. She describes how food is frequently used for the purpose of communication. There are people, she proposes, whose need to communicate distress can only be voiced via eating behaviour. The power of their emotions can mean that their eating behaviour becomes destructive.

The picture Ogden paints is of eating behaviour as a vastly more complex issue than conventional psychological theory proposes. Our reasons for eating and our food choices are driven by emotional experience and association that defy simple explanation. If we wish to understand the individual's eating behaviour, she suggests, we must be willing to explore the meanings with which it is invested. This theme will echo through the whole of this book.

The next two chapters focus on AN, and in very different ways, suggest new approaches to the vexing problem of AN, and its consequences.

Carolina Lopez, Marion Roberts, Ana Sepulveda and Janet Treasure address their chapter, 'Using an Evidence-Based Approach to Develop New Tailored Treatment for Anorexia Nervosa', to the continuing difficulty of identifying an effective treatment for AN and the hope offered by recent neuroscientific research and work with carers. They begin with a brief outline of the failure so far to develop a treatment based on established risk factors. Their review is followed by an outline of the variables that Schmidt and Treasure have identified as relevant to the onset and maintenance of AN:

Underlying factors:
• compulsive traits, rigidity and perfectionism
• high anxiety and avoidance
Maintaining factors:
• close others react with features of high expressed emotion (overprotection and criticism) and behaviours that inadvertently enable the AN behaviours
• biological and psychological changes which are perceived to be positive for the individual

In the rest of the chapter they describe their work on two of these factors. They give an account of how they have translated neuropsychological findings on compulsive traits, rigidity and perfectionism into treatment and then outline a 'training programme for carers' to develop helpful patterns of communication.

Using new evidence on impaired flexibility and cognitive style they have identified deficits in cognitive flexibility among those with AN, those recovered from AN and the healthy sisters of those with AN suggesting that this deficit may be an underlying trait of eating disorders and therefore, a possible target for treatment. In addition they have shown that people with AN show weak central coherence, that is, a bias towards local processing of information over integrating information into a broader context. Those with AN have been found to perform better in tasks requiring attention to detail and poorer in those benefiting from global processing.

Building on the ideas of cognitive re-mediation therapy (CRT) they have incorporated strategies to modify these traits. CRT for anorexia encourages patients to reflect on their cognitive functioning and trains them in new cognitive strategies in the belief that these strategies can be transferred to everyday behaviour. Interventions of this kind have been used in both in-patient and out-patient settings with good results. The major innovation in this treatment is that attention is focused on changing *how* the patient thinks rather than *what* she thinks.

In the second part of the chapter the authors describe the degree of stress experienced by carers and the consequent patterns of interpersonal reactions that maintain the illness. A collaborative programme between health professionals and carers has developed workshops which focus on a range of carers' needs and is based on a written manual. Other strategies using DVDs and the internet are being developed. Evaluation of these interventions is in progress. AN is known often to have disruptive and damaging effects on family functioning. Lopez and her colleagues are seeking to modify these effects by offering help and support to the carers.

The same theme of modifying the damaging effects of AN on other family members inspires the following chapter, 'Eating Disorders: Breaking the Intergenerational Cycle through Group Therapy: The Effects of the Group, Experience'. Sarah Barnett, Julia Buckroyd and Karen Windle address the increased risk of developing eating disorders to the children of mothers with eating disorders. They describe a research project which attempted to modify that risk by offering group therapy to the mothers. They begin the chapter with a review of the literature in a number of areas relevant to the study. This review shows how the relationship with the mother is central to the child's healthy development and that eating disordered mothers suffer from a condition which is likely to interfere with their ability to parent appropriately. The response the authors propose is group therapy which has as its aim, not only improvement in the mothers' condition, but also changes in the way they parent, to help them nurture their children more effectively. Their chapter focuses on the outcomes of the group process and its effects on the participants.

Three sessions have been selected from the 19 sessions for which the group ran: the first, the tenth and the last. In the discussion of the first session Barnett and her colleagues show how useful it was in creating an initial sense of mutual understanding, that all the participants were mothers. Since the ages of their children ranged from babies of a few months to 13 years, there was also a range of experience of mothering in the group, which enabled some mothers to offer advice and support on mothering to those with less experience. This normalising exchange quickly led to a freedom to share how their eating disorder had affected them when they were pregnant and the expression of feelings of shame and guilt about what their illness might have done to the developing baby. The mutual empathy created by this sharing led to further disclosure of their difficulties and their isolation in the face of these difficulties. These were feelings and experiences which they said they had not previously been able to share.

Even within this first session the authors show how the sense of trust between the participants had developed to the point where they were able to begin to acknowledge how their eating behaviour might be affecting their children. They show how the group members struggled between wanting to care appropriately for them yet felt the urge to continue their own dysfunctional behaviour and even pass on their attitudes to the children.

The tenth session was at the mid-point of the group and focused on how their own mothers had influenced them and how they felt they had influenced their children in turn. Group members began to be much more aware of how they had often unconsciously modelled their behaviour on their mothers'. They could also begin to dare to identify the limitations of their mothers' capacity to love and value them. They started to see that their behaviour needed to change if they were not to repeat their own experience.

The final session highlighted how little continuous care group members had experienced during their illness and how difficult it would be to find a situation in which they could continue the work they had begun in the group. They recognised how much change had occurred during the lifetime of the group. They had become more confident and much more aware of their relationships with their children.

This snapshot of the group process demonstrates how well participants used the group but also illustrates how much development was needed for these women. It suggests that a group intervention of this kind may be highly relevant to modifying the inter-generational transmission of eating disorders.

The next two chapters focus on BN. Glenn Waller begins his chapter, 'Current Thinking on Working with People with Bulimia Nervosa and Bulimic Disorders', with a discussion of the problems of diagnosis of bulimia. He describes how not only have the criteria for bulimia nervosa changed since the concept was first devised by Russell in 1979, but also how it has become steadily more apparent that diagnoses in eating disorders are not fixed and that many patients, presenting for treatment, do not fulfil the current diagnostic criteria. This confused situation has by no means been resolved and has led to a polarisation of professional opinion between those who would like to have narrower definitions of more subtypes of eating disorders and those who think, as does Waller himself, that there are more significant underlying commonalities. In Waller's view the central characteristics of bulimic disorders remain bingeing and compensation; destructive thought patterns about eating, weight and shape; emotional factors; and the physical consequences of the behaviour. Even when these commonalities are identified it is impossible to estimate prevalence among young adult females with any degree of confidence.

In this rather unsatisfactory state of affairs, Waller goes on to describe what he calls the most 'explicit' formulation of bulimic disorders, that is, the cognitive behavioural model. He provides a 'hot-cross bun' model that shows the inter-relationship between the four elements of cognitions, emotions, behaviour and physiology and then proceeds to identify the specific characteristics in the bulimic disorders of each of these components. He identifies the most important cognitions as 'overvalued ideas about the importance of controlling body shape and weight'. He proposes that bulimic behaviours are triggered by specific emotional states, especially anxiety, loneliness and anger. The behaviours serve to provide a short-term solution to unwanted feelings. The behaviours themselves are most obviously binge eating and purging or other compensations, together with behaviour relating to body shape and size. Finally the physiological consequences of bulimic disorders are described and the importance of medical support stressed. These four factors interrelate and collectively maintain the condition.

Taking this model as his starting point, Waller goes on to map out a strategy for treatment. Once risk is assessed, the therapy begins with an exploration of motivation. Waller emphasises the absolute need for collaboration in the treatment between patient and therapist. He briefly discusses a number of possible therapeutic approaches but identifies CBT as the most successful. The complications presented by patients with comorbid psychiatric conditions are considered. In all cases Waller recommends the formulation of an individual treatment programme. In conclusion he comments that despite advances in understanding, many patients still fail to benefit and urges continued attention to the improvement of treatment outcomes.

Emma Corstorphine focuses her chapter, 'Addressing Emotions in the Eating Disorders: Schema Mode Work', on one aspect of the many elements of treatment for BN outlined by Waller. She describes the difficulty faced by the clinician who works with patients who use their bulimic behaviour to protect them from distress and difficult feelings. Corstorphine identifies a continuum of severity in those who have difficulties with affect regulation. Those at the less severe end of the continuum, who can consciously acknowledge their experience of emotions, can often make use of existing psychological interventions. For those whose dissociation from their feelings is more profound, Corstorphine proposes a treatment based on Young's schema mode model (2003). She identifies a particular mode, the detached protector, as a maladaptive coping mode characterised by emotional withdrawal, disconnection, isolation and behavioural avoidance. This mode functions to shut off emotions in order to protect the individual from the pain of feeling. Corstorphine contends that the action of the detached protector renders therapeutic attempts to connect the eating disordered patient with her feelings ineffective. Standard therapeutic interventions, which depend on the patient's awareness of this connection, thus become useless.

In the rest of her chapter Corstorphine discusses in detail how the patient can be helped to understand that the detached protector has evolved in a situation where the child needed to block the pain of experience, but also to understand that awareness of emotions is necessary for effective interaction in the adult world. She builds on the substantial research that has been carried out, especially in the last 15 years, in the fields of attachment and trauma. The work of neuroscientific researchers such as Alan Schore (2003a, 2003b) has vastly expanded our understanding of the mechanisms by which poor parenting and early trauma translate into dissociative disorders and addictions and can also clearly be seen in severe cases of disordered eating.

Corstophine outlines an intervention, which will modify the action of the detached protector sufficiently to allow the patient access to thoughts and feelings, so that specific eating disorder treatments can then be utilised. The process she recommends has the following stages:

- identification
- formulation
- objectification
- monitoring
- construction of a development pathway
- negotiation
- counterattacking

Each of these stages is described and the processes illustrated with clinical vignettes. Corstorphine does not disguise the difficulty of an intervention which requires the patient to modify a coping strategy which has probably served her well. Therapists working with dissociative disorders are very familiar with the difficulties she describes. The clinician is asking the patient to increase her awareness of feelings when she has devised a strategy devoted to their concealment. This process will arouse frustration as patients struggle to become aware of the mechanism and then anxious about how they will tolerate their emotions in its absence. The clinician will undergo an equivalent process of doubt, frustration and anxiety. Where patient and clinician can collaborate to understand the purpose and process of the intervention, there is the possibility of therapeutic success.

The next section contains five chapters, which explore in different ways a psychological understanding of overeating. Attention to psychological issues is new in terms of the treatment of obesity but the failure of existing methods of weight management has led to a search for innovative methods of treatment. Despite the diversity of the following chapters there are a number of common denominators. There is agreement that conventional dieting and behavioural approaches to overweight do not deliver maintained weight loss. There is agreement that there are psychological issues involved in obesity especially where binge eating is involved. Finally, there is agreement that early attachment experience and a history of trauma are relevant to current eating behaviour.

We begin this section with a chapter by Julia Buckroyd and Sharon Rother entitled, 'Psychological Group Treatment for Obese Women'. The authors begin their chapter with a brief review of the existing responses to obesity and their limitations. They go on to identify a range of reasons why permanent weight loss is so difficult. They list the toxic environment of food in western societies, the reduction in effort, a genetic predisposition, physiological mechanisms and the problems of lifestyle change. However, their chapter focuses on yet another factor: the psychological uses of food that maintain psychic equilibrium for a substantial minority of obese people. They then identify some of the wide range of literature in the past 15 years which has suggested that some obese people are using food for affect management. They consider some of the evidence linking these two factors and demonstrate that stress of various kinds promotes overeating.

They continue by showing that binge eating is common among obese people and is associated with weight regain. They then describe some of the substantial literature which suggests that there are increased risks for obesity among those with poor attachment history and a history of trauma. They draw attention to the biochemical mechanisms that may be at work to produce a soothing effect in response to overeating. They interpret all of this literature to suggest that a substantial minority of obese people are using food for affect management as a result of difficult childhood experiences. The authors then propose that the literature further identifies specific deficits in the psychological functioning in the group of obese people that they have identified. These are a lack of an emotional language, poor self-esteem and difficulties in either self-soothing or creating relationships that will support them.

They suggest that any intervention to treat obesity in this subgroup that they have identified needs to address these deficits. They report the results of a pilot study based on these insights which produced maintained weight loss in 75% of completers after nine months. They go on to give preliminary results for a further study incorporating the same principles which demonstrated maintained weight loss in 39% of completers at six months. They continue by discussing what can be learned from their research experience so far and, in particular, a range of ways in which the subgroup of obese people can be identified with a view to offering therapeutic treatment.

They conclude with a brief discussion of the literature which suggests that the development of treatments should focus less on particular modalities and more on the delivery of generic features of therapy which have been shown to be responsible for most of the therapeutic effect.

The section continues with a chapter from Patricia Goodspeed Grant which generates qualitative data and draws on the experience of obese people themselves. She describes a qualitative study which explored how morbidly obese people attending a weight-loss programme give meaning to their eating behaviour. The author begins her chapter, 'Food for the Soul: Social and Emotional Origins of Comfort Eating in the Morbidly Obese', with a review of the literature on weight loss. She highlights how the dominant medical discourse on obesity has excluded from consideration the social, cultural and psychological aspects of eating behaviour. She proposes that the failure of conventional medical exhortations to eat less and exercise more should lead us to take far more interest in the meanings that obese people themselves ascribe to their eating behaviour.

She reports a study in which she interviewed 11 morbidly obese people recruited from a weight-loss clinic and asked them to talk about their memories and associations to food, meals and eating. Her objective was to deepen knowledge of how social and cultural factors contribute to overeating. Her findings were codified into four major themes. Overeating was seen as arising from emotional hunger; mistaking emotional hunger for physical hunger; using food to solve problems; and lack of attention to social well-being. Goodspeed Grant illustrates these themes with vivid quotations from her participants. She shows how, far from lacking discipline and motivation to lose weight, her participants were desperate for help. However, many of them had lost any hope that they could achieve permanent weight loss. All of them had previously lost substantial amounts of weight and regained it. They had considerable insight into the psychological origins of their eating behaviour, but very little idea about how it might change.

She concludes that a different and much better psychologically informed approach is necessary if severely obese people are to be enabled to lose weight permanently. She proposes that a counselling intervention must, first of all, recognise that the problematic eating behaviour was originally adopted for self-medication and that the issue to be addressed is not one of eating behaviour but one of a lack of social support to manage stress. She goes on to suggest that the emotional pain and hunger behind overeating need to be resolved and that the individual's self-concept and self-efficacy need to be developed.

The next chapter, 'Cognitive Behaviour Group Therapy for Obesity and Binge Eating Disorder', describes an intervention which is inspired by many of the same perceptions and understandings which underlie work by Buckroyd and Rother and the chapter by Seamoore and her colleagues. Saskia Keville,

Verity Byrne, Madeleine Tatham and Gerry McCarron describe the thinking behind the evolution of a cognitive behavioural group therapy for obesity and binge eating disorder. They begin by outlining the evidence that suggests that psychological factors such as deficits in emotional regulation and poor self-esteem and self-efficacy, may act as both triggers and maintenance factors for binge eating. They then go on to present a theoretical rationale for their group intervention based on an understanding of binge eating as a means of managing life and emotional experience. They conceptualise the development of binge eating with a diagram which shows how early learning experiences create enduring themes relating to self, others, the world and emotions. Those negative and fearful themes lead in turn to rules and assumptions that suggest that binge eating can help people manage their lives. They go on to show how specific triggers may activate the operation of binge eating behaviour.

The authors then show how a number of CBT theorists have identified similar developmental trajectories which lead patients to adopt avoidant coping strategies. They suggest that flexibility of coping strategies, such as adaptive and action-based strategies, is useful in enabling acceptance of emotional experience rather than avoidance or suppression of it.

The intervention and its aims are then described. The authors emphasise that although they wish to reduce bingeing and enable weight loss, they also intend to target the underlying causes of the disordered eating. They present a session-by-session outline of an 18-session group intervention which explores food choice, triggers to emotional eating, strategies to change eating behaviour and attention to anxiety, depression, self-esteem, body image and assertiveness.

The authors then turn to discussing the value of group as opposed to individual treatment for the obese people with whom they worked. They describe the format of each session and how the group process was structured. The first six sessions of the group are closely related to eating behaviour and its management. The following eight sessions deal, in detail, with coping styles and how avoidant and suppressive strategies can be modified and more helpful mechanisms developed. The final sessions address the ending of the group and relapse prevention. They conclude with a plea for treatment strategies for binge eating, which take more notice of underlying psychological issues and for treatments that aim for more than a quick fix.

As a feminist psychoanalytic theorist, Colleen Heenan presents a very different approach to the same problem. She argues in her chapter, 'A Feminist, Psychotherapeutic Approach to Working with Women who Eat Compulsively', that women's eating problems demonstrate ways in which their conscious and unconscious gendered feelings about themselves are split off and projected on to their own bodies. Disordered eating is one of the ways in which women attempt to negotiate and express their identities within their paradoxical social position in contemporary western society. They are not just consumers but also objects of consumption.

Her chapter explores material from a feminist psychodynamic therapy group for women with a variety of eating problems, focusing on how interweaving both discursive and unconscious approaches to understanding the gendered function of weight, can facilitate change. Feminist psychodynamic therapists work with the concept that the body is an interface between conscious and unconscious mind within both an internal and a social world. This framework enables the client to understand the connections between socially constructed frameworks of femininity, emotions and bodily sensations, rather than to act on them through some form of bodily abuse.

This approach is based on Heenan's adaptation of Susie Orbach's *Fat is a Feminist Issue* (1978) a therapeutic model for working with compulsive eaters. While arguing that a feminist psychoanalytic framework is crucial for this work, she suggests that it is essential to combine it with cognitive and behavioural therapeutic interventions in order to provide a structure in which food, eating and body size come to be seen as meaningful.

In the last chapter Deborah Seamoore, Julia Buckroyd and David Stott report on a psychological intervention with a group of obese women. They begin their chapter, 'Changes in Eating Behaviour Following Group Therapy for Women who Binge Eat: A Pilot Study', with a literature review which demonstrates that binge eating and compulsive eating may be a significant problem in the obese population. They show that there is higher incidence of binge eating among women, associated with subjective distress and poor prognosis for weight control and comment that despite attendant health risks, researched clinical responses have not been developed.

They then describe a before and after uncontrolled pilot study which was carried out to evaluate the effectiveness of group therapy for women who binge eat and eat compulsively. Participants attended a weekly integrative therapy group for six months. Measurements before and after the group intervention were taken using the Binge Eating Scale and Clinical Outcomes in Routine Evaluation inventories. Before and after interviews were also conducted, which were then thematically analysed for changes in eating behaviour. Following the group intervention, all participants demonstrated changes in eating behaviour measured by the Binge Eating Scale and the overall effect from baseline to one year demonstrated statistical significance. Qualitative data revealed four categories that underpinned reduction in binge eating: changes in dichotomous thinking; awareness of eating behaviour; detachment from food; and dietary changes.

This very interesting piece of research deserves further attention and replication. It is particularly noteworthy because it shows not only changes in eating behaviour, but also reduction in weight. The integrative model of group therapy used in this study warrants further research and refinement for this population.

These five chapters together provide ample evidence to support the need for the further development of treatments for obesity that incorporate attention to the emotional history of the obese person. Much more work needs to be done on identifying whether all obesity is driven by emotional issues or whether, as much of the research suggests, binge eating provides a simple test for identifying psychogenic overeating. The continued rise in the prevalence of obesity suggests the limitations of conventional treatments which assume that eating behaviour can be changed without reference to psychological factors or emotional history.

REFERENCES

O'Brien, M.O. & Houston, G. (2007). *Integrative Therapy: A Practitioner's Guide, 2nd edition*. London: Sage.

Orbach, S. (1978). *Fat is a Feminist Issue*. London: Arrow.

Schore, A.N. (2003a). *Affect Dysregulation and Disorders of the Self*. New York: W.W. Norton.

Schore, A.N. (2003b). *Affect Regulation and the Repair of the Self*. New York: W.W. Norton.

CHAPTER 1

THE MANY MEANINGS OF FOOD AND THEIR IMPACT ON EATING BEHAVIOUR

JANE OGDEN, *University of Surrey, UK*

This chapter will explore why we eat what we eat and will describe biological models of eating behaviour, psychological models and those which emphasise the many and varied meanings associated with food. It will highlight how choosing what to eat relates to far more than being hungry, as food is a complex issue for most people. It will also explore why food only becomes a problem for a minority of people.

BIOLOGICAL MODELS OF EATING

When asked why and when they eat, most people describe their eating in terms of hunger, fullness and taste, saying 'I like eating it', 'it tastes nice', 'I was hungry' and 'I couldn't eat anymore'. Such explanations are in line with a more biological model of eating behaviour which suggests that food choices are governed by innate preferences and the biological sensations of hunger and satiety. Research shows that newborn babies innately prefer certain foods and have been shown to prefer sweet-tasting substances (Desor et al., 1973) and salt (Denton, 1982), and to reject bitter tastes (Geldard, 1972). Beauchamp and Moran (1982) reported however, that babies who were accustomed to drinking sweetened water drank more than those who were not. It seems that even the apparently inherent preference for sweet tastes may be modified by familiarity.

In terms of hunger and satiety, the psychophysiology of food intake highlights the role of three main neurotransmitters which influence appetite and are situated either in the central or the peripheral nervous system. These are serotonin, catecholamines and peptides. Blundell et al. (1989) suggested that these three neurotransmitters influence appetite in different ways: the serotonin

Psychological Responses to Eating Disorders and Obesity: Recent and Innovative Work.
Edited by J. Buckroyd and S. Rother. © 2008 John Wiley & Sons, Ltd

pathways influence the feeling of fullness within a meal; catacholamines influence satiety between meals thereby triggering hunger; peptides influence the reward and hedonic properties of food.

However, people eat differently according to their culture, ethnicity and family history. Given the enormous cultural diversity of food preferences it is generally accepted that food choice is more complex than simply a matter of innate preferences, or the biological drives of hunger and satiety. This has been clearly argued by Rozin: 'there is no doubt that the best predictor of the food preferences, habits and attitudes of any particular human would be information about his ethnic group ... rather than any biological measure that one might imagine' (Rozin, 1982). To reflect this perspective psychological models of eating have been developed.

PSYCHOLOGICAL MODELS OF EATING

Psychological models of eating behaviour emphasise factors such as cognitions, exposure, social and associative learning and control. They provide a framework to understand why we eat what we eat and are useful tools for research and informing interventions.

One psychological approach emphasises the importance of cognitions in predicting food intake. Most research using cognitive approaches have drawn upon social cognition models, particularly the Theory of Reasoned Action (TRA) and the Theory of Planned Behaviour (TPB) (e.g. Ajzen, 1988). These models have been applied to eating behaviour both as a means to predict it and as central to interventions to change it. They focus on cognitions such as attitudes, perceived behavioural control, subjective norms and behavioural intentions. Shepherd and Stockley (1985), for example, used the TRA to predict fat intake and reported that attitude was a better predictor than subjective norms. Similarly, attitudes have also been found to be the best predictor of table salt use (Shepherd & Fairleigh, 1986), eating in fast-food restaurants (Axelson et al., 1983), the frequency of consuming low-fat milk (Shepherd, 1988) and healthy eating (Povey et al., 2000).

Research has also pointed to the role of perceived behavioural control in predicting behaviour, particularly in relation to weight loss (Schifter & Ajzen, 1985) and healthy eating (Povey et al., 2000).

Recent studies have also explored the role of ambivalence in predicting behaviour (Thompson et al., 1995). Sparks et al. (2001) have applied the concept of ambivalence to eating behaviour, incorporated it into the TPB and assessed whether it predicted meat or chocolate consumption. In line with previous TPB studies, the results showed that attitudes per se were the best predictor of the intention to consume both meat and chocolate. The results also showed that the relationship between attitude and intention was weaker in those participants with higher ambivalence. This implies that holding both positive and negative attitudes to a food makes it less likely that the overall attitude will be translated into an intention to eat it.

In contrast, a developmental approach to eating behaviour emphasizes the importance of learning and experience and focuses on the development of food preferences in childhood. Birch highlights how food choices are related to our 'ability to learn about the consequences of eating [and] to learn to associate food cues with the consequences of ingestion in order to control food intake' (Birch, 1999).

The development of food preferences can be understood in terms of exposure, social learning and associative learning. The theory of exposure simply describes the impact of familiarity on food preferences. Human beings need to consume a variety of foods in order to have a balanced diet and yet show fear and avoidance of novel foodstuffs (neophobia). This has been called the 'omnivore's paradox' (Rozin, 1976). Young children will show neophobic responses to food but must come to accept and eat foods which may originally appear threatening. Research has shown that mere exposure to novel foods can change children's preferences. Birch and Marlin (1982) gave two-year-old children novel foods over a six-week period. One food was presented 20 times, one 10 times, one 5 times whilst one remained novel. The results showed a direct relationship between exposure and food preference and indicated that a minimum of about 8 to 10 exposures was necessary before preferences began to shift significantly. From this perspective we simply prefer foods with which we are more familiar.

Social learning describes the impact of observing other people's behaviour on one's own behaviour and is sometimes referred to as 'modelling' or 'observational learning'. An early study explored the impact of 'social suggestion' on children's eating behaviours and arranged to have children observe a series of role models with eating behaviours different to their own (Duncker, 1938). The models chosen were other children, an unknown adult and a fictional hero. The results showed a greater change in the child's food preference if the model was an older child, a friend or the fictional hero. The unknown adult had no impact on food preferences. The impact of social learning has also been shown in an intervention study designed to change children's eating behaviour using video-based peer modelling (Lowe, Dowey & Horne, 1998). This series of studies used video material of 'food dudes' who were older children enthusiastically consuming refused food, which was shown to children with a history of food refusal. The results showed that exposure to the 'food dudes' significantly changed the children's food preferences and specifically increased their consumption of fruit and vegetables. Food preferences therefore change through watching others eat.

Parental attitudes to food and eating behaviours are also central to the process of social learning. Olivera et al. (1992) for example, reported a correlation between mothers' and children's food intakes for most nutrients in pre-school children and suggested targeting parents to try to improve children's diets. Contento *et al.* (1993) found a relationship between mothers' health motivation and the quality of children's diets. Brown and Ogden (2004) reported consistent correlations between parents and their children in terms of reported snack food intake, eating motivations and body dissatisfaction.

The final mechanism explored from a developmental perspective is associative learning, that is, the impact of contingent factors on behaviour. Some research has examined the effect of rewarding eating behaviour as in 'if you eat your vegetables I will be pleased with you'. Birch *et al.* (1980), for example, gave children food in association with positive adult attention, compared with more neutral situations. This was shown to increase food preference. Rewarding eating behaviour seems to improve food preferences. Other research has explored the impact of using food as a reward. For these studies gaining access to the food is contingent upon another behaviour as in 'if you are well behaved you can have a biscuit'. Birch *et al.* (1980) presented children with foods either as a reward, as a snack or in a non-social situation (the control). The results showed that food acceptance increased if the foods were presented as a reward but that the more neutral conditions had no effect. This suggests that using food as a reward increases the preference for that food.

The relationship between food and rewards, however, appears to be more complicated than this. Lepper *et al.* (1982) told children stories about children eating imaginary foods called 'hupe' and 'hule' in which the child in the story could only eat one if he/she had finished the other. The results showed that the food which was used as the reward became the least preferred one. These examples are analogous to saying 'if you eat your vegetables you can eat your pudding'. Although parents use this approach to encourage their children to eat vegetables, the evidence indicates that this may be increasing their children's preference for pudding even further as pairing two foods results in the 'reward' food being seen as more positive than the 'access' food.

Central to these associations between food and rewards is a role for parental control over eating behaviour. Some research has addressed the impact of control, as studies indicate that parents often believe that restricting access to food and forbidding children to eat food are good strategies to improve food preferences (Casey & Rozin, 1989). Birch (1999) reviewed the evidence for the impact of imposing any form of parental control over food intake and argued that it is not only the use of foods as rewards which can have a negative effect on children's food preferences but also attempts to limit a child's access to foods. She concluded from her review that 'child feeding strategies that restrict children's access to snack foods actually make the restricted foods more attractive' (Birch, 1999, p. 11). When food is made freely available children chose more of the restricted than the unrestricted foods particularly when the mother is not present (Fisher *et al.*, 2000). Parental control may then have a detrimental impact upon a child's eating behaviour.

In contrast, however, some studies suggest that parental control may actually reduce weight and improve eating behaviour. Wardle *et al.* (2002) suggested that 'lack of control of food intake [rather than higher control] might contribute to the emergence of differences in weight' (p. 453). Similarly, Brown and Ogden (2004) reported that greater parental control was associated with higher intakes of healthy snack foods. Ogden, Reynolds and Smith (2006b) explored whether these contradictory results illustrated that parental control was more complex than often thought. They examined the effect of differentiating between 'overt control' which can be detected by the child (e.g. being firm about how much your child should eat) and 'covert control' which cannot be detected by the child (e.g. not buying unhealthy foods and bringing them into the house). The results showed that these different forms of control did differently predict snack food intake and that whilst higher covert control was related to decreased intake of unhealthy snacks, higher overt control predicted an increased intake of healthy snacks.

The final psychological perspective which impacts upon eating behaviour is the focus on dieting and Restraint Theory (Herman & Polivy, 1989; Ogden, 2003). Dieting is the conscious attempt to control food intake cognitively. Dieting, however, may not only be a consequence of obesity, but also a cause. There is evidence that dieting is often characterised by periods of overeating, precipitated by factors such as lowered mood and eating a high calorie food (Herman & Polivy, 1989; Ogden, 2003). The process of denial and self-control makes food more attractive and creates a situation in which the individual becomes increasingly preoccupied with eating. There is also some evidence that overeating is reflected in weight gain, particularly in women. French *et al.* (1994) reported the results from a cross-sectional and longitudinal study of 1,639 men and 1,913 women who were involved in a worksite intervention study for smoking cessation and weight control. The cross-sectional analysis showed that a history of dieting, current dieting and previous involvement in a formal weight loss programme were related to a higher body weight in both men and women. Similarly, the prospective analysis showed that baseline measures of involvement in a formal weight loss programme and dieting, predicted increases in body weight at follow up. However this was for women only. Klesges, Isbell and Klesges (1992) reported similar results in their study of 141 men and 146 women who were followed up after one year. The results showed that the dieting men and women were both heavier than their non-dieting counterparts at baseline. Higher baseline weight and higher restraint scores at baseline also predicted greater weight gain at follow up in women.

Implicit within these models are the many meanings associated with food. While cognitive models emphasise our beliefs about foods, these beliefs are reflections of what food means to us and whether a food is attractive, a treat, healthy or boring. We learn to associate certain foods with pleasure or with a celebration and we learn that although some foods will make us feel good about ourselves, others can make us feel guilty. Food choice therefore takes place within a network of meanings which we learn, adopt and encode throughout our lives. Similarly, by trying to control our own food intake or that of others, through dieting, we are assigning meanings to some foods such as unhealthy, guilt ridden and naughty. Other foods are considered to be acceptable, good for us and permitted.

Frequently however, psychological theories of eating behaviour neglect these meanings and make them implicit rather than explicit within their descriptions of food choice. This complex array of meanings is explicitly described by Todhunter (1973):

> Food is prestige, status and wealth. . . . It is a means of communication and interpersonal relations, such as an 'apple for the teacher' or an expression of hospitality, friendship, affection, neighbourliness, comfort and sympathy in time of sadness or danger. It symbolises strength, athleticism, health and success. It is a means of pleasure and self-gratification and a relief from stress. It is feasts, ceremonies, rituals, special days and nostalgia for home, family and the 'good old days'. It is an expression of individuality and sophistication, a means of self-expression and a way of revolt. Most of all it is tradition, custom and security. . . . There are Sunday foods and weekday foods, family foods and guest foods; foods with magical properties and health and disease foods (Todhunter, 1973, p. 301).

The remainder of this chapter will focus on the complex social and cultural meanings of food, which are illustrated in Figure 1.1. In particular it will explore the meanings of food in terms of emotional roles, conflict, social roles and health. It will draw upon the experiences of people who either are obese or have been obese, who were interviewed as part of a series of studies about their relationship with food and the impact of behavioural, medical and surgical management of obesity on this relationship (Ogden & Clementi; submitted; Ogden et al., 2006; Ogden & Sidhu, 2006).

Meaning of food

- Comfort
- Boredom
- Sexuality
- Pleasure
- Control
- Celebration
- Treat

- Denial
- Guilt
- Family love
- Religion
- Culture
- Power
- Social power

Figure 1.1 The meanings of food

THE MANY MEANINGS OF FOOD

Emotional Roles

Food plays a central role in people's emotional lives in terms of how they manage their emotions and how eating is moderated by their emotional state. In the 1970s Schachter and colleagues developed the emotionality theory of eating behaviour and argued that people became obese or overweight because they ate for emotional reasons more than thinner people (Schachter & Rodin, 1974). From this perspective the obese were considered to eat when they were upset, bored, anxious or for comfort whereas the non-obese were seen to eat because of hunger. Bruch (1974) described how people with eating disorders used food as a means to regulate their emotions and often ate because they interpreted the internal signals of emotional need as hunger. This is reflected in the words of one woman from our studies who said: *I use it so much to control my emotions although of course it never does and makes it worse. It's not a friend but it's an emotional support. . . . I have a sort of love–hate relationship with food.*

However, much research indicates that it is not just those with obesity or eating disorders who eat for emotional reasons but that most people do. Most people at times eat as a means to manage their emotions and for the majority, different foods are encoded with meanings such as comfort, pleasure, boredom, upset and relief and are central to celebration and the need for indulgence (Bordo, 1990). These meanings are learned from our childhood through the processes of reward and association and provide us with a rich set of cognitions about food. They are not always straightforward and often generate conflicts for the individual.

Food and Conflict

Food is therefore strongly linked with our emotional lives and can be used as a means of emotional regulation. This process, however, generates a range of conflicts. Food can be associated with opposite sets of meanings: eating versus denial; guilt versus pleasure; health versus pleasure; self-control versus out of control.

Eating versus denial

Charles and Kerr (1987) studied 200 young mothers in an urban area of northern England and concluded that whereas women have to provide healthy and nutritious foods for their families, they are expected to deny themselves food in order to remain thin and sexually attractive. This conclusion is reflected in the work of Murcott (1983) who argued that although food planning and providing takes up a large part of a woman's day, a woman is also aware that she must remain thin and desirable. There is further evidence for this conflict from a content analysis of 48 issues of magazines for men and magazines for women (Silverstein *et al.*, 1986). The results showed that there were 1,179 food advertisements in the women's magazines and only 10 in the men's; 359 advertisements for sweets and snacks in the women's magazines and only one in the men's; and 63 advertisements for diet foods in the women's magazines and only one in the men's. The message to women was: 'Think about food all the time but stay slim!' (Silverstein *et al.*, 1986). Lawrence (1984) also described this conflict in her analysis of her patients: 'Eating is a source of pleasure, but not often for the people who have the primary responsibility for providing it. Women take control of food, whilst simultaneously denying themselves the pleasure of it' (p. 31). Further as Orbach stated: 'Women have occupied this dual role of feeding others while needing to deny themselves' and 'Women must hold back their desires for the cakes they bake for others and satisfy themselves with a brine canned tuna salad with dietetic trimmings' (1986, p. 60). Food therefore communicates and embodies a conflict, particularly for women, between eating and denial.

Guilt versus pleasure

Some foods such as chocolate and cakes are also associated with a conflict between pleasure and guilt. For example the advertising slogans, 'forbidden fruit' and 'naughty but nice', describe the paradox of having and regretting eating. The concept of 'sins of the flesh' indicates that both eating and sex are at once pleasurable and guilt-ridden activities. Research has explored the feelings and experiences of individuals who consider themselves to be addicted to chocolate and indicates that those describing themselves as 'chocoholics' reported eating chocolate in secret and craving chocolate but feeling guilty afterwards (Hetherington & MacDiarmid, 1993). Chernin (1992) described her own feelings towards food and how she experienced both the need for food and the subsequent self-loathing. She wrote that she could not 'make it as far as lunch without eating a pound of candy'. She said 'I ran from bakery to bakery, from street stall to street stall. . . . I bought a pound of chocolate and ate it as I ran'. Unable to wait her turn any longer in a queue for a hot dog behind a man who has just ordered his, she reported 'I suddenly dart forward, grab the plate and begin to run . . . I run with a sudden sense of release' (p. 58). Similarly, Levine (1997) described in her book, *I Wish I Were Thin I Wish I Were Fat*, how 'I still feel as if I am sneaking food when I eat something I love. And I still feel guilty when I let it get the better of me' (p. 19). These sweet foods represent pleasure and fulfil a need. Their consumption is then followed by guilt and feelings of 'shame', feeling 'self-conscious', 'frantic' and 'perverse'. Food is therefore a forum for conflicts between guilt and pleasure. As one woman from our studies said: *I constantly feel guilty when I'm eating something. Like I'll eat a big bar of chocolate and then I'll feel guilty. I'll eat a packet of crisps and wish I hadn't.*

Health versus pleasure

At times food can also generate a conflict between health and pleasure. Van Otterloo and Van Ogtrop (1989) explored the eating behaviour of families in the Netherlands and concluded that a desire to feed their children and husbands healthy foods can create conflict in women, as unhealthy foods are often preferred. Similarly, Murcott (1983) concluded from her study of 40 young women and mothers in Wales, that on the one hand women are responsible for the health of their family while on the other they wish to please them and show them love by providing foods to their taste. Further as Lawrence (1984) argued: 'Good nourishing food is what every mother knows her children need. She also knows that it is usually the last thing they want. Give them junk food and they will love you. But you will also have to live with the guilt about their teeth, their weight, their vitamins' (p. 30).

Food and self-control

Food also represents self-control and at times generates a conflict between control and the lack of control. Fasting, food refusal and the hunger artists of the nineteenth century were and are received with a sense of wonder. As Gordon (1999) argued: 'Hunger artists had no moral or religious agenda ... their food refusal was a sheer act of will and self-control for its own sake' (p. 195). Crisp (1984) compared the anorexic to the ascetic in terms of her 'discipline, frugality, abstinence and stifling of the passions' (p. 210). Bruch (1974) described the anorexic as having an 'aura of special power and super human discipline'. Ogden (1997) argued that over the past few decades, diet has become the perfect vehicle for self-control. Following an examination of psychological and sociological texts over the twentieth century, she suggested a shift in the model of the individual from a passive responder, to an interactive individual, to a late twentieth century self who is reflexive and intra active. Such an individual is characterised by self-control. This focus on self-control is epitomised by the interest in eating behaviour, as diet becomes the vehicle for control and the anorexic reflects the ultimate self-controlling intra-active individual.

In contrast to control, however, much eating behaviour is also characterised by episodes of lack of control and overeating. In particular, research has identified how although dieters intend to eat less as a means to lose weight, they often overeat in response to a range of factors, including anxiety, alcohol and eating something they feel they should not have (see Ogden, 2003 for a review). In line with this, restraint theory suggests that dieting and bingeing are causally linked and that 'restraint not only precedes overeating but contributes to it causally' (Polivy & Herman, 1983). This suggests that attempting not to eat, paradoxically increases the probability of overeating – the specific behaviour dieters are attempting to avoid. Furthermore, although those with anorexia manage to control their eating much of the time, many are prone to episodes of bingeing and overeating. Those with bulimia often switch between episodes of restriction and then periods of loss of control over their food intake. Food is therefore related to issues of control with some showing strict control but the majority showing both control and episodes when this control is lost. As one of our interviewees said: *I've got a lot of control in my life so you'd think I'd be able to control my eating but I can't. Maybe it's because I'm so controlled everywhere else that I'm not controlling my eating.* Another described how trying to control her diet made her eating worse: *It's like being a kid and being told that you can't eat that. When you've got to be an adult you can do exactly what you want. . . . I mean if they told you to eat It, you wouldn't.*

Food is therefore embedded with meaning and often linked to our emotions and ways in which we manage how we feel. For many, however, this can generate conflicts as the meanings are sometimes in opposition to each other. These meanings are often generated as we interact with our social worlds.

Social Roles

The meaning of food has also been explored as central to social roles and social interaction. In particular, food is a common tool for communication within the family. The dinner table is often the only place where the family gets together; the family meal can become the forum for sharing the day's experiences. In addition, the types of foods eaten and the way in which they are cooked can create a sense of group identity, as in 'The birthday party' and 'The Sunday lunch'. As one of our interviewees said: *Being Latin, we talk about food; we sit around the table, the whole family . . . It's also the way I was programmed from when I was a kid. You have to finish everything on your plate, so I would overcook, I would put everything on the plate and I would eat it.* Some studies have therefore examined the meaning of the meal as a social interaction.

The meal as love

Charles and Kerr (1987) explored the meaning of the meal and suggested that sweet foods are often used to pacify children and to maintain family harmony. They also concluded that healthy and tasty food is a sign of family love and the determination to please and satisfy the different family members. Lawrence argued that 'Food is the medium through which women demonstrate our love and concern for our children, lovers, husbands and friends' and that 'Taking care over the preparation of food is an act of love' (1984, p. 29).

Food and sexuality

Some food is linked with sex and sexuality. Advertisements for ice cream offer their product as the path to sexual fulfilment; chocolate is often consumed in an erotic fashion. The bestselling book, *The Joy of Sex*, by Alex Comfort (1974) was named after the *Joy of Cooking* (Rombauer & Rombauer Becker, 1931) and was subtitled, *A Gourmet Guide to Love Making*. This interrelationship between food and sex permeates many cultures and many times. Rites of passage ceremonies depicting the onset of sexuality, involve practices such as washing with the blood of a goat and killing the first animal (see Fiddes, 1990).

Similarly, eating meat is considered to arouse sexual drives. Cecil (1929) described how a captain of a slave ship stopped eating meat to prevent him from lusting after female slaves. Similarly, low meat diets were recommended in the nineteenth and twentieth centuries to discourage masturbation in young males (Punch, 1977). Further, sexual language describing women or sex is often derived from animals or food such as 'beaver', 'bird', 'bitch', 'chick', 'lamb', 'meat market', 'beef' and 'beefy' (Fiddes, 1990). At a more prosaic level 'going out for dinner', 'a dinner for two' and 'a candle-lit dinner' are frequent precursors to sex. Explanations for the association between eating and sex tend to highlight the biological similarity between the two. They are both 'a basic drive for survival' and 'both perpetuate life, that both may be pleasurable and that both imply vulnerability by breaching normal bodily boundaries' (Fiddes, 1990). But such explanations are essentially biologically reductive and neglect the power of society to construct its own social meanings. Food therefore embodies statements about sex and symbolises the individual as a sexual being.

Power relations

Food can also reflect power relations within a family. Delphy (1979) reported that in nineteenth-century rural France, men regularly received larger amounts of food than women, children or the infirm elderly and that if poultry or meat was available it was reserved for the men. Millett (1969) described how 'In nearly every patriarchal group it is expected that the dominant male will eat first or eat better and even when the sexes feed together, the male shall be served by the female' (p. 48). Charles and Kerr (1987) examined the distribution of food within English families and argued that food allocation reflected the power relations and sexual divisions within a family with larger portions of meat particularly being given to men; the children and women had subsidiary positions in the family hierarchy. Murcott (1983) similarly concluded from her study that the cooked dinner 'symbolises the home, a husband's relation to it, his wife's place in it and their relationship to one another' and that the denial of food both maintained a thinner body and fulfilled a woman's role as the provider for others.

Food as religious identity

Meanings associated with religion and religious identity are also embedded in food. Starr Sered (1988) examined cooking behaviour amongst Middle Eastern Jewish women. She argued that much of their food embodies Jewish symbols and that their rituals of food preparation create a sense of holiness in their daily domestic work. Further, she argued that the women consider that feeding others represents Jewish identity, tradition, law and holiness. Eating food, preparing food and providing food for others therefore become a medium through which holiness can be communicated within the family. A similar use of food can be seen across all religions, with food forming a central part of religious celebrations and the avoidance of food often being seen as a religious duty or act.

Food as social power

Food is also a symbol of social status. Powerful individuals eat well and are fed well by others and as Wolf (1990) argued, 'Food is the primal symbol of social worth' (p. 189). Early sociological writers such as Engels and Marx regarded food as an essential component of human subsistence and its absence as an illustration of inequality (see Mennell, Murcott & van Otterloo, 1992). Food is a statement of social status and an illustration of social power. In parallel, food avoidance also serves to regain control over the social world. When political prisoners need to make a social statement they refuse to eat and initiate a hunger strike. Bobby Sands, for example, a political prisoner in Northern Ireland in the 1980s, refused food to illustrate his political point. He was voted a member of parliament by his local constituency just before he died. Similarly, the suffragettes in the early twentieth century turned to hunger strikes as a political protest over gender inequalities. Lady Constance Lytton (1869–1923) for example, was imprisoned in Liverpool for 14 days following a suffragette demonstration. In protest, she started to scratch the words 'Votes for Women' on her body; went on a hunger strike and was promptly force fed on eight occasions (Lytton, 1914). She told the wardress, 'We are sorry if it will give you trouble; we shall give as little as possible; but our fast is against the government and we shall fight them with our lives not hurting anyone else' (p. 260). She argued that the 'government had been petitioned in every other way' (p. 262). As Gordon (1999) stated, 'Historically the hunger strike has been employed by the socially oppressed as a means of embarrassing or humiliating those in control and ultimately extracting concessions from them' (p. 194). Orbach (1986) regarded eating disorders as a form of 'hunger strike' and Wolf stated 'in the public realm, food is status and honor' (p. 189). The presence of food therefore represents a social power and the refusal of food is a powerful tool for regaining control over the political world.

Food and Health

The final area that is central to understanding the meaning of food is health. Food is seen as being healthy or unhealthy, necessary for life or an indulgence. Nowadays we consider that for a diet to be healthy it needs to be low in fat and include lots of fruit and vegetables and complex carbohydrates such as brown bread and brown pasta. Freshly prepared meals are considered healthier than processed pre-prepared food. Fast food and snacks are considered necessary evils if consumed only occasionally. Salt and alcohol are recommended in only minimal amounts, whereas foods such as oily fish, oats, broccoli, green tea and cranberries are often seen as 'super foods' with almost magical qualities. The nature of a healthy diet however, has not always been the same and if ever there was an area where science has varied in its recommendations, then diet must be that area. Fibre, for example, has at times been a must for a healthy digestion, whereas at other times too much fibre has been linked with gastro-intestinal problems. After Eyton's 'The F plan diet' was launched by the media in 1982 recommending a high-fibre diet, sales of bran-based cereals rose by 30%, wholewheat bread rose by 10%, wholewheat pasta rose by 70% and baked beans rose by 8%. Similarly, advice fluctuates as to whether margarine or butter is better and whether children can drink too much or too little fruit juice.

The nature of a good diet has therefore changed over the years. *The Family Oracle of Good Health* published in the UK in 1824 is a good illustration of this. It recommended that young ladies should eat the following at breakfast: 'plain biscuit (not bread), broiled beef steaks or mutton chops, under done without any fat and half a pint of bottled ale, the genuine Scots ale is the best' or if this was too strong it suggested 'one small breakfast cup . . . of good strong tea or of coffee – weak tea or coffee is always bad for the nerves as well as the complexion'. Dinner is later described as similar to breakfast with 'no vegetables, boiled meat, no made dishes being permitted much less fruit, sweet things or pastry . . . the steaks and chops must always be the chief part of your food'. Similarly in the 1840s Dr Kitchener recommended in his diet book a lunch of 'a bit of roasted poultry, a basin of good beef tea, eggs poached . . . a sandwich – stale bread – and half a pint of good home brewed beer' (cited in Burnett, 1989, p. 69). How food and health are linked has changed over time but at each point in time, different foods have been and are embedded with meanings associated with health.

Food, however, is also associated with danger and threat. Over the past few decades there have been several major food scares which have caught the imagination of the general public and have resulted in dramatic changes in eating behaviour. In December 1988 Edwina Curry, the then junior health minister in the UK, said on television, 'Most of the egg production in this country, sadly, is now infected with salmonella' (ITN, 1988). Egg sales then fell by 50% and by 1989 were still only at 75% of their previous levels. Similarly massive publicity about the health risks of beef in the UK between May and August 1990 resulted in a 20% reduction in beef sales. One study examined the public's reactions to media coverage of 'food scares' such as salmonella, listeria and BSE and compared it to reactions to coverage of the impact of food on coronary heart disease. The study used interviews, focus groups and an analysis of the content and style of media presentations (MacIntyre *et al.*, 1998). The authors concluded that the media has a major impact upon what people eat and how they think about food. People can associate food with risk and danger. In part this reflects media representations of scientific evidence but Douglas (1966) in her book, *Purity and Danger*, described how substances which cross body boundaries can be seen as threats to the system. In a similar vein, Armstrong (1993), in his history of public health, described how dangers in the nineteenth century were considered to be in the spaces between people, but dangers in the twentieth century were those which crossed the spaces into bodies. From this perspective, perhaps we see food as potentially dangerous because it is something that we put into our bodies. When the media offers us evidence that food is dangerous we quickly believe and assimilate this viewpoint and change our behaviour accordingly.

In Summary

Why we eat what we eat is related to far more than just innate taste preferences or hunger. Food choice is a product of our cognitions, of familiarity and of our expectations and experiences. Furthermore, these processes provide us with a rich set of meanings about food relating to our emotional states, conflict, our social interactions and health. And these meanings influence how much we eat, what we eat and how we feel about food. But if these meanings are available and encoded by the majority, why do only the minority of people develop eating-related problems?

FOOD AS A FORUM FOR COMMUNICATION

Central to all the meanings of food is the role that food can play in communication. Food can be used to make statements such as: 'Who am I?', 'How am I feeling?', 'What do I feel about you?' and 'How do you make me feel?'. People can use food to make statements about their emotions ('I am fed up', 'I am bored'); they can make statements about how they feel about other people ('I love you', 'I appreciate you'); and they can make statements about how others make them feel ('I feel sexy', 'I feel caring'). They can also use food to make statements about how things are going wrong ('I am unhappy', 'I feel unloved'). This is particularly the case when people develop eating disorders such as anorexia and lose weight through food avoidance. From a psychoanalytic perspective, it has been argued that the avoidance of food has two central meanings: first it says 'This is an area in which I am in control'. Secondly it says 'I am only a little child, I cannot live by myself, I have to be looked after' (Dare & Crowther, 1995). Family systems theory also describes how symptoms such as not eating can be communicative acts (Eisler, 1995) and suggests that a symptom appears when a person 'is in an impossible situation and is trying to break out of it' (Haley, 1973, p. 44). Similarly, psychoanalytic psychotherapy for eating disorders describes the development of a focal hypothesis by the therapist involving an analysis of 'the use the patient makes of the symptoms in current personal relations' (Dare & Crowther, 1995, p. 298).

Food and weight are therefore currently embedded with a range of meanings and offer a forum for communication for an individual to make statements

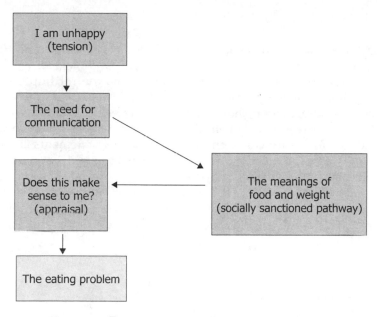

Figure 1.2 Food and the socially sanctioned pathway

about themselves to the world. So why do only some people develop problems with food if all of us use food in this way? Perhaps only some people have the need to use food for communication in ways that are problematic. Perhaps only the minority have tensions, conflicts or issues that require food to be used in ways that are detrimental to health. As I have argued elsewhere (Ogden, 2007) the meanings associated with food (and weight) offer up a socially sanctioned pathway for the expression of such tensions, conflicts or issues. In particular, I have suggested that because food and its meanings are so apparent and central to our contemporary world, the way we eat or do not eat can be read by others in ways that enables them to understand what we are trying to say. When people stop eating and lose weight they provide a recognisable sign that something is wrong; when people overeat and gain weight, they signal that they are in a state of tension. Accordingly, some people have problems which need to be communicated; the socially sanctioned pathway created by the meanings attached to food (and weight) generates a forum through which they can be expressed. This model is illustrated in Figure 1.2.

A multitude of meanings are embedded in food. For the majority these meanings are a central part of the ways in which we eat and use food in our day-to-day lives. Food is part of our attempts to regulate our emotions and is at the core of our interactions with others. Food can, however, offer a socially sanctioned pathway for the communication of tensions or issues. In doing so eating behaviour can become damaging, pathological and destructive.

CONCLUSION

Biological models of eating behaviour emphasise taste, hunger and fullness but food intake seems to be much more a product of psychological factors such as cognitions, learning, experiences, expectations and control. Implicit within such a psychological analysis are the many meanings of food in terms of its role in emotional regulation, the conflicts it generates, its central role in social interaction and its relationship to health. Furthermore, these many meanings offer food as a forum for communication for making statements about who we are, how we feel about others and how they make us feel. For most people this results in the unproblematic day-to-day process of food choice, food preferences and eating behaviour. For a minority, however, this forum also offers up a socially sanctioned pathway for communicating tensions, conflicts and issues, which can result in eating becoming a more destructive and damaging form of behaviour.

REFERENCES

Ajzen, I. (1988). *Attitudes, Personality and Behavior*. Chicago, IL: Dorsey Press.

Armstrong, D. (1993). Public health spaces and the fabrication of identity. *Sociology*, 27, 393–410.

Axelson, M.L., Brinberg, D. & Durand, J.H. (1983). Eating at a fast-food restaurant – a social-psychological analysis. *Journal of Nutrition Education*, 15, 94–8.

Beauchamp, G.K. & Moran, M. (1982). Dietary experience and sweet taste preference in human infants. *Appetite*, 3, 139–52.

Birch, L.L. (1980). Effects of peer model's food choices and eating behaviors on preschooler's food preferences. *Child Development*, 51, 489–96.

Birch, L.L. (1999). Development of food preferences. *Annual Review of Nutrition*, 19, 41–62.

Birch, L.L. & Marlin, D.W. (1982). I don't like it; I never tried it: effects of exposure on two-year-old children's food preferences. *Appetite*, 23, 353–60.

Birch, L.L., Zimmerman, S. & Hind, H. (1980). The influence of social affective context on preschool children's food preferences. *Child Development*, 51, 856–61.

Blundell, J.E., Hill, A.J. & Lawton, C.L. (1989). Neurochemical factors involved in normal and abnormal eating in humans. In R. Shepherd (ed.), *Handbook of the Psychophysiology of Human Eating* (pp. 85–112). Chichester: John Wiley & Sons, Ltd.

Bordo, S. (1990). Reading the slender body. In M. Jacobus, E.F. Keller & S. Shuttleworth (eds), *Body/Politics: Women and the Discourses of Science*. New York: Routledge.

Brown, J. & Ogden, J. (2004). Children's eating attitudes and behaviour: a study of the modelling and control theories of parental influence. *Health Education Research: Theory and Practice*, 19, 261–71.

Bruch, H. (1974). *Eating Disorders: Obesity, Anorexia and the Person Within*. New York: Basic Books.

Burnett, J. (1989). *Plenty and Want: a Social History of Food in England from 1815 to the Present Day*, 3rd edition. London: Routledge.

Casey, R. & Rozin, P. (1989). Changing children's food preferences: parents' opinions. *Appetite*, 12P, 171–82.

Cecil, R.D. (1929). *The Stricken Deer; or, The Life of Cowper*. London: Constable.

Charles, N. & Kerr, M. (1987). Just the way it is: gender and age differences in family food consumption. In J. Brannen & G. Wilson (eds), *Give and Take in Families: Studies in Resource Distribution*. London: Allen and Unwin.

Chernin, K. (1992). Confessions of an eater. In D.W. Curtin & L.M. Heldke (eds), *Cooking, Eating, Thinking: Transformative Philosophies of Food*. Indianapolis: Indiana University Press.

Comfort, A. (1974). *Joy of Sex. A Gourmet Guide to Lovemaking*. London: Quartet. 2

Contento, I.R., Basch, C., Shea, S. *et al.* (1993). Relationship of mothers' food choice criteria to food intake of pre-school children: identification of family subgroups. *Health Education Quarterly*, **20**, 243–59.

Crisp, A.H. (1984). The psychopathology of anorexia nervosa: getting the 'heat' out of the system. In A.J. Stunkard & E. Stellar (eds), *Eating and its Disorders*. New York: Raven Press.

Dare, C. & Crowther, C. (1995). Psychodynamic models of eating disorders. In G. Szmukler, C. Dare & J. Treasure (eds), *Handbook of Eating Disorders: Theory, Treatment and Research*. Chichester: John Wiley & Sons, Ltd.

Delphy, C. (1979). Sharing the same table: consumption and the family. In C. Harris (ed.), *The Sociology of the Family: New Directions for Britain*. Sociological Review Monograph 28, Keele: University of Keele.

Denton, D. (1982). *The Hunger for Salt*. Berlin: Springer-Verlag.

Desor, J.A., Maller, O. & Turner, R.E. (1973). Taste and acceptance of sugars by human infants. *Journal of Comparative and Physiological Psychology*, **84**, 496–501.

Douglas, M. (1966). *Purity and Danger: An Analysis of the Concepts of Pollution and Taboo*. London. Routledge & Kegan Paul.

Duncker, K. (1938). Experimental modification of children's food preferences through social suggestion. *Journal of Abnormal Social Psychology*, **33**, 489–507.

Eisler, I. (1995). Family models of eating disorders. In G. Szmukler, C. Dare & J. Treasure (eds), *Handbook of Eating Disorders: Theory, Treatment and Research*. Chichester: John Wiley & Sons, Ltd.

Fiddes, N. (1990). *Meat: a Natural Symbol*. London: Routledge.

Fisher, J.O., Birch, L.L., Smiciklas-Wright, H. & Piocciano, M.F. (2000). Breastfeeding through the first year predicts maternal control in feeding and subsequent toddler energy intakes. *Journal of the American Diet Association*, **100**, 641–6.

French, S.A., Jeffery, R.W., Forster, J.L. *et al.* (1994). Predictors of weight change over two years among a population of working adults: the healthy worker project. *International Journal of Obesity*, **18**, 145–54.

Geldard, F.A. (1972). *The Human Senses*. New York: John Wiley & Sons, Inc.

Gordon, R.A. (1999). *Eating Disorders: Anatomy of a Social Epidemic* (2nd edition). Oxford, England: Blackwell.

Haley, J. (1973). *Uncommon Therapy: the Psychiatric Techniques of Milton H. Erickson, M.D.* Boston, MA; Norton.

Herman C.P. & Polivy, J.A. (1988). Restraint and excess in dieters and bulimics. In K.M. Pirke & D. Ploog (eds), *The Psychobiology of Bulimia*. Berlin: Springer-Verlag.

Hetherington, M.M. & MacDiarmid, J.I. (1993). 'Chocolate addiction': a preliminary study of its description and its relationship to problem eating. *Appetite*, **21**(3), 233–46.

Klesges, R.C., Isbell, T.R. & Klesges, L.M. (1992). Relationship between dietary restraint, energy intake, physical activity, and body weight: a prospective analysis. *Journal of Abnormal Psychology*, **101**, 668–74.

Lawrence, M. (1984). *The Anorexic Experience*. London: The Women's Press.

Lepper, M., Sagotsky, G., Dafoe, J.L. & Greene, D. (1982). Consequences of superfluous social constraints: effects on young children's social inferences and subsequent intrinsic interest. *Journal of Personality and Social Psychology*, **42**, 51–65.

Levine, M.J. (1997). *I Wish I Were Thin I Wish I Were Fat*. New York: Fireside.

Lowe, C.F., Dowey, A. & Horne, P. (1998). Changing what children eat. In A. Murcott (ed.), *The Nation's Diet: the Social Science of Food Choice*. Harlow: Longman.

Lytton, C. (1914). *Prisons and Prisoners*. London: Heinemann.

MacIntyre, S., Reilly, J., Miller, D. & Eldridge, J. (1998). Food choice, food scares and health: the role of the media. In A. Murcott (ed.), *The Social Science of Food Choice*. London: Longman.

Mennell, S., Murcott, A. & van Otterloo, A.H. (1992). *The Sociology of Food: Eating, Diet and Culture*. London: Sage.

Millett, K. (1969). *Sexual Politics*. London: Virago.

Murcott, A. (1983). Women's place: cookbooks' images of technique and technology in the British kitchen. *Women's Studies International Forum*, **6**(1), 33–9.

Ogden, J. (1997). Diet as a vehicle for self control. In L. Yardley (ed.), *Material Discourses of Health and Illness*. London: Routledge.

Ogden, J. (2003). *The Psychology of Eating: From Healthy to Disordered Behaviour*. Oxford: Blackwell.

Ogden, J. (2007). Symptom onset and the socially sanctioned pathway: the example of diet. *Health: An International Journal of Health, Illness and Medicine*, **11**, 7–27.

Ogden, J. & Clementi, C. (2007). The experience of being obese and the many consequences of stigma, submitted for publication.

Ogden, J., Clementi, C. & Aylwin, S. (2006). Having obesity surgery: a qualitative study and the paradox of control. *Psychology and Health*, **21**, 273–93.

Ogden, J., Reynolds, R. & Smith, A. (2006). Expanding the concept of parental control: a role for overt and covert control in children's snacking behaviour. *Appetite*, **47**, 100–6.

Ogden, J. & Sidhu, S. (2006). Adherence, behaviour change and visualisation: a qualitative study of patient's experiences of obesity medication. *Journal of Psychosomatic Research*, **61**, 545–52.

Olivera, S.A., Ellison, R.C., Moore, L.L. *et al.* (1992). Parent–child relationships in nutrient intake: the Framingham Children's Study. *American Journal of Clinical Nutrition*, **56**, 593–8.

Orbach, S. (1986). *Hunger Strike: the Anorectic's Struggle as a Metaphor for Our Age*. London: Faber & Faber.

Polivy, J. & Herman, C.P. (1985). Dieting and bingeing. A causal analysis. *American Psychologist*, **40**, 193–201.

Povey, R., Conner, M., Sparks, P. *et al.* (2000). The theory of planned behaviour and healthy eating: examining additive and moderating effects of social influence variables. *Psychology and Health*, **14**, 991–1006.

Punch, M. (1977). *Progressive Retreat: a Sociological Study of Dartington Hall School*. Cambridge: Cambridge University Press.

Rombauer, I.S. & Rombauer Becker, M. (1931). *Joy of Cooking* (1946 edition). London: Dent.

Rozin, P. (1976). The selection of foods by rats, humans, and other animals. In P. Rosenblatt, R.A. Hinde, C. Beer & E. Shaw (eds), *Advances in the Study of Behavior, volume 6*. New York: Academic Press.

Rozin, P. (1982). Human food selection: the interaction of biology, culture and individual experience. In L.M. Barker (ed.), *The Psychobiology of Human Food Selection*. Bridgeport, CN: AVI.

Schachter, S. & Rodin, J. (1974). *Obese Humans and Rats.* Chichester: John Wiley & Sons, Ltd.

Schifter, D.A. & Ajzen, I. (1985). Intention, perceived control, and weight loss: an application of the theory of planned behavior. *Journal of Personality and Social Psychology,* 49, 843–51.

Shepherd, R. (1988). Belief structure in relation to low-fat milk consumption. *Journal of Human Nutrition and Dietetics,* 1, 421–8.

Shepherd, R. & Farleigh, C.A. (1986). Preferences, attitudes and personality as determinants of salt intake. *Human Nutrition: Applied Nutrition,* 40A, 195–208.

Shepherd, R. & Stockley, L. (1985). Fat consumption and attitudes towards food with a high fat content. *Human Nutrition: Applied Nutrition,* 39A, 431–42.

Silverstein, B., Peterson, B. & Purdue, L. (1986). Some correlates of the thin standard of physical attractiveness of women. *International Journal of Eating Disorders,* 5, 898–905.

Sparks, P., Conner, M., James, R. *et al.* (2001). Ambivalence about health-related behaviours: an exploration in the domain of food choice. *British Journal of Health Psychology,* 6, 53–68.

Starr Sered, S. (1988). Food and holiness: cooking as a sacred act among Middle Eastern Jewish women. *Anthropological Quarterly,* 61(3), 129–39.

Thompson, M., Zanna, M. & Griffin, D. (1995). Let's not be indifferent about (attitudinal) ambivalence. In R.E. Perry & J.A. Krosnick (eds). *Attitude Strength: Antecedents and Consequences.* Hillsdale, NJ: Erlbaum.

Todhunter, E.N. (1973). Food habits, food faddism and nutrition. In M. Rechcigl (ed.), *Food, Nutrition and Health: World Review of Nutrition and Dietetics, 16* (pp. 186–317). Basel: Karger.

Van Otterloo, A.H. & Van Ogtrop, J. (1989). *The Regime of Plenty, Fat and Sweet: Talking With Mothers on Food and Health.* Amsterdam: VU-Uitgeverij.

Wardle, J., Sanderson, S., Guthrie, C.A. *et al.* (2002). Parental feeding style and the intergenerational transmission of obesity risk. *Obesity Research,* 10, 453–62.

Wolf, N. (1990). *The Beauty Myth: How Images of Beauty are Used Against Women.* London: Vintage.

PART II

ANOREXIA NERVOSA

USING AN EVIDENCE-BASED APPROACH TO DEVELOP NEW TAILORED TREATMENT FOR ANOREXIA NERVOSA

CAROLINA LOPEZ, *University of Chile*
MARION ROBERTS, *King's College London, UK*
ANA SEPULVEDA, *Institute of Psychiatry, UK*
and
JANET TREASURE, *South London Maudsley Hospital NHS Trust, UK*

INTRODUCTION

The evidence base for treatment of anorexia nervosa is extremely limited. There was no study graded 'A' in the recent NICE guidelines and only one study reached the 'B' quality criteria (NICE, 2004). Many treatments that have been tested as studies of efficacy have been 'off the peg', that is, treatments designed for other purposes and adapted to 'fit' anorexia nervosa, rather than purposively tailored to match the relevant aetiological factors (both antecedent and maintaining). In allied fields of psychiatry such tailoring of treatment based on established risk factors has been found to be beneficial. Nemeroff and collaborators (Nemeroff *et al.*, 2003) reported that people with depression and childhood trauma responded better to psychotherapy alone than to pharmacotherapy alone. Furthermore, combining psychotherapy with pharmacotherapy only made a small contribution to psychotherapy alone in those with childhood abuse.

Technological advances in understanding brain function make it more possible to move from the simple clinical description of thoughts, feelings and behaviours of broad syndromes, to a more specific aetiological definition based on the causal, pathophysiological factors. These improvements in treatment for psychiatric disorders should in turn lead to treatment being more tailored to the individual's needs.

It is possible that non-specific elements such as attention, positive regard and a good therapeutic alliance are responsible for any effects seen so far. Few, if any studies, have examined the mediators of change. With a few exceptions

Psychological Responses to Eating Disorders and Obesity: Recent and Innovative Work.
Edited by J. Buckroyd and S. Rother. © 2008 John Wiley & Sons, Ltd

there has been no attempt to find reasons for negative results such as lack of power, floor or ceiling effects, fidelity or adherence problems, therapist effects and possible subgroup/moderator effects, etc.

THE CURRENT EVIDENCE BASE

As can be seen in Appendix 2.1, only 15 randomised controlled trials (RCTs) for anorexia nervosa have been undertaken over the last two decades. Three of them have been done since the NICE guidelines were published. Indeed one trial completed since the NICE guidelines even questioned whether it was possible to use such a methodological approach for this condition, as the acceptability of some treatments was so low (Halmi *et al.*, 2005). In addition to this paucity of data, inconsistent styles of reporting outcome variables make it difficult to generalise findings across studies. The most consistent subgroup of RCTs investigate various forms of family therapy in the adolescent population. Large gains in BMI (as measured by effect size) for the groups receiving family therapy are seen across all trials. The completion rate is also high for this treatment modality in adolescents.

There is less certainty about treatment for adults. The overall outcome is worse and there is little difference between the types of therapy (family or individual, CBT or dynamic). One surprising finding was that a non-specific supportive form of treatment outperformed CBT. This, if replicated, might have important repercussions in terms of understanding the process of change in anorexia nervosa; so far other treatment trials have shown little difference between more specialist treatments. However, there is some evidence that routine psychiatric treatment has a poorer outcome (Dare *et al.*, 2001) so these results are not merely a placebo response. Even with these limited findings it remains true that such treatments are simply being borrowed, rather than specifically developed for the purpose of treating anorexia nervosa.

UNDERSTANDING THE CAUSAL AND MAINTAINING FACTORS THAT UNDERPIN THE PATHOPHYSIOLOGY OF ANOREXIA NERVOSA

There has been a call for sophisticated refutable theories in eating disorders that capture the underlying mechanisms of onset and maintenance (Cooper, 2005). Maintenance factors are particularly important as a focus for treatment interventions. These are variables that predict symptom persistence over time among initially symptomatic individuals. Schmidt and Treasure (2006) have detailed a theoretical model of the maintenance of anorexia nervosa including inter- and intra-personal factors.

The argument is that four broad factors impact on outcome.

Two dispositions that precede the onset:

1. Compulsive traits, rigidity and perfectionism.
2. High anxiety and avoidance.

Two consequences of severe starvation:

1. Close others react with features of high expressed emotion (overprotection and criticism) and behaviours that inadvertently enable the anorexia nervosa behaviours.
2. Biological and psychological changes which are perceived to be positive for the individual. A detailed discussion of how medical consequences can perpetuate anorexia nervosa is given in Treasure and Szmukler (1995).

Crane and colleagues have undertaken a systematic review to test the above theory in part and examine the evidence for the role of compulsive traits, rigidity and perfectionism as a mediator or moderator in the treatment of anorexia nervosa (Crane *et al.*, 2007). There were 11 prospective longitudinal studies and over 50% found that obsessive-compulsive personality disorder (OCPD) traits were associated with a negative outcome in anorexia nervosa. Within the 12 RCTs, three RCTs suggested that these traits may moderate outcome and five RCTs found that OCPD traits were reduced after treatment. This suggests that treatment focused on these traits may be of value in the management of eating disorders.

TAILORING TREATMENT FOR INDIVIDUALS

In this chapter, we present two aspects of treatment currently being developed as part of the Maudsley model of individual treatment for adults with anorexia nervosa (see Figure 2.1). Both of these aspects are at the forefront of treatment research and findings to date show promising results. Firstly we explore the neuropsychological profile of people with anorexia nervosa and how neuropsychological findings can be translated into treatment (addressing the first factor impacting outcome detailed by Schmidt and Treasure – compulsivity, rigidity and perfectionism). Secondly we outline a 'training' programme for carers, in order to reduce the high expressed emotion environments that are often a consequence of starvation and instead to develop helpful patterns of communication (factor 3 of Schmidt and Treasure's model, above).

Cognition Applied to Clinical Interventions in Eating Disorders

In recent years the neuropsychology of mental health disorders has been gaining more attention. In the eating disorders there has been a substantial

Maudsley Model of Individual Therapy for AN

PROCESS

SOCRATIC	MOTIVATIONAL	ROGERIAN

DOMAIN

relationships	emotions	thinking style	eating/weight risks

TECHNIQUES

ACCEPTANCE	PROBLEM SOLVING	GOAL SETTING	FORMULATION	EDUCATION	MONITORING	PROS & CONS	DECENTERING	RULES

Figure 2.1 The Maudsley model of individual therapy for anorexia nervosa: processes, domains and techniques. Highlighted are the areas involved in the treatment described in this chapter

increase in the empirical investigations into neuropsychological profile in the last 20 years. Evidence from neuropsychological studies in anorexia has consistently found a number of functional anomalies (Kemps *et al.*, 2006; Lena *et al.*, 2004; Southgate *et al.*, 2005). Of particular interest at the moment are difficulties in set-shifting (Tchanturia *et al.*, 2004a; Tchanturia *et al.*, 2002) and weak central coherence (Gillberg *et al.*, 2007; Lopez *et al.*, in press).

There has been evidence in a laboratory setting of impaired flexibility in cognitive style using a variety of set-shifting tasks. Set-shifting is one of the most important executive functions which concerns the capacity to shift back and forth between multiple tasks, operations or mental sets (Miyake *et al.*, 2000). Problems in set-shifting may manifest in a variety of forms related to cognitive inflexibility (e.g. concrete and rigid approaches to problem solving and stimulus-bound behaviour) and response inflexibility (e.g. perservative or stereotyped behaviours). Tchanturia and collaborators (Tchanturia *et al.*, 2004a) found set-shifting to be significantly impaired in patients with AN ($n = 34$) compared to matched healthy controls. This deficit in cognitive flexibility is found to persist among recovered AN (Roberts *et al.*, 2007; Tchanturia *et al.*, 2004b; Tchanturia *et al.*, 2002). Holliday *et al.* (2005) found that healthy sisters of those with AN also displayed marked impairment on set-shifting tasks compared to healthy controls. The presence of this trait among healthy sisters implicates set-shifting or cognitive inflexibility as a possible endophenotype (underlying trait) of eating disorders, therefore a possible target for treatment.

In addition to poor set-shifting, people with anorexia have been found to show weak central coherence: a bias towards local processing of information over integrating information into a broader context (Frith, 1989; Happe & Frith,

2006). This is one of the core features of the cognition in autism spectrum disorders. This trait became of great interest in eating disorders following a study by Gillberg and collaborators (Gillberg et al., 1996) who found a similar cognitive profile, in terms of weak central coherence, in people with anorexia nervosa and those with autism and Asperger syndromes. This group also found that more than 20% of the anorexia nervosa group could be described as having a disorder from the autism spectrum. There is further evidence in favour of the weak central coherence account in anorexia nervosa, from studies looking at general cognitive functioning (Mathias & Kent, 1998; Sours, 1969; Southgate et al., in press; Strupp et al., 1986).

More recently, a small number of studies have specifically examined weak central coherence specifically, using a hypothesis driven approach (Tokley & Kemps, 2007; Lopez et al., in press). Overall, people with anorexia nervosa have been found to perform better in tasks requiring attention to detail and poorer in those benefiting from global processing (e.g. object assembly). This group has also shown a lack of global advantage in open-ended tasks such as the Rey–Osterrieth Complex Figure (Lopez et al., in press).

Bridging neuroscience evidence and clinical practice

Empirical evidence for these biases in information-processing styles (poor set-shifting ability and weak central coherence) have started to be included as specific targets in the treatment of anorexia nervosa. This novel approach, translating neuroscience-based evidence into treatment of eating disorders, is founded on the experience of cognitive re-mediation therapy (CRT) in the area of brain injury and psychosis (Delahunty & Morice, 1993; Wykes & Reeder, 2005). The hypothesis behind this approach is that cognitive anomalies underpinning the OCPD traits could act as maintaining factors for eating disorder psychopathology, through its influence in a variety of interpersonal and emotional variables (Schmidt & Treasure, 2006; Treasure et al., 2005).

As mentioned before, the new Maudsley model of individual treatment for people with anorexia has included interventions focused on underlying cognitive processing traits such as perfectionism and rigidity. These strategies are aimed at either improving or re-mediating cognitive functioning, or moderating processing biases that may affect the outcome in the treatment of eating disorders. By exercising and strengthening cognitive flexibility, for example, patients with anorexia nervosa seem to be able to transfer this ability to their day-to-day life and eating difficulties, by introducing flexibility in incremental amounts. Our group has pioneered the research in this area. Tchanturia and collaborators have introduced CRT to people with severe anorexia as a pre-therapy intervention in the in-patient setting (Davies & Tchanturia, 2005; Tchanturia et al., 2006a).

CRT for anorexia in the present form, targets both weak central coherence and set-shifting difficulties, with the aim of improving cognitive processing as well as enhancing the patients' meta-cognitive ability. Patients are encouraged to reflect on their own cognitive functioning and to adjust it accordingly in everyday situations when their natural tendency may not be advantageous to them. CRT is delivered in 10 individual sessions in a twice-a-week format. Each session lasts between 30 and 45 minutes and has a semi-structured design. Therapists encourage patients to go through a number of cognitive exercises that train cognitive strategies involved in flexibility of thinking and the ability to see the gestalt.

Motivational strategies are employed in order to enhance reflection and practice in out-of-session behavioural experiments. The rationale is that practising cognitive strategies will improve cognitive performance in specific tasks but, more importantly, training will eventually be transferred to day-to-day routines, thus improving general functioning. Case reports indicate that CRT is a valued intervention and an effective method to increase flexibility (Tchanturia *et al.*, 2006a; Tchanturia *et al.*, 2006b). Exercises based on the central coherence account were more recently added as part of a pilot study in CRT. Preliminary results indicate that both flexibility and global processing improved after 10 sessions of CRT.

As described above, CRT corresponds to an intensive module of cognitive remediation that has been mainly used in the in-patient setting with severe cases of anorexia. As an alternative intervention for out-patient settings, Treasure and collaborators have developed a three-session intervention module using individualised feedback of neuropsychological assessment akin to that used for CRT (targeting cognitive flexibility [set-shifting] and weak central coherence). The aim of this intervention is to translate the outcome of the assessment into an individual formulation.

Each session has specific aims as follows:

- Session 1 involves a neuropsychological assessment.
- Session 2 is centred on motivational feedback from the patient's neuropsychological results and individual formulation.
- Session 3 is a review session where targets and strategies to moderate local bias and rigidity are discussed (e.g. behavioural experiments, problem solving).

This module is offered to those individuals who are extreme on the traits mentioned above, that is they have a strong bias towards detail-focused processing; have difficulty in processing the whole; and/or have cognitive flexibility impairments. The assessment results are summarised in a friendly, visual format using bar charts (see Figure 2.2) where patients can compare their performance with a clinical sample (other people suffering from an eating disorder) and a healthy comparison group in each task they have done.

The therapist uses this feedback as a base to encourage the patient to reflect on where this information-processing bias emerges, examine how it interferes

How quickly can you find the hidden shapes ?

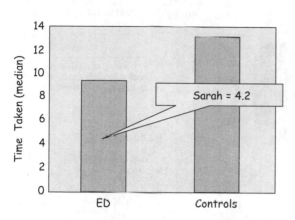

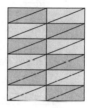

If you are able to do this task quickly, then it suggests you are good at picking up on detail.

Time taken to find hidden figure

Figure 2.2 An example of the graphical feedback given to patients. The graphs detail their performance on each neuropsychological task in relation to a clinical and a healthy control group. The therapist uses a motivational approach to generalise the findings of an enhanced focus on detail onto more general areas of functioning

with their quality of life and consider strategies to transcend this bias in general aspects of life, and in relation to food and shape/weight. This intervention is offered as a 'pre' therapy procedure, following patients' initial psychiatric assessment and before commencing the standard Maudsley model of individual treatment. This module fits well in the out-patient setting and has proved to be acceptable and of great value according to patient feedback. The neuropsychological assessment informs the wider aspects of treatment and is generalised to goal setting in the other domains. Rather than setting goals that might be aimed at changing the content of the thinking, goals are set that change the 'how' of thinking.

A small clinical vignette is given in Figure 2.3 that illustrates how, when working on setting goals to improve nutrition, the therapist encourages the patient to step back from her rigid rules about food and to consider food in the context of a fuel which will allow her to function and attain more global goals.

The Interpersonal Aspects of Anorexia Nervosa

The interpersonal dimension is an additional component in Schmidt and Treasure's model of maintenance of anorexia nervosa (2006). Integration of the

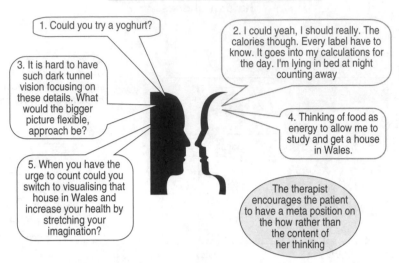

Figure 2.3 This excerpt from therapy comes from the early phase of treatment of a 35-year-old woman with anorexia nervosa who had been rapidly losing weight before treatment began. The therapist in this early phase was working on nutritional goals urgently as the patient was in the high clinical risk category and met many of the criteria for requiring inpatient care. The therapist was using some of the techniques of motivational interviewing and eliciting from the patient goals relating to her thinking style. The patient indicates that any change in eating behaviour will lead to increased anxiety and rumination about rules relating to the calorie content of food

close interpersonal network into treatment for anorexia nervosa may improve the outcome in all cases and not just for adolescents. Indeed the NICE guidelines recommended that families should be included in the treatment (2004). However, these guidelines also noted the scarcity of evidence regarding family interventions and called for further research. A variety of specific and nonspecific interventions for families have been developed (Asen & Schmidt, 2005).

Parents or other carers also have their own unmet needs in the domains of 'information about eating disorders', 'support from other people/ organisations' and 'information received from a general practitioner' (Haigh & Treasure, 2003), which contribute to the stress they experience in their caring role (Treasure *et al.*, 2007a; Treasure *et al.*, 2005b).

In the Maudsley model of treatment, carers are actively involved, with the aim of reducing the role of interpersonal maintaining factors. In addition, separate interventions have been developed for carers themselves as a means of reducing their distress and sharing information and skills to help them support the individual with an eating disorder.

The interpersonal factors that serve to maintain eating disorder symptoms

Unhelpful attributions about the illness and high expressed emotion are core components of the interpersonal maintenance factors (Treasure *et al.*, 2001; Whitney *et al.*, in press; Whitney *et al.*, 2005).

These have been merged into a model of stress and coping in parents of people with eating disorders (Treasure *et al.*, 2007a; Treasure *et al.*, 2005b). This model has distinguished several factors that contribute to carer stress:

- Misattributions about the illness which produce unhelpful emotions and behaviours.
- Lack of information or help with their caring role.
- Disorder-related problems (eating disorders symptoms).
- The stigma, role strain, and the quantity (time of face-to-face contact) and quality of the interaction with the person with an eating disorder (overprotection, hostility and criticism).
- Accommodation to the symptoms in an effort to keep the peace at home or in order to ensure that some eating takes place (Treasure *et al.*, 2007a).

The aim of treatment is to unlock some of these patterns of interpersonal reactions that maintain the illness. In Figure 2.4 we illustrate how conversations

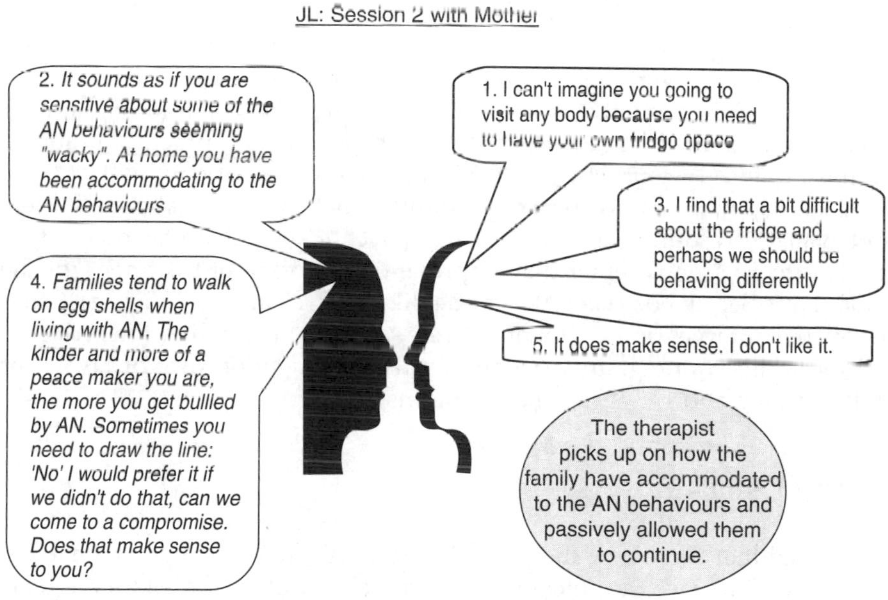

JL: Session 2 with Mother

2. It sounds as if you are sensitive about some of the AN behaviours seeming "wacky". At home you have been accommodating to the AN behaviours

1. I can't imagine you going to visit any body because you need to have your own fridge space

3. I find that a bit difficult about the fridge and perhaps we should be behaving differently

4. Families tend to walk on egg shells when living with AN. The kinder and more of a peace maker you are, the more you get bullied by AN. Sometimes you need to draw the line: 'No' I would prefer it if we didn't do that, can we come to a compromise. Does that make sense to you?

5. It does make sense. I don't like it.

The therapist picks up on how the family have accommodated to the AN behaviours and passively allowed them to continue.

Figure 2.4 This cartoon depicts part of the conversation with the family of JL described in Figure 2.3. This conversation led on from a discussion about how the individual, JL, could get more support and counteract the isolation that had followed when anorexia nervosa developed. The mother is speaking with the therapist in this extract

with family members can explore how the family may condone or allow eating behaviour rules and regulations. The family is encouraged to carry out a functional analysis of its role in reinforcing or extinguishing the abnormal behaviours.

Implementing a collaborative family intervention

The Eating Disorders Research Unit (EDU) at the Institute of Psychiatry (London) has carried out various studies aimed at examining the impact of implementing a *collaborative programme* between formal (doctors, nurses, etc.) and informal (closest relatives) carers on treatment outcome. Workshops for carers were introduced which focused on the following areas:

* understanding behavioural change
* communication skills
* emotional processing
* problem solving
* interpersonal relationships
* managing difficult behaviours

Elements from cognitive behavioural therapy and motivational interviewing were incorporated as theoretical and practical bases in the teaching. The workshops were offered to all carers of someone with an eating disorder (including all diagnostic categories) and delivered fortnightly in six two-hour sessions. Sessions were supported by a written manual used throughout the workshops. This manual was written in collaboration with a carer and a recovered eating disorder patient. It offers a theoretical and practical rationale for the training (Treasure *et al.*, 2007b). The workshops fulfil some of the carers' needs (emotional and practical support, information about eating disorders and available resources, and reduction of psychological distress and guilt). It remains to be seen whether they improve the outcome of treatment for the patient (see Sepulveda *et al.*, 2007 for details; see Treasure *et al.*, 2007a). Other innovative interventions involving carers, aimed at extending their accessibility to skills training, are currently under investigation (use of DVDs for skills training and web-based interventions).

CONCLUSIONS

It is hoped that these new theoretically driven approaches that we have described will improve the outcome and acceptability of treatment for anorexia nervosa, especially in the adult group for which treatment is so poor. Early intervention produces profound benefits in terms of long-term outcome; the main problem is how to deliver the effective treatments widely. New methods of dissemination in which parents and other carers are engaged with the process will be an important next step.

REFERENCES

Asen, E. & Schmidt, U. (2005). Multi-family group treatments. *Journal of Family Therapy, Special Edition*.

Ball, J. & Mitchell, P. (2004). A randomized controlled study of cognitive behaviour therapy and behavioural family therapy for anorexia nervosa patients. *Eating Disorders: The Journal of Treatment and Prevention*, **12**, 303–14.

Channon, S., de Silva, P., Hemsley, D. & Perkins, R. (1989). A controlled trial of cognitive-behavioural and behavioural treatment of anorexia nervosa. *Behaviour Research and Therapy*, **27**(5), 529–35.

Cooper, M.J. (2005). Cognitive theory in anorexia nervosa and bulimia nervosa: progress, development and future directions. *Clinical Psychology Review*, **25**(4), 511–31.

Crane, A.M., Roberts, M.E. & Treasure, J. (2007). Are obsessive-compulsive personality traits associated with a poor outcome in anorexia nervosa? A systematic review of randomised controlled trials and naturalistic outcome studies. *International Journal of Eating Disorders*, **40**(7), 581–8.

Dare, C., Eisler, I., Russell, G.F., Treasure, J. & Dodge, E. (2001). Psychological therapies for adults with anorexia nervosa. *British Journal of Psychiatry*, **178**, 216–21.

Davies, H. & Tchanturia, K. (2005). Cognitive remediation therapy as an intervention for acute anorexia nervosa: a case report. *European Eating Disorders Review*, **13**, 1–6.

Delahunty, A. & Morice, R. (1993). *Training Programme for the Remediation of Cognitive Deficits in Schizophrenia*. Albury, NSW: Department of Health.

Eisler, I., Dare, C., Hodes, M., Russell, G.F., Dodge, E. & Le Grange, D. (2000). Family therapy for adolescent anorexia nervosa: the results of a controlled comparison of two family interventions. *Journal of Child Psychology and Psychiatry*, **11**(6), 727–36

Frith, U. (1989). *Autism. Explaining the Enigma*. Oxford: Blackwell.

Geist, R., Heinmaa, M., Stephens, D., Davis, R. & Katzman, D.K. (2000). Comparison of family therapy and family group psychoeducation in adolescents with anorexia nervosa. *Canadian Journal of Psychiatry*, **45**, 173 8.

Gillberg, I., Gillberg, C., Rastam, M. & Johansson, M. (1996). The cognitive profile of anorexia nervosa: a comparative study including a community-based sample. *Comprehensive Psychiatry*, **37**(1), 23–30.

Gillberg, I., Rastam, M., Wentz, E. & Gillberg, C. (2007). Cognitive and executive functions in anorexia nervosa ten years after onset of eating disorder. *Journal of Clinical and Experimental Neuropsychology*, **29**(2), 170–8.

Gowers, S., Norton, K., Halek, C. & Crisp, A. (1994). Outcome of outpatient psychotherapy in a random allocation treatment study of anorexia nervosa. *International Journal of Eating Disorders*, **15**, 165–77.

Haigh, R. & Treasure, J. (2003). Investigating the needs of carers in the area of eating disorders: development of the Carers' Needs Assessment Measure (CaNAM). *European Eating Disorders Review*, **11**, 125–41.

Halmi, K., Agras, S., Crow, S. *et al.* (2005). Predictors of treatment acceptance and completion in anorexia nervosa. *Archives of General Psychiatry*, **62**, 776–81.

Happe, F. & Frith, U. (2006). The weak coherence account: detail-focused cognitive style in autism spectrum disorders. *Journal of Autism and Developmental Disorders*.

Holliday, J., Tchanturia, K., Landau, S., Collier, D.A. & Treasure, J. (2005). Is impaired set-shifting an endophenotype of anorexia nervosa? *American Journal of Psychiatry*, **162**(12), 2269–75.

Kemps, E., Tiggermann, M., Wade, T. & Ben-Tovim, D. (2006). Selective working memory deficits in anorexia nervosa. *European Eating Disorders Review*, **14**(2), 97–103.

Le Grange, D., Eisler, I., Dare, C. & Russell, G. F. (1992). Evaluation of family treatments in adolescent anorexia nervosa: a pilot study. *International Journal of Eating Disorders*, **12**, 347–57.

Lena, S.M., Fiocco, A.J. & Leyenaar, J.K. (2004). The role of cognitive deficits in the development of eating disorders. *Neuropsychological Review*, **14**(2), 99–113.

Lock, J., Agras, W., Bryson, S. & Kraemer, H.C. (2005). A comparison of short- and long-term family therapy for adolescent anorexia nervosa. *Journal of the American Academy of Child & Adolescent Psychiatry*, **7**, 632–9.

Lopez, C., Tchanturia, K., Stahl, D., Booth, R. & Treasure, J. (in press). An examination of the concept of central coherence in women with anorexia nervosa. *International Journal of Eating Disorders*.

Mathias, J. & Kent, P. (1998). Neuropsychological consequences of extreme weight loss and dietary restriction in patients with anorexia nervosa. *Journal of Clinical and Experimental Neuropsychology*, **20**(4), 548–64.

McIntosh, V.V.W. Jordan, J., Carter, F.A., Luty, S.E., McKenzie, J.M., Bulik, C.M., Frampton, C.M.A. & Joyce, P.R. (2005). Three psychotherapies for anorexia nervosa: a randomized, controlled trial. *American Journal of Psychiatry*, **162**(4), 741–7.

Miyake, A., Freidman, N.P., Emerson, M.J., Wizki, A.H., Howerter, A. & Wager, T.D. (2000). The unity and diversity of executive functions and their contributions to complex 'frontal lobe' tasks: a latent variable analysis. *Cognitive Psychology*, **41**(49–100).

Nemeroff, C.B., Heim, C.M., Thase, M.E. *et al.* (2003). Differential responses to psychotherapy versus pharmacotherapy in patients with chronic forms of major depression and childhood trauma. *Proceedings of the National Academy of Sciences of the United States of America*, **100**(2), 14293–6.

NICE. (2004). *National Clinical Practice Guideline: Eating Disorders: Core Interventions in the Treatment and Management of Anorexia Nervosa, Bulimia Nervosa, and Related Eating Disorders*. London: National Institute for Clinical Excellence.

Pike, K.M., Walsh, T., Vitousek, K., Wilson, T. & Bauer, J. (2003). Cognitive behavioural therapy in the 23 posthospitalisation treatment of anorexia nervosa. *American Journal of Psychiatry*, **160**, 2046–9.

Roberts, M.E., Tchanturia, K., Stahl, D., Southgate, L. & Treasure, J. (2007). A systematic review and meta-analysis of set shifting ability in eating disorders. *Psychological Medicine*, **37**(8), 1075–84.

Robin, A.L., Siegel, P.T., Moye, A.W., Gilroy, M., Dennis, A.B. & Sikand, A. (1999). A controlled comparison of family versus individual therapy for adolescents with anorexia nervosa. *Journal of the American Academy of Child & Adolescent Psychiatry*, **38**(12), 1482–9.

Russell, G.F., Szmukler, G., Dare, C. & Eisler, I. (1987). An evaluation of family therapy in anorexia nervosa and bulimia nervosa. *Archives in General Psychiatry*, **44**, 1047–56.

Schmidt, U. & Treasure, J. (2006). Anorexia nervosa: valued and visible. A cognitive-interpersonal maintenance model and its implications for research and practice. *British Journal of Clinical Psychology*, **45**(3), 343–66.

Sepulveda, A.R., Lopez, C., Todd, G., Whitaker, W. & Treasure, J. (2007). Implementing family intervention in an eating disorder service following a skills training: a pilot study. *Journal of Advanced Nursing*, **57**.

Serfaty, M., Turkington, D., Heap, M., Ledsham, L. & Jolley, E. (1999). Cognitive therapy versus dietary counselling in the outpatient treatment of anorexia nervosa: effects of the treatment phase. *European Eating Disorders Review*, **7**, 334–50.

Sours, J.A. (1969). The anorexia nervosa syndrome: phenomenologic and psychodynamic components. Clinical heterogeneity in four cases. *Psychiatric Quarterly*, **43**(2), 240–56.

Southgate, L., Tchanturia, K. & Treasure, J. (2005). Neuropsychological studies in eating disorders: a review. In P. Swain (ed.), *Progress in Eating Disorders*. New York: Nova Science.

Southgate, L., Tchanturia, K., & Treasure, J. (in press). Information processing bias in anorexia nervosa. *Psychiatry Research*.

Strupp, B.J., Weingartner, H., Kaye, W.H. & Gwirstman, H. (1986). Cognitive processing in anorexia nervosa. A disturbance in automatic information processing. *Neuropsychobiology*, **15**, 89–94.

Tchanturia, K., Anderluh, M., Morris, R. *et al.* (2004a). Cognitive flexibility in anorexia nervosa and bulimia nervosa. *Journal of the International Neuropsychological Society*, **10**, 513–20.

Tchanturia, K., Davies, H., Schmidt, U. & Treasure, J. (2006a). *Cognitive Remediation Flexibility Module For Anorexia Nervosa*. London: King's College London.

Tchanturia, K., Morris, R., Anderluh, M., Collier, D., Nikolaou, V. & Treasure, J. (2004b). Set shifting in anorexia nervosa: an examination before and after weight gain, in full recovery and relationship to childhood and adult OCPD traits. *Journal of Psychiatric Research*, **38**(5), 545–52.

Tchanturia, K., Morris, R., Surguladze, S. & Treasure, J. (2002). An examination of perceptual and cognitive set shifting tasks in acute anorexia nervosa and following recovery. *Journal of Eating and Weight Disorders*, **7**(4), 312–15.

Tchanturia, K., Whitney, J., & Treasure, J. (2006b). Can cognitive exercises help treat anorexia nervosa? *Journal of Eating and Weight Disorders* **11**(4).

Tokley, M. & Kemps, E. (2007). Preoccupation with detail contributes to poor abstraction in women with anorexia nervosa. *Journal of Clinical and Experimental Neuropsychology*, **29**(7), 734–41.

Treasure, J., Murphy, T., Szmukler, G., Tood, G., Gavan, K. & Joyce, J. (2001). The experience of caregiving for severe mental illness: a comparison between anorexia nervosa and psychosis. *Social Psychiatry and Psychiatric Epidemiology*, **36**(7), 343–7.

Treasure, J., Sepulveda, A.R., Whitaker, W., Todd, G., Lopez, C. & Whitney, J. (2007a). Collaborative care between professionals and non-professionals in the management of eating disorders: a description of workshops focused on interpersonal maintaining factors. *European Eating Disorders Review*, **15**, 15–24.

Treasure, J., Smith, G. D., & Crane, A. M. (2007b). *Skills-Based Learning for Caring for a Loved One with an Eating Disorder*. London: Routledge.

Treasure, J. & Szmukler, G. (1995). Medical complications of chronic anorexia nervosa. In G. Szmukler, C. Dare & J. Treasure (eds), *Handbook of Eating Disorders* (pp. 197–220). Chichester: John Wiley & Sons, Ltd.

Treasure, J., Tchanturia, K. & Schmidt, S. (2005a). Developing a model of the treatment for eating disorder: using neuroscience research to examine the how rather than the what of change. *Counselling and Psychotherapy Research*, **5**, 187–90.

Treasure, J., Whitaker, W., Whitney, J. & Schmidt, U. (2005b). Working with families of adults with anorexia nervosa. *Journal of Family Therapy*, **27**, 158–70.

Wallin, U., Kronovall, P. & Majewski, M-L. (2000). Body awareness therapy in teenage anorexia nervosa: outcome after 2 years. *European Eating Disorders Review*, **8**, 19–30.

Whitney, J., Haigh, R., Weinman, J. & Treasure, J. (in press). Caring for people with eating disorders: factors associated with psychological distress and negative caregiving appraisals in carers of people with eating disorders.

Whitney, J., Murray, J., Gavan, K., Todd, G., Whitaker, W. & Treasure, J. (2005). Experience of caring for someone with anorexia nervosa: qualitative study. *British Journal of Psychiatry*, **187**, 444–9.

Wykes, T. & Reeder, C. (2005). *Cognitive Remediation Therapy for Schizophrenia: Theory and Practice*. New York: Routledge.

Appendix 2.1 Randomised controlled trials for psychotherapy treatments of anorexia nervosa

RCT	N	Age (SD)	Baseline BMI/ABW	Intervention	Pre/Post BMI/ABW effect size	Treatment completers	'Good' outcome
Halmi et al. (2005)	122 (AN)	24.8 (6.8)	17.8 (1.7)	Cognitive behavioural therapy	—	43.0%	—
				Fluoxetine	—	27.0%	—
				CBT + Fluoxetine	—	41.0%	—
Lock et al. (2005)	86 (AN)	12–18	17.1 (1.4)	Short-term family therapy (n = 44)	1.40	95.4%	—
				Long-term family therapy (n = 42)	1.22	83.3%	—
McIntosh et al. (2005)	56 (AN)	17–40	17.3 (1.1)	Cognitive behavioural therapy (n = 19)	0.60	63.0%	—
				Interpersonal psychotherapy (n = 21)	0.44	57.0%	—
				Specialist supportive clinical management (n = 16)	1.10	69.0%	—
Ball & Mitchell (2004)	16 (ANR) 9 (AN-BP)	18.01 (2.97)	16.26	Cognitive behavioural therapy (n = 9)	1.74	69.0%	60.0%
				Behavioural family therapy (n = 9)	1.78	75.0%	(Total)
Pike et al. (2003)	33 (AN)	26.1 (6.2) 24.3 (6.9)	16.0 (2.1) 15.2 (1.5)	Cognitive behavioural therapy	—	77.8%	44.0%
				Nutritional counseling	—	26.7%	7.0%
Dare et al. (2001)	84 (AN)	26.3 (6.7)	15.4 (1.6)	Focal psychotherapy (n = 21)	—	57.1%	33.3%
				Family therapy (n = 21)	—	76.2%	36.4%
				Cognitive analytic therapy (n = 21)	—	62.0%	9.0%
				Routine treatment (n = 21)	—	62.0%	5.3%
Eisler & Dare (2000)	40 (AN)	15.5 (1.6)	74.3% (9.8)	Conjoint family therapy	—	85.0%	26.0%
				Separated family therapy	—	75.0%	47.6%
Geist et al. (2000)	25 (AN)	14.3 (1.5) 14.9 (1.7)	74.9 (9.2) 77.2 (11.1)	Family therapy (n = 12)	2.94	—	—
				Family group psychoeducation (n = 13)	2.68	—	—
Wallin et al. (2000)	23 (ANR) 3 (AN-BP)	NR	15.45 (1.75)	Body awareness therapy + Family therapy	—	—	61.5%
				Family therapy	—	—	69.2%
Robin et al. (1999)	37 (AN)	14.5	15.9	Behavioural family systems therapy (n = 19)	2.61	—	—
				Ego-oriented individual therapy (n = 18)	0.90	—	—

Appendix 2.1 (*Continued*)

RCT	N	Age (SD)	Baseline BMI/ABW	Intervention	Pre/Post BMI/ABW effect size	Treatment completers	'Good' outcome
Serfaty et al. (1999)	25 (AN)	22.1 (6.6)	16.6	Cognitive therapy (n = 25)	0.81	92.0%	—
				Dietary advice (n = 10)	N/A	0.0%	—
Gowers et al. (1994)	40 (AN)	21.2 (5.12) 21.9 (4.460)	15.52 (1.44) 15.84 (1.67)	Outpatient psychotherapy (n = 20)	2.05	75.0%	60.0%
				Control – one-off assessment (n = 20)	0.48	N/A	—
Le Grange et al. (1992)	18 (AN)	15.33 (1.81)	77.9 (7.62)	Family therapy- conjoint (n = 9)	1.23	—	—
				Family counseling – separated (n = 9)	2.83	—	—
Channon et al. (1989)	24 (AN)	23.8 (6.28)	15.3	Cognitive behavioural therapy (n = 8)	—	100.0%	—
				Behavioural therapy (n = 8)	—	87.5%	—
				Control (n = 8)	—	75.0%	—
Russell et al. (1987)	57 (AN) 23 (BN)	21.8 (7.1)	69.6 (13.0)	Family therapy (n = 36)	—	63.4%	22.0%
				Individual therapy (n = 37)	—	68.4%	16.2%

Note: — Insufficient data in paper to allow calculation.

CHAPTER 3

EATING DISORDERS: BREAKING THE INTERGENERATIONAL CYCLE THROUGH GROUP THERAPY — THE EFFECTS OF THE GROUP EXPERIENCE

SARAH BARNETT, *Private Practice*

and

JULIA BUCKROYD AND KAREN WINDLE, *University of Hertfordshire, UK*

INTRODUCTION

The research described in this chapter was undertaken to explore the effectiveness of a group therapy intervention in helping mothers recover from their own eating disorder (ED) in order to prevent or mitigate the perpetuation of transgenerational eating disorders in their children. There is now a greater understanding of the importance of the mother–child dyad in relation to the development of an ED (Patel *et al.*, 2002; Thompson, 1999). If the mother recovers, then the difficulties in the attachment behaviour between the mother and child can perhaps be repaired. The recovery of the mother also protects the child from exposure to disordered eating behaviour and thus reduces the risk of the child introjecting this behaviour. These changes can break the transgenerational cycle.

BACKGROUND

The relationship between mother and child during infancy and the early years is one of the most important factors in the development of the child's personality (Bowlby, 1990; Fonagy, 2001; Greenberg, 1999). Green and Goldwyn (2002) believe that the child's repeated experiences within the attachment relationship are a primary social experience and a template for later emotional regulation. At birth the infant depends entirely on the maternal presence to develop its instinctual and primal needs (Schore, 2003; Sidoli, 1988).

Psychological Responses to Eating Disorders and Obesity: Recent and Innovative Work.
Edited by J. Buckroyd and S. Rother. © 2008 John Wiley & Sons, Ltd

The first phases of an infant's development are bound up with feeding and nurturing; the next stages involve introjecting perceptions and attitudes; then learning to separate, becoming an individual (Palazzoli, 1985). The capacities for self-care are not innate, but evolve within the context of the responsive handling of the mother. The mother plays an essential role in the regulation of the infant's psychobiological states and the mother–child dyad affects the formation of the attachment bond between them (Schore, 2003). If this handling has been absent or distorted and the opportunity to internalise the functions of self-care have not been available, there is a likelihood of a damaged sense of knowing and understanding the body (Turp, 1999). If the developmental stages of infancy and early childhood have not been successfully negotiated and the infant has not been effective in having her needs adequately met, she becomes unable to identify her own functions, needs and emotions, becoming reliant on the mother to do so. This can result in limited development of her own 'body identity' (Bruch, 1985) or sense of self and makes the mother both indispensable and invasive. Recreating the same relationship with food as with the mother – that which is desired yet feared – may increase the risk of an eating disorder for the child (Ward *et al.*, 2000a). It is not surprising therefore that the treatment of an eating disorder may often focus on the mother–daughter dyad. The inability of the mother to be sufficiently emotionally and psychologically available for the child can be as damaging as being physically removed from her (Rutter, 1977). The resultant insecurity of the child can be seen in both anxious/ambivalent and avoidant attachment patterns, both of which are recognisable in EDs (Ward *et al.*, 2000).

Previous research has concluded that children of mothers with an ED are at high risk of developing an ED themselves (Agras, Hammer & McNicholas, 1999; Hodes, Timimi & Robinson, 1997; Scourfield, 1995; Stein, 1995; Stein *et al.*, 1994; Strober *et al.*, 2000; Van den Broucke, Vandereycken & Norre, 1997; Waugh & Bulik, 1999). The mother–child relationship can be the starting point of the transmission of the disorder and creates a repetitive cycle (Colahan & Senior, 1997). As growing children gradually start to develop the conceptual skills they need to make sense of and represent their own personal experiences, they are likely to appropriate behaviours, perspectives and understandings that they have witnessed from their main care givers (Patel *et al.*, 2002; Thompson, 1999).

RISK FACTORS

To look at the possibility of prevention, the risk factors surrounding the development of an eating disorder need be identified. These risks are a combination of genetic, environmental and sociocultural influences (Schmidt, 2002; Vandereycken & Noordenbos, 1998). The result of genetic research is as yet inconclusive and the correlation between what is inherited, learned, or is a response to environmental and sociocultural conditions, is a complex question.

Schore states that, 'the genetic specification of neuronal structure is not sufficient for the optimally function nervous system – the environment also has
a powerful effect on the structure of the brain' (Schore 2003, p. 72). Genetic
vulnerability by itself is not sufficient to cause illness, but an accumulation of
genes and environmental factors will increase the risks (Collier, 2002; Schmidt,
2002; Vandereycken & Noordenbos, 1998). Anorexic genetic traits are usually
described as obsessional, inhibited, compliant, restrained and perfectionist.
Bulimic genetic traits have been described as impulsive, interpersonally sensitive and anxious. The most common trait is an acute lack of self-esteem
(Wonderlich, 2002). If eating disordered aetiology is a combination of genetic
and adverse environmental factors (Strober et al., 2000) the probability of
transmission is considerable. If the mother continues to be affected by her
own eating disorder, then her relationship with her child may become distorted (Van den Broucke et al., 1997). The child can then face well-established
risks of becoming affected (Duncan & Reder, 2000; Seifer, 2003).

PREVENTION

Fingeret et al. (2006) did a meta-analysis of ED prevention research. Their findings were that targeting 'at risk' groups for prevention programmes had better
outcomes. Yet despite the recognition of the significant part mothers play in
the development of an eating disorder in their child (Evans & Le Grange,
1995; Stein & Woolley, 1996; Strober et al., 2000) this evidence has not been adequately incorporated into preventive treatment. The hypothesis that mothers
can play a significant part in the primary prevention of an eating disorder for
the child has not been satisfactorily tested. It is important to look at repeating
family interactions from a transgenerational perspective as it has been found
that eating disordered patients show serious parenting difficulties. (Van den
Broucke et al., 1997; Vandereycken, 2002; Woodside & Shekter-Wolfson, 1990).
Such research could have significant implications for future prevention programmes. Further research is needed on the significance of maternal eating
disorders for the child's development and psychopathology (Hodes, 2000).

DEMOGRAPHICS

As EDs are a secret illness with a great deal of shame and guilt attached,
the demographics of EDs in the population are difficult to assess as there are
many cases unreported (Eating Disorders Association, 2000; Schmidt et al.,
2004). However, in 2004 it was estimated that 1% of women in the UK between the ages of 15–30 suffered from anorexia nervosa and 2% suffered from
bulimia nervosa (Mind, 2004). The Eating Disorders Association (2000) suggested that there could be as many as 1.15 million sufferers in the UK. In order
to reduce the prevalence, prevention programmes directed at the children of
ED mothers need to be accessed while the child is still young.

EATING DISORDERS AND GROUP THERAPY

Group therapy has been found to be an effective intervention for EDs (Wanlass *et al.*, 2005; Reiss, 2002). Within the group environment there are more opportunities to correct unhelpful experiences originating in the family. ED patients have the opportunity of readjusting their accustomed way of interacting with others (Willis, 1999). Being part of a group with a female facilitator enables re-enactment of the mother–daughter relationship within the transference. Other group members can be used to play out past and present scenarios with siblings (Glover-Reed & Garvin, 1996).

A group can offer a forum for sharing experiences with which other group members can identify (Gold, 2001; Polivy, 1981; Protinsky & Marek, 1997). The group is able to develop a system of 'shared norms' which encourages a climate of mutual support and collaboration (Brunori, 2004). New interpersonal learning can be achieved by feedback and modelling (MacKenzie & Harper-Giuffre, 1992). Bion (1994) believed that the culture developed in the group will influence each individual member and the individual member will influence the group, creating a cycle of contribution. This is an important concept for the ED patient as mutuality has usually been absent in their emotional growth (Lunt *et al.*, 1989).

AIMS AND OBJECTIVES

A research project responding to these considerations was carried out to explore the possibility of prevention or mitigation of transgenerational EDs by evaluating a group therapy intervention for mothers with an ED who have children under the age of 13 (Barnett *et al.*, 2005).

The objectives of the research were:

- To conduct a group intervention in a healthcare setting.
- To investigate the possibility of primary prevention of an ED for the child.
- To aid the recovery of the mother from her ED.
- To help the mother nurture her child/children more effectively.
- To assess if a group therapy intervention is suitable for meeting the above aims.
- To develop a protocol from the group therapy that could be used by other therapists within a healthcare setting.

This chapter presents the outcomes of the group process and its effects on the participants.

THE RESEARCH GROUP

The main source of recruitment was specialist in-patient and community mental health units. Patients from these settings are more seriously ill than those found in primary care and have a longer duration of illness (Barnett *et al.*, 2006). In the original design of this project, recruitment from primary care was expected. Unfortunately referrals from this source were not forthcoming. The complex psychopathology and ambivalence of those who were recruited from secondary care increased the risk of drop out (Willis, 1999). During the lifetime of the group there was a 50% drop out. When EDs become chronic, it is more difficult for the sufferers to accept help (Slade, 1997).

The group started with eight mothers who were white, British and aged between 24 and 44 years (mean 33.5). The age of the onset of their ED ranged between 13 and 18 years (mean 15.75 years) making the average duration of the ED 17.75 years. Their body mass index (BMI) ranged from 15 to 22.5 (mean 18.4). The mothers, between them, had 15 children of which 10 were girls and five boys. The children's ages ranged from one month to 12 years (mean 7.75 years).

Exclusion criteria were drug or alcohol problems, severe depression or major psychiatric disorder, for example schizophrenia, bipolar disorder.

The group ran for 19 weekly sessions each of 1.5 hours. The Clinical Outcomes in Routine Evaluation (CORE) Questionnaire (Mellor-Clark *et al.*, 2001) and the Eating Disorders Inventory (EDI) (Garner, 1991) were administered, together with a semi-structured interview at the beginning and end of the group and at six- and 12-month follow-up. All the interviews and the group sessions were taped, transcribed verbatim and thematically analysed using NU*IST (Richards, 2002).

The protocol of the group was semi-structured using self-psychological (Goodsitt, 1997), psychodynamic (Herzog, 1995) and cognitive behavioural therapy (Garner *et al.*, 1997) methods. Each session was allocated a theme developed from the previous pilot study (Barnett *et al.*, 2006). Each session commenced with either an exercise or a video; some of the exercises included art therapy (Dokter, 1995). After each exercise or video, time was given to allow the participants to explore their responses. The group was a closed group as this encouraged the members to feel safe with one another (Wanlass *et al.*, 2005; Reiss, 1992).

THE ANALYSIS

The analysis presented will be of the first (session 1), middle (session 10) and last session (session 19). These abstracts illustrate the content and process of the group as a whole.

First Group Session

The initial purpose of the group was to provide a forum for the articulation of participants' problems and concerns, without the risk of judgement (Brunori, 2004). It has been acknowledged that mixing adolescent and adult ED clients is detrimental to the progress of the group and that neither party feel that their needs are met (Wanlass *et al.*, 2005). In this case all participants were adults. During the first session of the group, the benefits of homogeneity within the group became rapidly evident. Not only was their illness common, but they were all mothers. These factors seemed to play an important part in their ability to understand one another.

'I don't think I'd be here now if I hadn't had the children. They're the reason to get on with everything'. Maggie

'Yeah! It's the children that keep me alive. Especially quite recent, I've had periods of hurting myself and stuff so [it's been difficult] coping with it all'. Joan

'I find that one of the things of coming out of hospital I found I almost got quite angry about, is that when you're not a mum a lot of the teenage girls in there. . . . I've been in there as a teenage girl. You can be incredibly selfish 'cos you've got no one else [to think about]'. Maggie

The advantages of being in a homogeneous group with other mothers were also evident as the mothers with younger children were able to share the normal worries of motherhood. The mothers with older children were then able to pass on their experience and to reassure. Being able to normalise their experiences was an important ingredient in repairing their damaged sense of self.

'Do you find that when you actually go out and you leave her with a baby sitter, you worry about her'? Sally

'Yeah, as I say I'm sort of, [my partner's] got her at the moment and I'm like, is everything all right, are you all right'? Pam

'You get a routine and you get used to it all'. Maggie

'Just make the most of it when they're that age'. Joan

This set the scene for further exploration. Women with eating disorders are often consumed with guilt and shame which leads to isolation (Garfinkel & Dorian, 2001). Their amazement at being able to fall pregnant and then their accompanying guilt about harming the baby, started to spill out. The group very quickly became the place where they were able to compare and share the experiences related to their illness without the accompanying feelings of being judged (Brunori, 2004).

'So I'm sort of in the same boat as these two. I was anorexic since I was fifteen and I was told I'd never have children, never. Of course I got a surprise as, well yeah, as you do'. Pam

'I found when I was pregnant, I'm ashamed to have been sick. But I was panicking, so I told them I had an eating disorder and he just said – I think to try and scare me – but it didn't. It was, "The only person you're going to hurt is yourself, 'cos your baby will drain every last bit of stuff from you". And I thought, oh that's okay then, because he didn't give a toss about me so as long as the baby's all right. And then he said, "Oh, some people are sick all the way through pregnancy" and I thought, oh well, that's okay, so I justified it in my head that I could naturally be sick every time anyway and then I'd eat an apple for the baby'. Maggie

'I've heard stories and things and when I first found out about it, I started to bleed. And that's when I started thinking, 'cos I was making myself sick in the beginning and when I had the bleed and they took me into hospital to have the emergency scan, is when I suddenly thought, I can't do this'. Sally

'I was anorexic when I fell pregnant with [my daughter] and to this day I still am. She was born at thirty weeks and she was like a tiny premature baby and I still feel that's my fault 'cos even when I fell pregnant, I decided well, I know I've got to eat now 'cos I'm pregnant. But I still feel that she was premature and that's because I couldn't provide properly for her because of what I was like'. Joan

'That's it. I know what you're saying. I'd had a miscarriage after my first baby and I put that down to the anorexia'. Maggie

Having a specific focus was found to benefit the clients, but it did not prevent other issues emerging (McFarland, 1995). The group members were able to empathise with each other and began verbalising their own feelings of inadequacy. This enabled them to disclose emotions and thoughts that they had felt were too emotive to be revealed.

'I've always been piggy in the middle. That's how I see myself, the piggy in the middle. I've got an older sister and a younger brother and I wasn't as academically able as they were and even to this day I still feel totally inferior to them'. Joan

'You feel like you have to apologise all the time. That's how I've felt all my life, that I'm a pain in the backside to everybody'. Maggie

'Did you basically think you was adopted'? Maggie

'Oh yeah! I used to believe that they weren't my parents and that I used to have some strange beliefs about them'. Joan

The therapy group provided the space and containment that the participants needed to divulge and experience feelings that were previously too dangerous and overwhelming for them (Hudson et al., 1999; Segercrantz, 2006). They admitted that this was the first time that they had felt safe enough to divulge their secrets. They were now able to talk about their abusive behaviour and the isolation that they felt.

'And I just feel very isolated and I feel that I don't have anyone to talk to about things. But I've been upsetting her [my surrogate mother] so much with my cutting and my eating that it's got to the point now where she'll just have a go at me, so that I just don't feel that I can talk to her now, either'. Jenny

'I can't make myself be sick. I have to take the laxatives and sometimes you haven't really eaten something, or even a little bit of apple sometimes. You've eaten that and you think oh, there's too much in me and I'll just, I don't, I just empty it out. When she's [my daughter] in bed, that's when I get the knife out, especially if I've had a bad time'. Lucy

Problem solving, enmeshment and conflict avoidance are all present in disturbed interactive patterns in the families of ED sufferers (Lattimore *et al.*, 2000). These together with a lack of adequate mirroring and an inability to communicate can all be reinacted within the group environment (Segercrantz, 2006) and the group can help to resolve these issues in a more constructive and positive way. This allowed the women, probably for the first time in their lives, to feel validated by others (Hudson *et al.*, 1999), which took them back to the first stage of building the sense of self which is so deficient (Kohut, 1985; Segercrantz, 2006).

'I'm glad you said it, that you can't remember your childhood, 'cos I was so nervous about coming today'. Pam

'Oh I don't know remember a lot and I don't remember a lot when I was ill either'. Jenny

'I don't remember hardly anything'. Joan

'I feel like I've had lots of different lives. And you forget and you don't remember then and you block it'. Maggie

'But yeah, I suppose I don't like to think about it either, really'. Jenny

When children have experience of rejection or unreliability, their expectation is that their caretaker is unavailable. They learn not to express their needs as they are unlikely to be met. Several studies have found that people with EDs are alexithymic and also suffer from depression and anxiety. They have a diminished capacity to articulate their experiences and are disconnected from their emotional functioning (Motebarocci *et al.*, 2006). This results in the development of a damaged self that feels unlovable, unacceptable and deserving of rejection (Dozier *et al.*, 1999). This had been the experience of most of the group.

'I think my eating habits got bad then because I felt unloved. I felt unloved; I didn't feel particularly good about myself. You know, I'd never been cuddled'. Jenny

'All I've ever wanted is my mum and dad's approval and never getting it. I didn't dare argue with my mum. Even now she frightens the life out of me'. Maggie

'My mum was anorexic so I grew up around my mum not eating a lot of food. I was always quite a plump little girl 'cos my dad used to give me the sweets and the chocolates, trying to make up for the fact that my mum couldn't take me out, or she couldn't even brush my hair, 'cos her hands were so bad with the arthritis'. Sally

Having a homogeneous group with both motherhood and an ED as common denominators helped the participants confront the possibility of a transgenerational link. The group allowed them to deal with the fear of passing on their ED to their children. They recognised that children mirror their main attachment figure and mimic negative as well as positive behaviour. This led them to acknowledge that their behaviour around food in front of their children was dysfunctional and could be repeated by the children.

'If we didn't go there [her mother's] she wouldn't have much of a dinner I don't think, because I just don't seem to be able to cook. So mum does dinner'. Lucy

'I didn't want my little girl to be like me'. Pam

'He's twelve, he's starting the teenage bit so he'll say, "Mum I'm not eating today, 'cos I'm getting fat"'. Joan

'They're picking up on things, you know'. Maggie

'They know what I'm going to be like if I do eat something. Finger down and I'll say that in the main, he is very aware of it. So it is the same with boys'. Joan

'But it was only since I've had the baby now that I realise I don't want this to pass on to her 'cos it was passed from my mum to me and I don't want it to carry on. I want to do something about it before she gets too old to actually realise that mummy's not eating her meals and having her ask, "Why aren't you having your dinner"? I don't want that to carry on'. Sally

'I look at her and I worry because I think to myself, you do that, you eat that, you're going to get fat. And I'm biting my tongue not too say that to her because I'm so worried that she's going to get fat and start worrying and things and I don't want her to get fat'. Lucy

The Mid Group Session 10

It has been acknowledged in previous research (Segercrantz, 2006) that the early stages of a group are beset by drop outs. This group was no exception. All four women that dropped out, with the exception of one, were negatively influenced by their partners. By the mid-group session, the remaining four participants settled down and became comfortable with one another. It is interesting to note that the literature identified that family dynamics stand a greater chance of being elaborated in a small group which is a closer model to the nuclear family (Brunori, 2004). The participants felt that a smaller group was more intimate and safer and that the drop outs could not have been committed enough to their recovery to complete the course.

Session 10 was the second session with the theme of modelling. Participants were asked to reflect on questions in relation to:

* Copying their mothers.
* Doing things with their children that their mothers did with them.
* Not doing things with their children that their mothers did with them.

- Awareness of their children mimicking them.
- Similarity to their mothers and their children's similarity to them.
- The use of mirrors through the generations.
- Body image and weight through the generations.

When this exercise was finished it was then opened out to discussion. One participant found it hard to contain the feelings that had emerged surrounding her mother.

> 'I found it hard to stop. I know I've got lots of issues there, a lot of anger as well. It still gets to me'. Maggie

The thoughts that emerged seemed to take her back to her childhood and enabled her to re-examine what her mother had made her feel. She was then able to look at how this affected her relationship with her own children.

> 'I'm never positive about me. I'm always the butt of my own jokes. And I know they [my children] humour me. It's a bit embarrassing sometimes. It's not until when I've brought a friend home that he [my son] openly realises how little self-confidence I've actually got'. Maggie

Stern (1994) believes that if the infant fails to involve the mother emotionally the infant then tries to win her by imitation and identification. This pattern then becomes repeated thereby creating the dysfunctional transgenerational cycle. One participant had blocked out most of her childhood and could only remember her mother as absent. This seemed to affect her ability to nurture her own child; she pushed her away. In this way she was repeating the behaviour she had been subjected to when she was a child.

> 'Mum was like this, in bed asleep or she was going to work, so I hardly ever saw her'. Lucy

> 'I've lost touch with being a mum. So it's hard to answer these questions because she'd [my daughter] be there, but I'd take no notice and I know that's horrible'. Lucy

Weston (1999) talks of the 'empty matrix' which is the emptiness that the anorexic and bulimic create because of the denial of their devouring needs.

There was a realization that their illness was connected to the lack of love and nurturing that had come from their mothers.

> 'It's almost made me kill myself to get her to say that she does actually care and that's something. I do know – that's my way, I suppose, of getting my mum to notice me, is to have an ongoing crisis'. Maggie

Some of the other participants also felt that their mothers had either been neglectful, abusive or absent. One was described as 'nondescript'. In their cases the negative experiences influenced them to manage motherhood in a different way.

'I was starting to tell my children off in the way that my mum did and I didn't like doing it. And I don't think at the time I was conscious of it, but since then I don't do that now. I make sure I give them lots of cuddles and tell them how lovely they are, which my mum never did'. Jenny

'I didn't know how to say, I love you. Nobody ever said that to me. I can't stop now with my kids, but until then I wouldn't have shown my emotions at all'. Maggie

By this stage of the group the participants had started to gain a better understanding of how much the family dynamics and their relationship with their mothers played a part in the continuation of their ED. It was a surprise to them that they still needed their mother's approval and they realised how intense the sibling rivalries were in their family. Being in the group helped them to uncover what they were feeling. For the first time they were coming to the realisation that being ill was the only way they could retain their mother's attention.

'It is a constant battle because I still need her approval, which is so stupid. My oldest sister shines 'cos she's outgoing and confident and a complete nutcase. My younger sister shines. She can be funny but she's a loud mouth, outrageously loud and very rude. And my only way of shining, I suppose, is by being ill. I think that's what I've realised'. Maggie

'I didn't think until, it was the last week, the way that I am. Certain things have just stuck 'cos I want my mum to think the best of me. I didn't realise that I was doing it, really. Didn't realise until I was with you last week when we was talking last week with the people I was with [the group]'. Joan

As the group felt more comfortable with each other they were able to talk about the fear and anger related to their partners. They felt their partners did not understand their illness. This fed their insecurities and self-loathing. Most of them had similar feelings which they had been containing for a considerable time. It was disclosed that their partners felt excluded and threatened by the group.

'Cos they don't know what's going on do they? They don't understand that other people experience it [ED]'. Joan

'The similarity to other people's problems, not just all the weird things that you do. Other people do it as well and it's part of the nature of the illness. It's not me being a selfish person trying to hurt'. Maggie

'[My husband] is very black and white, you know. He'll say, well it's up to you. You choose to do something or you don't. It's very hard for men to understand'. Jenny

Near the end of the session they returned to modelling which was the original theme of this group. Many authors (Kohut, 1985; Patel *et al.*, 2002; Thompson,

1999; Winnicott, 1965) writing on the mother–daughter dyad, have recognised that the infant can begin to respond by repeating or mirroring the mother. If the mother's actions and re-actions are inadequate or dysfunctional the infant (and later the child) will internalise and mirror the dysfunction and fail to develop in a real and natural way.

The mothers began to realise that saying the right things to their children was not enough. They started to understand that children learn by example and if their mothers are saying one thing and doing another the messages are confusing.

> 'Very occasionally I do a Sunday dinner and I sit there and "You've got to eat your dinner". "But you're not going to eat all yours". "Yeah", I said, "Well, I put too much on my plate"'. Joan

The Final Group

As the end of the group was drawing nearer, it became evident that the participants were only just starting the therapeutic process and needed to be supported for a longer period if they were to maintain their recovery. This was as a result of the length and severity of their ED. A great deal of time was spent in trying to find a suitable continuation for the work of the existing group. This search highlighted the absence of specialist services in out-patient care. Fewer than half of ED sufferers in the UK receive specialist treatment and there is a recognised lack of specialist ED services (Eating Disorders Association, 2005). The mothers themselves recognised the difficulty of getting care and also the frustrations of continuous care never being available to them.

> 'I wanted someone to talk too and there was nowhere to go. There was nothing else I could do, 'cos I've been in a crisis like this before and you get these really stupid people say[ing] things to me [like], "Unless you try and kill yourself . . .", basically. You might as well just kill yourself anyway. But it's just so, you know, you get the help and then you get to trust in somebody and then they're taken away. And all they say to you is that the NHS can't provide, you know, they can't keep the people'. Joan

In the penultimate session the participants were asked to write a letter to each other which they were to read out in the final session. During the first part of the final session we reviewed what had been done in the group, going over the themes. The mothers were surprised at how much the group had made them aware of their behaviour and how much change had occurred during the lifetime of the group.

> 'I feel a little bit more confident, a lot more than I was. It's made me realise that I can do more than I thought I could do'. Maggie

> 'I think I know, I think I am much more aware, of why I am like I am, I think. I think that certainly, coming to the group's helped me realise more how much the children do take in, even when you think they don't'. Jenny

One of the mothers stated that, before the group, she had not realised that she made a distinction between her sons and her daughter. The group made her aware that she fed her children in a different way.

'But I was doing that sub-consciously. I wasn't really aware that I was making such a distinction'. Joan

The letters that the group wrote to one another showed a remarkable depth of empathy and perception. Being able to understand one another so completely helped them to understand themselves, as they were able to see a mirror image. Although they were well prepared for the ending they were frightened of letting go, but believed that maybe for the first time they were capable of completing their recovery.

'I feel quite sad, a bit scared actually. I think it's the first time I've ever felt something working for me and it's ending'. Maggie

'It's 'cos it's – you really want to do this and you want to do it and you've got to believe in, that you will do it'. Joan

CONCLUSION

It is important that ED mothers are made aware of the possible dangers to their children and the risks that surround the impairment of the natural and healthy development of their child (Van den Broucke et al., 1997). If a child develops anorexia, there are long term risks involving growth, fertility and osteoporosis (Bryant-Waugh & Lask, 2002).

McFarland (1995) believed that hope is one of the major benefits of group therapy for the ED sufferer and develops the necessary ego strengths by recognising the resources needed to make changes. Running a group solely for mothers with EDs seemed to enable them to feel understood without explanation. They could then accept feedback and criticism which facilitated their development (Polivy, 1981). Each participant agreed that knowledge and understanding played an integral part in instigating a desire to work on ways to change.

When eating disorders become embedded and chronic, treatment becomes a very lengthy and expensive process, often resulting in repeated hospitalisation (Schmidt et al., 2004). If these disorders can be prevented or ameliorated then we are not only helping the individual but are also lessening the financial burden on the health service. Although the sample was small the results of the pilot and the main study are an encouraging start to developing a useful intervention that could in time lead to the prevention of some cases of this dangerous and destructive illness.

REFERENCES

Agras, S., Hammer, L. & McNicholas, F. (1999). A prospective study of the influence of eating disordered mothers on their children. *International Journal of Eating Disorders*, **25**(3), 53–61.

Barnett, S., Buckroyd, J. & Windle, K. (2005). Eating disorders from parent to child: mothers' perception of transgenerational effect. *Counselling and Psychotherapy Research*, **5**(3), 203–11.

Barnett, S., Buckroyd, J. & Windle, K. (2006). Using group therapy to support eating disordered mothers with their children: the relevance for primary care. *Primary Health Care*, **7**(1), 39–49.

Bion, W.R. (1994). *Experiences in Groups and Other Papers*. London: Routledge.

Bowlby, J. (1990). *Child Care and the Growth of Love*. London: Penguin.

Bruch, H. (1985). Four decades of eating disorders. In D.M. Garner & P.E. Garfinkel (eds), *Handbook of Psychotherapy for Anorexia Nervosa and Bulimia*. New York: Guilford Press.

Brunori, L. (2004). Analysis of the therapeutic course of an eating disorders group. *Group Analysis*, **37**(3), 387–400.

Bryant-Waugh, R. & Lask, B. (2002). Childhood-onset eating disorders. In C.G. Fairburn & K.D. Brownell (eds), *Eating Disorders and Obesity. A Comprehensive Handbook*, 2nd edition. New York: Guilford Press.

Colahan, M. & Senior, R. (1997). Family patterns in eating disorders: going round in circles, getting nowhere fasting. In G. Szmukler, C. Dare & J. Treasure (eds), *Handbook of Eating Disorders: Theory, Treatment and Research*. Chichester: John Wiley & Sons, Ltd.

Collier, D.A. (2002). Molecular genetics of eating disorders. In C.G. Fairburn & K.D. Brownell (eds), *Eating Disorders and Obesity. A Comprehensive Handbook*, 2nd edition. New York: Guilford Press.

Dokter, D. (1995). *Arts Therapies and Clients with Eating Disorders*. London: Jessica Kingsley.

Dozier, M., Stovall, K.C. & Albus, K.E. (1999). Attachment and psychopathology in adulthood. In J. Cassidy & P.R. Shaver (eds), *Handbook of Attachment. Theory, Research and Clinical Applications*. New York: Guilford Press.

Duncan, S. & Reder, P. (2000). Children's experience of major psychiatric disorder in their parent. In P. Reder, M. McClure & A. Jolley (eds), *Family Matters: Interfaces Between Child and Adult Mental Health*. London: Routledge.

Eating Disorders Association (2000). *The Need for Action in 2000 and Beyond*. EDA Press.

Eating Disorders Association (2005). *Getting Better: Is the Quality of Treatment for Eating Disorders in the UK Getting Better?* www.edauk.com.

Evans, J. & Le Grange, D. (1995) Body size and parenting in eating disorders: a comparative study of the attitudes of mothers toward their children. *International Journal of Eating Disorders*, **18**(1), 39–48.

Fingeret, M.C., Warren, C.S., Cepeda-Benito, A. & Gleaves, D.H. (2006). Prevention series. eating disorder prevention research: a meta-analysis. *Eating Disorders*, **14**, 191–213.

Fonagy, P. (2001). *Attachment Theory and Psychoanalysis*. New York: Other Press.

Garfinkel, P.E. & Dorian, B.J. (2001). Improving understanding and care for the eating disorders. In R.H. Striegel-Moore & L. Smolak (eds), *Eating Disorders: Innovative Directions in Research and Practice*. Washington, DC: American Psychological Association.

Garner, D.M. (1991). *Eating Disorder Inventory-2 (EDI-2): Professional Manual.* Odessa, FL: Psychological Assessment Resources.

Garner, D.M., Vitousek, K.M. & Pike, K.M. (1997) Cognitive behavioural therapy for anorexia nervosa. In D.M. Garner & P.E. Garfinkel (eds), *Handbook of Treatment for Eating Disorders,* 2nd edition. New York: Guilford Press.

Glover-Reed, B. & Garvin, C.D. (1996). Feminist thought and group psychotherapy: feminist principles as praxis. In B. DeChant (ed.), *Women and Group Psychotherapy: Theory and Practice.* New York: Guilford Press.

Gold, B. (2001). Group-analytic psychotherapy in the treatment of eating disorders. In T. Hindmarch (ed.), *Eating Disorders: A Multiprofessional Approach.* London: Whurr Publishers.

Goodsitt, A. (1997). Eating disorders: a self-psychological perspective. In D.M. Garner & P.E. Garfinkel (eds), *Handbook of Treatment for Eating Disorders,* 2nd edition. New York: Guilford Press

Green, J. & Goldwyn, R. (2002). Annotation: attachment disorganisation and psychopathology: new findings in attachment research and their potential implications for developmental psychology in childhood. *Journal of Child Psychology and Psychiatry,* 43(7), 835–46.

Greenberg, M.T. (1999). Attachment and psychopathology in childhood. In J. Cassidy & P.R. Shaver (eds), *Handbook of Attachment. Theory, Research and Clinical Applications.* New York: Guilford Press.

Herzog, D.B. (1995). Psychodynamic psychotherapy for anorexia nervosa. In C.G. Fairburn & K.D. Brownell (eds), *Eating Disorders and Obesity. A Comprehensive Handbook,* 2nd edition. New York: Guilford Press.

Hodes, M. (2000). The children of mothers with eating disorders. In P. Reder, M. McClure & A. Jolley (eds), *Family Matters: Interfaces Between Child and Adult Mental Health.* London: Routledge.

Hodes, M., Timimi, S. & Robinson, P. (1997). Children of mothers with eating disorders: a preliminary study. *European Eating Disorders Review,* 5(1), 11–24.

Hudson, I., Ritchie, R., Brennan, C. & Sutton-Smith, D. (1999). Consuming passions: groups for women with eating problems. *Group Analysis,* 32, 37–51.

Kohut, H. (1985). *Self Psychology and the Humanities: Reflections on a New Psychoanalytic Approach.* London: W.W. Norton.

Lattimore, P.J., Wagner, H.L. & Gowers, S. (2000). Conflict avoidence in anorexia nervosa: an observational study of mothers and daughters. *European Eating Disorders Review,* 8(5), 355–68.

Lunt, P., Carosella, N. & Yager, J. (1989). Daughters whose mothers have anorexia nervosa: a pilot study of three adolescents. *Psychiatric Medicine,* 7(3), 101–10.

MacKenzie, R.K. & Harper-Giuffre, H. (1992). *Group Psychotherapy for Eating Disorders.* Washington, DC: American Psychiatric Press.

McFarland, B. (1995). *Brief Therapy and Eating Disorders.* California: Jossey-Bass.

Mellor-Clark, J., Connell, J., Barkham, M. & Cummins, P. (2001). Counselling outcomes in primary health care: core system data profile. *European Journal of Psychotherapy, Counselling and Health,* 4(1), 65–86.

Mind Information (2004). *How Common is Mental Distress.* www.mind.org.

Motebarocci, O., Codispoti, M., Surcinelli, P. *et al.* (2006). Alexithimia in female patients with eating disorders. *Eating and Weight Disorders,* 11, 14–21.

Palazzoli, M.S. (1985). *Self-Starvation.* New York: Jason Aronson.

Patel, P., Wheatcroft, R., Park, R.J. & Stien, A. (2002). The children of mothers with an eating disorder. *Clinical Child and Family Psychology Review,* 5(1), 1–19.

Polivy, J. (1981). Group therapy as an adjunctive treatment for anorexia nervosa. *Journal of Psychiatric Treatment and Evaluation*, **3**, 279–83.

Protinsky, H. & Marek, L.I. (1997). Insights into the treatment of eating disorders: a qualitative approach. *Family Therapy*, **24**(2), 63–9.

Reiss, H. (1992). Group psychotherapy for eating disorders. In J.S. Rutan (ed.), *Psychotherapy for the 1990s*. New York: Guilford Press.

Reiss, H. (2002). Integrative time-limited group therapy for bulimia nervosa. *International Journal of Group Psychotherapy*, **52**, 1–25.

Richards, L. (2002). *Using N6 in Qualitative Research QSR*. Melbourne: International Pty. Ltd.

Rutter, M. (1977). *Maternal Deprivation Reassessed*. London: Penguin.

Schmidt, U. (2002). Risk factors for eating disorders. In C.G. Fairburn & K.D. Brownell (eds), *Eating Disorders and Obesity. A Comprehensive Handbook*, 2nd edition. New York: Guilford Press.

Schmidt, U., Waller, G. & Treasure, J. (2004). Entry into specialist services for the eating disorders: audit of clinical pathways through primary and secondary care. http://web1.iop.kcl.ac.uk/IoP/Departments/PsychMed/EDU/AuditStudy.shtml.

Schore, A.N. (2003). *Affect Dysregulation and Disorders of the Self*. New York: Norton.

Scourfield, J. (1995). Anorexia by proxy: are the children of anorexic mothers an at-risk group? *International Journal of Eating Disorders*, **18**(4), 371–4.

Segercrantz, U. (2006). Treating bulimics in groups. *Group Analysis*, **39**(2), 257–71.

Seifer, R. (2003). Young children with mentally ill parents. In S.S. Luthar (ed.), *Resilience and Vulnerability. Adaptation in the Context of Childhood Adversities*. Cambridge, MA: Cambridge University Press.

Sidoli, M. (1988). Disintegration and reintegration in the first two weeks of life. In M. Sidoli & M. Davies (eds), *Jungian Child Psychotherapy: Individuation in Childhood*. London: Karnac Books.

Slade, P. (1997). Prospects for prevention. In G. Szmukler, C. Dare & J. Treasure (eds), *Handbook of Eating Disorders: Theory, Treatment and Research*. Chichester: John Wiley & Sons, Ltd.

Stein, A. (1995). Eating disorders and childrearing. In C.G. Fairburn & K.D. Brownell (eds), *Eating Disorders and Obesity. A Comprehensive Handbook*, 2nd edition. New York: Guilford Press.

Stein, A. & Woolley, H. (1996). The influence of parental eating disorders on young children: implications of recent research for some clinical interventions. *Eating Disorders*, **4**(2), 139–46.

Stein, A., Woolley, H., Cooper, S.D. & Fairburn, C.G. (1994). An observational study of mothers with eating disorders and their infants. *Journal of Child Psychology and Psychiatry*, **35**, 733–48.

Stern, D. (1994). One way to build a clinical relevant baby. *Infant Mental Health Journal*, **15**(1), 9–25.

Strober, M., Freeman, R., Lampert, C. *et al.* (2000). Controlled family study of anorexia nervosa and bulimia nervosa: evidence of shared liability and transmission of partial syndromes. *American Journal of Psychiatry*, **157**, 393–401.

Thompson, R.A. (1999). Early attachment and later development. In J. Cassidy & P.R. Shaver (eds), *Handbook of Attachment. Theory, Research and Clinical Applications*. New York: Guilford Press.

Turp, M. (1999). Encountering self-harm in psychotherapy and counselling practice. *British Journal of Psychotherapy*, **15**(3).

Van den Broucke, S., Vandereycken, W. & Norre, J. (1997). *Eating Disorders and Marital Relationships*. London: Routledge.

Vandereycken, W. (2002). Families of patients with eating disorders. In C.G. Fairburn & K.D. Brownell (eds), *Eating Disorders and Obesity. A Comprehensive Handbook*, 2nd edition. New York: Guilford Press.

Vandereycken, W. & Noordenbos, G. (1998). *The Prevention of Eating Disorders*. London: The Athlone Press.

Wanlass, J., Moreno, K.J. & Thomson, H.M. (2005). Group therapy for eating disorders: a retrospective case study. *Journal for Specialists in Group Work*, **30**, 47–66.

Ward, A., Ramsay, R. & Treasure, J. (2000a). Attachment research in eating disorders. *British Journal of Medical Psychology*, **73**, 35–51.

Ward, A., Ramsay, R., Turnbull, S. *et al.* (2000). Attachment patterns in eating disorders: past in the present. *International Journal of Eating Disorders*, **28**, 370–6.

Waugh, E. & Bulik, C.M. (1999). Offspring of women with eating disorders. *International Journal of Eating Disorders*, **25**(2), 123–33.

Weston, M.D. (1999). Anorexia as a symbol of an empty matrix dominated by the dragon mother. *Group Analysis*, **32**, 71–85.

Willis, S. (1999). Group analysis and eating disorders. *Group Analysis*, **32**, 21–35.

Winnicott, D.W. (1965). *The Family and Individual Development*. London: Tavistock.

Wonderlich, S.A. (2002). Personality and eating disorders. In C.G. Fairburn & K.D. Brownell (eds), *Eating Disorders and Obesity. A Comprehensive Handbook*, 2nd edition. New York: Guilford Press.

Woodside, D.B. & Shekter-Wolfson, L.F. (1990). Parenting by patients with anorexia nervosa and bulimia nervosa. *International Journal of Eating Disorders*, **9**(3), 303–9.

PART III

BULIMIA NERVOSA

CHAPTER 4

CURRENT THINKING ON WORKING WITH PEOPLE WITH BULIMIA NERVOSA AND BULIMIC DISORDERS

GLENN WALLER, *North West London NHS Foundation Trust*

BULIMIA NERVOSA AND BULIMIC DISORDERS

Since the label of 'bulimia nervosa' was first applied (Russell, 1979) it has become clear that this diagnosis is anything but the 'variant' of anorexia nervosa that Russell proposed. There are more bulimics than anorexics (e.g., Hoek, 2002) and it is clear that not all bulimics have a history of low weight. In many ways, we have progressed much further in our understanding and treatment of bulimic disorders in the past 30 years than in our capacity to work with low-weight anorexics. This chapter will review clinical and academic progress to date, so that we can identify both success and areas that require further research. My focus will be on evidence-based and evidence-generating approaches to the psychopathology and treatment of bulimia nervosa, as I see it as disrespectful to our patients to work in frameworks that are not evidence-related or capable of being tested.

DIAGNOSIS OF BULIMIA NERVOSA

At present, bulimia nervosa is diagnosed using the following criteria: normal weight; binge eating and compensating; and extreme concerns about eating, weight and shape (American Psychiatric Association, 1994; World Health Organisation, 1992). The distinction from anorexia nervosa of the bingeing/purging subtype is largely a matter of body mass index. However, the past decade has seen a slow move away from certainty about diagnostic criteria. Since bulimia nervosa was first identified, there have been substantial changes to the criteria, and there is still a lack of concordance across diagnostic schemes (e.g., American Psychiatric Association, 1980, 1987, 1994; World Health Organisation, 1992). Secondly, the validity of assessment is limited by

Psychological Responses to Eating Disorders and Obesity: Recent and Innovative Work.
Edited by J. Buckroyd and S. Rother. © 2008 John Wiley & Sons, Ltd

the subjective nature of some of those criteria, despite efforts to define them in robust ways. In bulimia nervosa, the key issue is how one defines binge eating. There is no objective criterion that allows us reliably and validly to differentiate a binge from an episode of overeating. We must therefore rely on clinicians' and patients' subjective judgements about quantity and loss of control. Such judgements have been shown to be flawed (Lawrence *et al.*, 2003). In fact, as the criteria for a binge have shifted over the years, they have become increasingly impossible to apply in any objective way.

Even if there were definite diagnostic indicators, many patients with bulimic disorders do not meet the full criteria for bulimia nervosa. Those patients fall into the broad category of 'atypical cases' or 'eating disorders not otherwise specified' (EDNOS) (e.g., Turner & Bryant-Waugh, 2004). Indeed, it appears that the majority of eating-disordered cases are 'atypical', with clinically significant pathology but without the full set of diagnostic criteria (e.g., Fairburn & Harrison, 2003). Fairburn *et al.* (2005) have shown that relaxing diagnostic criteria does little to redress the dominance of the EDNOS group. To add to the confusion, individuals change diagnosis without regard to the assumption that they will not. Many patients vary in presentation over time – passing through phases of restrictive and bulimic behaviours, changing weight, and using different behaviours (Fairburn & Harrison, 2003). Given this lack of a robust diagnosis, current clinical recommendations are to consider 'atypical' bulimic patients to be equivalent to full-blown cases when treating them (National Institute for Clinical Excellence, 2004).

The future of diagnosis in the eating disorders remains unclear, especially as preparations begin for DSM-V. At present, the field is divided between those who wish to subdivide the eating disorders still further (e.g., purging disorder, exercise disorder) in order to find a 'slot' for every patient, and those who argue that it is hard or impossible to justify the subgrouping of the eating disorders (Fairburn *et al.*, 2003, 2005; Waller, 1993, 2005). In terms of bulimia nervosa and the bulimic disorders, the key remains the behaviours of bingeing and compensation (e.g., restriction, purging, exercise); the underlying cognitions regarding eating, weight and shape; the emotional factors that drive the behaviours; and the physiological consequences of the eating behaviours.

Epidemiology of Bulimia Nervosa

The difficulties in diagnosing bulimic disorders make it impossible to give precise figures on the numbers of cases. Prevalence and incidence figures vary widely, according to the methodologies and definitions used in different studies. Hoek (2002) suggests a point prevalence rate of 1% among young adult females in westernised cultures, compared with a point prevalence for anorexia of 0.28%. These figures clearly represent an underestimate of bulimic cases when atypical presentations are included (e.g. those who do not binge and purge frequently enough to meet full criteria for the diagnosis).

There is some evidence that the incidence of bulimia rose in the early 1990s, but that it has fallen again in more recent years. In contrast, anorexia nervosa has had a relatively stable incidence over that time period (Currin *et al.*, 2005; Fombonne, 1995, 1996). We lack good evidence that the nature and prevalence of the eating disorders has changed over time. Without evidence for an alternative hypothesis, the simplest conclusion must be that changes in the incidence of bulimia can be explained by better case identification. Similarly, it is parsimonious to assume that 'atypical' cases have always been under the noses of clinical researchers, but that they have been ignored (or explicitly rejected from consideration) because they failed to fit our criteria.

MODELS OF BULIMIC DISORDERS

There are many formulations of bulimia nervosa and of bulimic behaviours (e.g., Cooper *et al.*, 2000; Fairburn, 1997; Fairburn *et al.*, 2003; Heatherton & Baumeister, 1991; McManus & Waller, 1995). The most explicit (and hence testable) are those based in the cognitive behavioural model. While they vary in focus and some specifics of content, these formulations have the common theme of being based in the 'hot-cross bun' model that underpins cognitive behavioural therapy. Figure 4.1 shows that model, with some examples of the cognitive, emotional, physiological and behavioural elements that contribute to individual case formulations. Each of these elements merits consideration, although it is also important to consider the broader domains of motivation (e.g., Geller, 2002) and interpersonal/social issues (e.g., Steiger *et al.*, 1999), which are relevant to all of these elements. Formulating the individual case (and hence planning treatment and evaluating outcome) requires that the clinician helps the patient to understand the role of each of these elements, and their interaction.

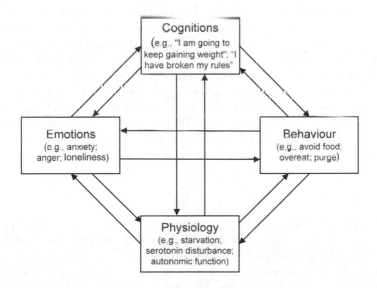

Figure 4.1 The CBT 'hot-cross bun' applied to eating disorders

Cognitions

The central cognitions in the eating disorders are overvalued ideas about the importance of controlling body, shape and weight (e.g., Fairburn *et al.*, 2003). While these beliefs are often presented as fear of weight gain, it is important to understand that they are more fundamentally a fear of weight gain *that is out of control*. (If the patient needs to gain weight to get to a physically stable state, the patient needs to understand that weight gain is necessary but that it can be controlled and stopped at a level that is compatible with the patient being safe and functional.) These beliefs drive negative self-perceptions and emotions, with their behavioural consequences (e.g., restricting intake because one believes that one is huge; binge eating to reduce negative emotional states). These behaviours are often safety behaviours, reducing short-term anxiety but resulting in worse outcomes in the longer term. However, it is also important to consider that there are relevant cognitions at a 'meta' level, such as beliefs about the unacceptability of emotional experience (e.g., Corstorphine, 2006), negative attributional biases (e.g., Morrison *et al.*, 2006), thinking biases (e.g., black and white thinking), and beliefs about the 'permissibility' of binge eating (e.g., Cooper *et al.*, 2000). There is also substantial evidence that patients with bulimic disorders have relatively pathological core beliefs (unconditional, schema-level thought patterns) and maintaining cognitive processes (e.g., Cooper, 1997, 2005; Waller *et al.*, 2007a). Each of these levels of cognition needs to be considered when formulating the individual case.

Emotions

While the literature on emotional states in bulimia nervosa stresses comorbidity with depressive states, depression can best be seen as a consequence of the eating disorders (due to physiological mechanisms, reduction in behavioural activation and reduction in positive reinforcement).There is stronger evidence that bulimic behaviours are triggered by other emotional states – particularly anxiety, loneliness and anger (e.g., Meyer *et al.*, 1998). These emotions can be driven by schema-level cognitions regarding the self, others and the world, as well as being consequences of the eating behaviours (e.g., anxiety regarding having overeaten). The bulimic behaviours are maintained because in the short term they reduce the impact of the immediate, intolerable emotional state, even though they result in longer term deterioration in self-esteem and mood.

Physiology

Bulimic eating behaviours have a number of physiological consequences, which enhance the risk of mortality and which worsen the individual's emotional and cognitive status. At the immediate level, purging behaviours can cause both mechanical damage (e.g., tears in the oesophagus) and imbalance in electrolytes (leading to cardiac problems, fits, etc.). However, the lack of balance in dietary intake also has important consequences. Most importantly, starvation and avoidance of carbohydrates can lead to imbalance in levels of serotonin, resulting in mood instability and depression. Good medical assessment and support is critical in such cases (e.g., Birmingham & Beumont, 2004; Kaplan & Garfinkel, 1993), and should never be overlooked.

Behaviours

The behaviours that typify bulimia nervosa and atypical bulimic cases are binge eating, purging (vomiting, taking laxatives, diuretics and diet pills) and other compensatory behaviours (restriction of intake, exercise). In addition to these bulimic behaviours, many patients engage in behaviours relating to body shape and acceptability. It is always important to consider the role of body checking, avoidance and comparison, along with the underlying cognitions (Mountford *et al.*, 2006; Reas *et al.*, 2002). Each of these can maintain the other eating behaviours.

It is important to enumerate these behaviours, as well as the disorder as a whole, so that the patient can be assisted to identify risk factors and to take action to avoid using the maladaptive behaviour. A useful method is the 'Newton's cradle' approach, where the chain of triggers, cognitions, emotions and behaviours can be established, and where the patient can be helped to consider alternatives to simply going along with the behaviour once the chain has been initiated (Waller *et al.*, 2007). However, where possible, it is more effective to identify factors that indicate a risk, so that the patient can intervene before the chain is initiated.

The risk factors are likely to be a combination of starvation, high levels of intolerable emotion, disinhibition (e.g., due to alcohol consumption) and exposure to food cues. The risks due to starvation and emotional arousal are the strongest, and the combination of the two is particularly potent. The other two factors make the behaviours more likely to have an impact, though they are less likely to trigger a bulimic behaviour in isolation. Figure 4.2 shows how these factors can be presented to the patient in a simple diagrammatic form.

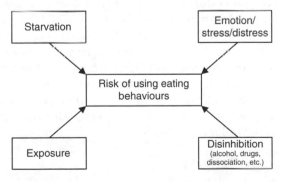

Figure 4.2 Risk factors for bulimic behaviours

TREATMENT OF BULIMIC DISORDERS

As with all eating disorders, the first issue to consider is the level of physical risk. Once the clinician is sure that the patient is physically stable and aware of the risks that the behaviours involve, it is possible to start the more psychotherapeutic work. That begins with ensuring that the patient is motivated to change. While such motivation is often better among bulimic patients than among anorexics, it should not be assumed that the patient and clinician have common goals in treatment, as the patient is likely to see more positive aspects to the bulimia than the clinician (e.g., Serpell & Treasure, 2002). The clinician stance is critical here (Geller *et al.*, 2001), since the clinician and patient need to work 'shoulder to shoulder', rather than 'head to head'. The patient needs to take on the role of therapist as soon as possible, guiding their own therapy between sessions, as 168-hour-a-week therapy is more likely to be effective than 1-hour-a-week therapy. The most useful single question for the clinician to ask is: 'How are we going to solve this?', rather than assuming that he or she can make the patient change or that the patient has sole responsibility for that change. The tools of motivational work are the same as those used in other eating disorders, such as motivational letters and pros and cons lists. As with all such cases, the use of a genuinely Socratic approach is vital if the patient is not to feel pushed into change.

Therapy Types

The effectiveness of specific treatments for the eating disorders has been reviewed in detail elsewhere (e.g., Berkman *et al.*, 2006; National Institute for Clinical Excellence, 2004; Fairburn & Harrison, 2003). Several treatments are worth considering when working with bulimia nervosa and atypical bulimic disorders. There is some evidence that antidepressant medication (especially fluoxetine) can reduce the symptoms, at least in the short term (e.g., Johnson *et al.*, 1996). However, the strongest evidence is with the psychological therapies. These include interpersonal psychotherapy (e.g., Fairburn *et al.*, 1995), dialectical behaviour therapy (e.g., Safer *et al.*, 2001), and structured, short-term focal psychotherapy with a behavioural element (Murphy *et al.*, 2005). However, the most powerful, fast-acting psychological therapy for the bulimic disorders is cognitive behavioural therapy (CBT) (Ghaderi, 2006; Waller *et al.*, 2005; Agras *et al.*, 2000; Fairburn *et al.*, 1995). This is an approach that focuses on the modification of cognitions, emotions and behaviours in parallel (while also focusing on physiological factors) based on the models of eating disorders and behaviours that are outlined above. This approach is detailed in existing CBT protocols based on models of the disorders (e.g., Fairburn *et al.*, 1993) and in therapies that are based on more individual formulations (e.g., Ghaderi, 2006; Waller *et al.*, 2007).

Format of Therapy Delivery

While most psychological therapies for the eating disorders are delivered in an individual, face-to-face setting, there is also evidence that other treatment formats can result in positive outcomes for bulimic disorders, although usually with lower levels of effectiveness than individual approaches. These include group work (e.g., Chen *et al.*, 2003; Leung *et al.*, 2000), guided self-help (Perkins *et al.*, 2006; Schmidt & Treasure, 1993), and new technologies such as the internet, computers and text messages (e.g., Robinson *et al.*, 2006). However, the majority of evidence regarding these different formats comes from CBT research, and it is unclear how these different formats would impact on other therapies.

Working with Comorbid Psychiatric Conditions

Many patients present with comorbid Axis I states (e.g., anxiety, depression, obsessive compulsive disorder, substance use) or Axis II states (e.g., borderline personality disorder, avoidant personality disorder) (e.g., van Hanswijck de Jonge *et al.*, 2003; Bulik, 2002). It is important to consider how to work with those states, using existing evidence-based methods. There is guidance about how to work with these disorders when they are comorbid with the eating disorders (e.g., Waller *et al.*, 2007; Hinrichsen & Waller, 2006). Critical issues are the development of an individual formulation (that determines whether the comorbid disorders are distinct or whether they have common roots or maintaining factors) and the associated planning and execution of a treatment programme, addressing the problems in parallel or in sequence.

CONCLUSIONS: THE FUTURE OF WORK WITH BULIMIC DISORDERS

Our understanding and treatment of the bulimic disorders has advanced substantially in the past three decades. Those advances have outstripped progress in the field of anorexia nervosa. However, there is still much to do, given that many patients still fail to benefit from any of the existing treatments that are on offer. Such developments are likely to take place within the framework of transdiagnostic and behaviour-oriented biopsychosocial models. The targets must be to continue to work on improving treatment outcomes and on making the transition from decent results in research settings to comparable results in routine clinical settings.

REFERENCES

Agras, W.S., Walsh, B.T., Fairburn, C.G. *et al.* (2000). A multicenter comparison of cognitive-behavioural therapy and interpersonal psychotherapy for bulimia nervosa. *Archives of General Psychiatry*, **57**, 459–66.

American Psychiatric Association (1980). *Diagnostic and Statistical Manual of Mental Disorders*, 3rd edition. Washington, DC: American Psychiatric Association.

American Psychiatric Association (1987). *Diagnostic and Statistical Manual of Mental Disorders*, 3rd edition – revised. Washington, DC: American Psychiatric Association.

American Psychiatric Association (1994). *Diagnostic and Statistical Manual of Mental Disorders*, 4th edition. Washington, DC: American Psychiatric Association.

Berkman, N.D., Bulik, C.M., Brownley, K.A. *et al.* (2006). *Management of Eating Disorders. Evidence Report/Technology Assessment No. 135. AHRQ Publication No. 06-E010.* Rockville, MD: Agency for Healthcare Research and Quality.

Birmingham, C.L. & Beumont, P.J.V. (2004). *Medical Management of Eating Disorders: A Practical Handbook for Healthcare Professionals.* Cambridge: Cambridge University Press.

Bulik, C.M. (2002). Anxiety, depression and eating disorders. In C.G. Fairburn & K.D. Brownell (eds), *Eating Disorders and Obesity: A Comprehensive Handbook*, 2nd edition (pp. 193–8). London: Guilford Press.

Chen, E., Touyz, S.W., Beumont, P.J. *et al.* (2003). Comparison of group and individual cognitive-behavioral therapy for patients with bulimia nervosa. *International Journal of Eating Disorders*, **33**, 241–54.

Cooper, M.J. (1997). Cognitive theory in anorexia nervosa and bulimia nervosa: a review. *Behavioural and Cognitive Psychotherapy*, **25**, 113–45.

Cooper, M.J. (2005). Cognitive theory in anorexia nervosa and bulimia nervosa: progress, development and future directions. *Clinical Psychology Review*, **25**, 511–31.

Cooper, M.J., Wells, A. & Todd, G. (2000). A cognitive model of bulimia nervosa. *British Journal of Clinical Psychology*, **43**, 1–16.

Corstorphine, E. (2006). Cognitive-emotional-behavioural therapy for the eating disorders: Working with beliefs about emotions. *European Eating Disorders Review*, **14**, 448–61.

Currin, L., Schmidt, U., Treasure, J. & Jick, H. (2005). Time trends in eating disorder incidence. *British Journal of Psychiatry*, **186**, 132–5.

Fairburn, C.G. (1997). Eating disorders. In D.M. Clark, & C.G. Fairburn (eds), *Science and Practice of Cognitive Behaviour Therapy* (pp. 209–38). Oxford: Oxford University Press.

Fairburn, C.G., Bohn, K., Cooper, Z. *et al.* (2005). Addressing the diagnosis of ED-NOS: the impact of adjusting the diagnostic criteria for anorexia nervosa and bulimia nervosa. Paper presented at the Eating Disorders Research Society Meeting, Toronto, Canada, September.

Fairburn, C.G., Cooper, Z. & Shafran, R. (2003). Cognitive behaviour therapy for eating disorders: A 'transdiagnostic' theory and treatment. *Behaviour Research and Therapy*, **41**, 509–28.

Fairburn, C.G. & Harrison, P. J. (2003). Eating disorders. *Lancet*, **361**, 407–16.

Fairburn, C.G., Marcus, M. & Wilson, G.T. (1993). Cognitive-behavioural therapy for binge-eating and bulimia nervosa: a comprehensive treatment manual. In C.G. Fairburn & G.T. Wilson (eds), *Binge-Eating: Nature, Assessment and Treatment* (pp. 361–404). New York: Guilford Press.

Fairburn, C.G., Norman, P.A., Welch, S.L. *et al.* (1995). A prospective study of outcome in bulimia nervosa and the long-term effects of three psychological treatments. *Archives of General Psychiatry*, **52**, 304–12.

Fombonne, E. (1995). Anorexia nervosa. No evidence of an increase. *British Journal of Psychiatry*, **166**, 462–71.

Fombonne, E. (1996). Is bulimia nervosa increasing in frequency? *International Journal of Eating Disorders*, **19**, 287–96.

Geller, J. (2002). What a motivational approach is and what a motivational approach isn't: reflections and responses. *European Eating Disorders Review*, **10**, 155–60.

Geller, J., Williams, K.D. & Srikameswaran, S. (2001). Clinician stance in the treatment of chronic eating disorders. *European Eating Disorders Review*, **9**, 374–80.

Ghaderi, A. (2006). Does individualization matter? A randomized trial of standardized (focused) versus individualized (broad) cognitive behavior therapy for bulimia nervosa. *Behaviour Research and Therapy*, **44**, 273–88.

Heatherton T.F. & Baumeister, R.F. (1991). Binge eating as escape from self-awareness. *Psychological Bulletin*, **110**, 86–108.

Hinrichsen, H. & Waller, G. (2006). The treatment of avoidant personality disorder in patients with eating disorders. In R.A. Sansone & J.L. Levitt (eds), *Personality Disorders and Eating Disorders: Exploring the Frontier* (pp. 213–30). New York: Routledge.

Hoek, H.W. (2002). Distribution of eating disorders. In C.G. Fairburn & K.D. Brownell (eds), *Eating Disorders and Obesity: A Comprehensive Handbook*, 2nd edition (pp. 233–7). New York: Guilford Press.

Johnson, W.G., Tsoh, J.Y. & Varnado, P.J. (1996). Eating disorders: efficacy of pharmacological and psychological interventions. *Clinical Psychology Review*, **16**, 457–78.

Kaplan, A.S. & Garfinkel, P.E. (1993). *Medical Issues and the Eating Disorders: The Interface*. Levittown, PA: Brunner/Mazel.

Lawrence, B., Campbell, M., Neiderman, M. & Serpell, L. (2003). Size really doesn't matter. *European Eating Disorders Review*, **11**, 397–404.

Leung, N., Waller, G. & Thomas, G. (2000). Outcome of group cognitive-behaviour therapy for bulimia nervosa: the role of core beliefs. *Behaviour Research and Therapy*, **38**, 145–56.

McManus, F. & Waller, G. (1995). A functional analysis of binge-eating. *Clinical Psychology Review*, **15**, 345–63.

Meyer, C., Waller, G. & Waters, A. (1998). Emotional states and bulimic psychopathology. In H. Hoek, M. Katzman & J. Treasure (eds), *The Neurobiological Basis of Eating Disorders* (pp. 271–89). Chichester: John Wiley & Sons, Ltd.

Morrison, T., Waller, G. & Lawson, R. (2006) Attributional style in the eating disorders. *Journal of Nervous and Mental Disease*, **194**, 303–5.

Mountford, V., Haase, A.M. & Waller, G. (2006). Body checking in the eating disorders: Associations between cognitions and behaviours. *International Journal of Eating Disorders*, **39**, 708–15.

Murphy, S., Russell, L. & Waller, G. (2005). Integrated psychodynamic therapy for bulimia nervosa and binge eating disorder: theory, practice and preliminary findings. *European Eating Disorders Review*, **13**, 383–91.

National Institute for Clinical Excellence (2004). *Eating Disorders: Core Interventions in the Treatment and Management of Anorexia Nervosa, Bulimia Nervosa and Related Eating Disorders. Clinical Guideline 9*. London: National Collaborating Centre for Mental Health.

Perkins, S.J., Murphy, R., Schmidt, U. & Williams, C. (2006). Self-help and guided self-help for eating disorders. *Cochrane Database Systematic Review*, **19** (3:CD004191).

Reas, D.L., Whisenhunt, B.L., Netemeyer, R. & Williamson, D.A. (2002). Development of the body checking questionnaire: a self-report measure of body checking behaviours. *International Journal of Eating Disorders*, **31**, 324–33.

Robinson, S., Perkins, S., Bauer, S. *et al.* (2006). Aftercare intervention through text messaging in the treatment of bulimia nervosa: Feasibility pilot. *International Journal of Eating Disorders*, **39**, 533–8.

Russell, G.F.M. (1979). Bulimia nervosa: an ominous variant of anorexia nervosa. *Psychological Medicine*, **9**, 429–48.

Safer, D.L., Telch, C.F. & Agras, W.S. (2001). Dialectical behavior therapy for bulimia nervosa. *American Journal of Psychiatry*, **158**, 632–4.

Schmidt, U. & Treasure, J. (1993). *Getting Better Bit(e) by Bit(e): Survival Kit for Sufferers of Bulimia Nervosa and Binge Eating Disorders*. Hove: Psychology Press.

Serpell, L. & Treasure, J. (2002). Bulimia nervosa: friend or foe? The pros and cons of anorexia nervosa. *International Journal of Eating Disorders*, **32**, 164–70.

Steiger, H., Gauvin, L., Jabalpurwala, S. *et al.* (1999). Hypersensitivity to social interactions in bulimic syndromes: relationship to binge eating. *Journal of Consulting and Clinical Psychology*, **67**, 765–75.

Turner, H. & Bryant-Waugh, R. (2004). Eating disorder not otherwise specified (EDNOS): profiles of patients presenting at a community eating disorder service. *European Eating Disorders Review*, **12**, 18–26.

van Hanswijck de Jonge, P., van Furth E.F., Lacey, J.H. & Waller, G. (2003). The prevalence of DSM-IV personality pathology among individuals with bulimia nervosa, binge eating disorder and obesity. *Psychological Medicine*, **33**, 1311–17.

Waller, G. (1993). Why do we diagnose different types of eating disorder? Arguments for a change in research and clinical practice. *Eating Disorders Review*, **1**, 74–89.

Waller, G. (2005). Psychological perspectives on atypical diagnoses in the eating disorders. In C. Norring & R. Palmer (eds), *EDNOS: Eating Disorders Not Otherwise Specified*. London: Routledge.

Waller, G., Cordery, H., Corstorphine, E. *et al.* (2007). *Cognitive-Behavioral Therapy for the Eating Disorders: A Comprehensive Treatment Guide*. Cambridge: Cambridge University Press.

Waller, G., Kennerley, H. & Ohanian, V. (2007a). Schema-focused cognitive behavioral therapy with eating disorders. In L.P. Riso, P.L. du Toit, D.J. Stein & J.E. Young (eds), *Cognitive Schemas and Core Beliefs in Psychiatric Disorders: A Scientist-Practitioner Guide* (pp. 139–75). New York: American Psychological Association.

Waller, G., Patient, E., Corstorphine, E. *et al.* (2005). Cognitive behaviour therapy for bulimic disorders: Effectiveness in non-research settings. Paper presented at the Eating Disorders Research Society Meeting, Toronto, Canada, September.

World Health Organisation. (1992). *ICD-10 Classification of Mental and Behavioural Disorders: Clinical Descriptions and Diagnostic Guidelines*. Geneva: World Health Organisation.

CHAPTER 5

ADDRESSING EMOTIONS IN THE EATING DISORDERS: SCHEMA MODE WORK

EMMA CORSTORPHINE, *Institute of Psychiatry, UK*

Concerns about eating, shape and weight are central, for the majority of people with eating disorders, to the maintenance of their problem. However, for a significant number, these cognitions are not the pivotal maintaining factor of their behaviour. Instead, for this subgroup, emotions seem to be the key feature in the perpetuation of their eating problems. These people have been described as having difficulties in distress tolerance (Linehan, 1993), also labelled mood intolerance (Fairburn *et al.*, 2003) or affect regulation problems (Corstorphine, 2006). Distress tolerance is the ability to endure and accept negative affect, so that problem solving can take place (Linehan, 1993). Poor distress tolerance involves high emotional vulnerability in combination with an inability to regulate emotion through adaptive means. It is a common feature of disorders characterised by impulsivity, such as bulimic disorders and borderline personality disorder. Such impulsive behaviours (e.g., bingeing and purging, self-harm, alcohol misuse) serve the function of temporarily blocking out awareness of intolerable affect – a necessary coping strategy for those with poor distress tolerance.

Affect regulation difficulties can be understood as existing on a continuum of severity (see Figure 5.1; Corstorphine 2006). A number of existing psychological interventions (e.g., dialectical behavioural therapy – Linehan, 1993; cognitive-emotional-behavioural therapy – Corstorphine, 2006) enable individuals to improve their affect regulation, but only if they are able to acknowledge consciously their experience of those emotions. For people with more severe difficulties, these approaches seem less effective, principally because the 'raw' materials for the interventions (emotions) are unavailable. Those at the far end of the affect regulation spectrum seem to experience such high emotional vulnerability and poor emotion regulation that they dissociate from their emotions to the extent that they deny the existence of any feelings (e.g.,

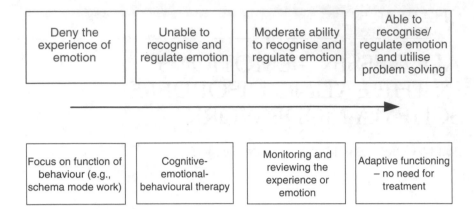

Figure 5.1 A continuum of affect regulation problems. The top row represents the level of function, the bottom row the level of intervention required
Source: Corstorphine, 2006

severe alexithymia, often manifesting as somatic features). This is a common feature of those presenting with multi-impulsive eating disorders (bulimia plus two additional impulsive behaviours, e.g., Fichter *et al.*, 1994). It may be useful to draw on aspects of Young *et al.*'s (2003) schema mode work in understanding and working with these people.

YOUNG'S SCHEMA MODE MODEL

A mode is the predominant state that we are in at a given point, and is made up of emotional states and coping responses that enable us to deal with our environment (Beck, 1996; Young *et al.*, 2003). We all flip from mode to mode over time depending upon our environment and interactions with others. For example, when at work we might engage a pragmatic, problem-solving mode that enables us to operate effectively in our surroundings. At home, we may flip into a more relaxed, emotional mode that allows us to interact with our family and enjoy our leisure time. Young *et al.* (2003) suggest that we all have the potential for a range of modes but our early experiences will determine the degree to which they are expressed.

Modes can be both adaptive and maladaptive, depending upon where on a spectrum of dissociation they lie (Young *et al.*, 2003). Where the level of dissociation is lower, the individual is able to experience simultaneously more than one mode. At work (and in work mode) a person may need to initiate a more emotional mode in order to show empathy for a colleague who is experiencing problems. Conversely, people may benefit from a shift into a pragmatic mode to resolve a problem while still feeling compassion towards the people they care for. At this end of the spectrum of dissociation the shift between modes is akin to the shift between moods, the process is more one of blending than of switching or replacing one state with another. At the other end of the continuum where the level of dissociation is higher, modes become increasingly cut off from one another; while experiencing one mode a person will find it difficult to consider that other modes exist. In dissociative identity disorder the different modes present themselves as separate personalities that are unaware of and/or have no memory of the others.

Young *et al.* (2003) use modes to differentiate between schemas as coping-related styles and traits (enduring, consistent patterns) and states (shifting patterns of activation and deactivation). They identify four sets of modes: the healthy adult mode, child modes, maladaptive parent modes and maladaptive coping modes. Together they represent the inborn emotional range of human beings. In early childhood the environment may suppress or enhance the development of these modes, but all human beings are born with the capacity to express all four. The mode that appears to be most relevant to those with affect regulation difficulties and therefore those with eating disorders (particular with multi-impulsive presentations) is the detached protector, one of the maladaptive coping modes.

THE DETACHED PROTECTOR

The detached protector is a maladaptive coping mode characterised by emotional withdrawal, disconnection, isolation and behavioural avoidance. It functions to shut off emotions in order to protect the individual from the pain of feeling. Young *et al.* (2003) describe it as a protective armour or wall behind which one or more of the other modes may hide. Within the eating disorders this mode seems most closely related to the alexithymic presentation of those with restrictive eating pathology, but also shares characteristics with the dissociative experiences described by those with bulimic pathology.

The concept of dissociation is helpful in understanding the detached protector mode: it provides a framework for understanding severity; when the level of dissociation is higher the problem is more severe as the detached protector is more cut off from the other parts of the self. Secondly, the concept of dissociation indicates the quality of this mode: dissociation is defined as the 'failure to process information that would normally be perceived in an integrated way (e.g. amnesia, depersonalisation) (Spiegal *et al.*, 1996). When in this mode patients report an inability to think, feel or behave in a clear or comprehensive way; instead their experiences are fragmented, 'woolly' or 'cloudy'. Finally, dissociation reflects the function that the detached protector serves. Dissociation enables the patient to escape from the awareness of intolerable experiences; the detached protector functions to cut off emotions, to act as a defence against intolerable feelings.

This mode of experience shares striking similarities to the instinctive freeze to a traumatic response often seen in those with post-traumatic stress event disorder (PTSD) (e.g. Rothschild, 1995). The altered sense of time, reduced sensations of pain and strong emotions that define the freeze reflex triggered in the absence of alternative coping strategies (e.g. fight or flight) have been described as a form of dissociation whereby the individual appears to enter an alternative state of reality and may be a predictor of PTSD (e.g. Bremmer *et al.*, 1992). The freeze reflex, like the detached protector, is a coping strategy intended to increase chances of survival (e.g. if the cause of the freeze is an attack, the attacker may lose interest when the prey appears lifeless) but when triggered outside the environment in which it was intended to function, exacts a high price.

Manifestations of the Detached Protector

Patients have described their experience of the detached protector in a number of ways that cluster in two groups, distinguished by the level of awareness at which the mode is activated. The first represents those for whom the detached protector mode is initiated as a preventive strategy, in anticipation of the experience of affect, or before the emotion has reached a conscious level of awareness. This has been described by Waller *et al.* (2007) as primary avoidance of affect. In our work, the detached protector has been described by patients as a 'bubble' protecting the individual from, or filtering out, emotional experience. The experience of the detached protector at this level has also been described as 'feeling like you are existing just as a brain' only able to connect to very intellectualised perspectives and striving to seek these out. Other patients describe the detached protector as a sheet of polythene that covers you from head to toe, or a large iron door that always remains bolted. Common to these patients is the experience of feeling 'zombified' and a wish to 'transcend emotions'. To this end, Sophie, a patient with a long history of emotional abuse, eating disordered pathology and self-harm, described a lifelong and ongoing quest to immerse herself in academia and philosophical thought and at university sought out courses that would enable her to develop this skill in preference to courses that she actually felt she would enjoy. The detached protector operating at this level, described frequently as alexithymic, is most often seen in those presenting with restrictive eating pathology.

The second cluster involves a detached protector mode that is triggered by the conscious experience of emotion, once it has reached an overwhelming level, a reactive strategy. This has been described by Waller *et al.* (2007) as secondary avoidance of affect. Here patients described the mode as a meat cleaver that is swung and severs the emotion; a surge of water that sweeps it away; or a blanket that smothers it. The detached protector operating at this level is most commonly seen in those patients presenting with bulimic and/or multi-impulsive pathology. It is important to note that the detached protector can exist at both levels of affective avoidance within one individual, with circumstances determining which type is engaged. If people can anticipate

Table 5.1 The detached protector

Detached protector thoughts	Detached protector feelings	Detached protector behaviours
I don't want to feel anything	Empty	Impulsive/compulsive behaviours
If I let myself feel my emotions I will lose control	Numb	Social withdrawal
I don't want to think about my problems because they upset me	Spacey	Excessive self-reliance
I feel like taking drugs/alcohol/bingeing to numb my feelings	Flat	Restriction and bingeing

the occurrence of negative affect they can prepare by activating the bubble (primary level of affective avoidance). However, this may not be possible and they will then have to rely on the meat cleaver (secondary level of affective avoidance). This pattern is commonly seen in those presenting with anorexia nervosa binge-purge subtype.

Drawing on the Patient's Reports

Table 5.1 describes the detached protector using the components of a traditional cognitive behavioural framework: thoughts, feelings and behaviours.

Origins of the Detached Protector

Young *et al.* (2003) suggest that the detached protector can be understood as the young child's attempt to adapt to living with unmet emotional needs in a harmful environment where it made sense to detach and not feel. However, although adaptive for the young child, in the wider adult world where the optimum strategy is to attend and respond to emotions, this mode becomes maladaptive.

A concept that seems particularly important to the development of the detached protector is the Invalidating Environment (Linehan, 1993). This is described as an environment in which the communication of emotion is ignored or responded to negatively and is typified in the following clinical examples of family responses to expressions of distress (Corstorphine 2006):

- 'If you can't show a happy face, don't show a face at all'
- 'Shut your temper in a drawer, I don't want to see it'
- 'Put your feelings in a bubble and let them float away forever'
- The expectation that an individual should sit an exam on the afternoon of her mother's death

Here the child receives the message that emotions are unnecessary, unhelpful, unimportant or worse still bad, risky or harmful. Instead of developing the ability to recognise, tolerate, accept and respond to emotions so that they can use them to navigate through their experiences, the child becomes skilled at blocking them out or dissociating from them, leaving them without a core part of a repertoire necessary to understand and interact with themselves, others and the world.

Formulating the Problem

Figure 5.2 shows a framework which can be used to develop an individualised formulation of how the detached protector interacts with the core eating pathology. It shows the detached protector operating at both levels of affective avoidance (primary and secondary) along with its hypothesised origins. It also highlights the temporary nature of its effect. In the longer term, the use of the detached protector reinforces the negative core belief that it has been developed to block; in the wider adult world in order to interact effectively we need to experience our emotions. The detached protector mode (primary level of avoidance e.g. through food restriction) may be used to protect people from the pain that is generated by the core belief that ultimately they will be left completely alone (abandonment). However, without awareness of their emotions – important indicators of how to react and interact with others – people will find it hard to form appropriate and secure attachments. The belief that they will be alone becomes a self-fulfilling prophecy that finds

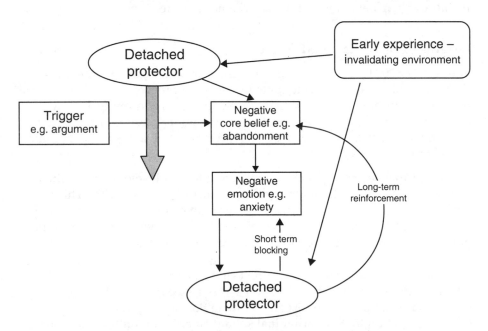

Figure 5.2 Framework for detached protector formulation

them alone. Someone using the detached protector at the secondary level of avoidance (e.g. through bingeing and purging) to protect from the distress created by a core belief of defectiveness, will experience some temporarily relief, but over a longer period the sense of defectiveness will be fuelled by the shame and guilt associated with their bulimic behaviour.

IMPLICATIONS FOR THERAPEUTIC INTERVENTIONS

Before looking in detail at the intervention itself, this section will consider why working with the detached protector may be necessary and when it may be appropriate to utilise such an approach.

Why Work with the Detached Protector?

The detached protector prevents access to the negative core beliefs that are maintaining the problem. For this reason it can be understood as a 'therapy interfering behaviour' (Linehan, 1993). Clinically, what is observed are patients who are inaccessible in sessions: they do not arrive, are late, or arrive and dissociate/zone out, or report having 'nothing to say'. They also struggle to complete homework assignments that require reflection on their internal experiences. Sophie's thought diary, for example, despite frequent and detailed discussion of its purpose and instruction as to how she should record her experiences, contained no record of her thoughts or feelings but instead was filled with brief, matter of fact descriptions or lists of what she had done that day. Sessions can also feel very flat and half-hearted and clinicians can be left feeling that their patients can't really be bothered and will soon disengage from treatment.

Addressing the detached protector also modifies the risk of behaviour substitution in this patient group (Coker *et al.*, 1993). If an emotion-blocking behaviour is addressed (or partially addressed) without consideration of its links to the detached protector, an alternative and equally maladaptive blocking behaviour will be substituted in its place. Although through the use of cognitive behavioural therapy a reduction was observed in Sophie's bingeing, for example, a gradual increase was seen in her impulsive self-harm. Behaviour substitution occurs when the detached protector is positively reinforcing in the short term and so prevents the development of more adaptive coping strategies, when one of its manifestations is removed. Unless the source is addressed, another develops in its place.

When to Work with the Detached Protector

In line with the current evidence base it is likely that a clinician may choose a disorder-specific treatment when working with a patient to address their eating disorder (e.g. cognitive behavioural therapy for bulimia nervosa).

However, if this patient has affect regulation problems these will interfere with the implementation of such interventions and consideration of alternative methods to address these, guided by a reformulation of the problem, may be necessary.

The detached protector can be seen as sitting at the far end of a continuum of affect regulation ability (see Figure 5.1). At the other end of this continuum are those individuals who are able to tolerate their emotions and so then attend and respond adaptively to them. Some people can reach an adaptive level of functioning via the process of monitoring their experience of emotions through the use of a diary and reviewing this with a clinician, in conjunction with some behaviour techniques to enhance their tolerance of emotions (e.g. dialectical behavioural therapy, Linehan, 1993). It can be helpful for those with moderate difficulties who are connected to their experience of emotions, but struggle with their expression (as a result of beliefs that emotions are risky or dangerous) to work to restructure these beliefs (e.g. via cognitive-emotional-behavioural therapy, Corstorphine, 2006).

Working with the detached protector becomes necessary when patients' affect regulation problems make it feel too dangerous for them to connect with their emotions in any way other than an intellectualised one. They can give an intellectualised description of emotions and their function but experientially have little or no knowledge of emotions. These patients often present in a cold and aloof way, offering matter of fact reports of extremely distressing material. They can often be dismissive of therapy and its relevance to them, Sophie commented, 'Yeah but that touchy-feely stuff just doesn't really resonate with me'. They will consistently endeavour to bring discussions back to an intellectual or practical level and appear baffled and sometimes annoyed if asked to reflect on their feelings. It is also not uncommon for the experience of certain emotions to be denied. Sophie was adamant that 'I just don't get angry. I guess genetically I don't have the capacity for it'.

INTERVENTION

The key aim of the intervention is to negotiate with the detached protector to stand back and allow the patient access to thoughts and feelings, so that specific eating disorder treatments can be utilised. This aim is achieved through a series of steps that will be outlined below:

- identification
- formulation
- objectification
- monitoring
- construction of a development pathway
- negotiation
- counteracting

Identification

The nature of the detached protector makes this seemingly straightforward initial task both essential and extremely challenging. The goal is to identify a vacuum where experience does not exist; to introduce awareness into a place that has been constructed for the sole purpose of escaping awareness. Clinicians will need to rely heavily on their own experience and reactions to the patient to guide them in this work dealing with the reduced experiential awareness of the patient. Questionnaires (e.g. Distress Tolerance Scale, Corstorphine *et al.*, 2006; Schema Mode Questionnaire, Young *et al.*, 2003) can be useful at this stage as they provide a framework on which to hang early discussions. Their tangible structure also seems to ground the work. Throughout the intervention, but particularly in these early stages, it is also important to discuss explicitly the challenges that this work presents. This will normalise what can be for the patient, an extremely frustrating process. Sophie referred to it as 'trying to get hold of emptiness'.

Formulation

The next step is to develop collaboratively a formulation of the detached protector and how it interacts with the core eating pathology, using the framework outlined in Figure 5.2. The aim of this phase is to communicate the idea that the detached protector is an innate coping strategy that has become overdeveloped as an adaptive response to early experiences. With time, as the environment and choices have shifted, it has become unhelpful, getting in the way of how life can be. The formulation also plays an important role in building and consolidating the patient's motivation to modify the influence of the detached protector. It is important to bear in mind that these patients are being asked to work towards getting in touch with their distress, the very thing that for so long they have being trying to avoid. They will therefore need a clear and robust rationale for doing this, which only a formulation that resonates with their experience can provide.

Objectification

This technique involves patients working to develop an image of the detached protector as an entity separate from themselves, complete with physical and psychological characteristics. This technique has been described elsewhere in the eating disorders literature (e.g. Mountford & Waller, 2006) as a way of facilitating cognitive behavioural therapy (CBT). Objectification encourages the individual to step back and gain some distance from the problem, which enables them to identify and monitor it from a different perspective. This in turn facilitates a reduction in the ego syntonic nature of the problem and increases awareness of its maladaptive aspects. This is similar to the process of decentring, a technique used in mindfulness-based treatments (e.g. Segal *et al.*, 2002). The individual is encouraged to practise intentionally disengaging from one mode of mind and engaging with another. It shares some features with the cognitive therapy technique of metacognitive monitoring, seeing thoughts as thoughts.

However, when using this technique with the detached protector mode, a note of caution should be sounded. Objectification relies on the person developing the skills to separate or distance themselves from the problem. This process has the potential to exacerbate the dissociative tendencies of the detached protector, unless patients are supported to remain connected to their experience. This can be done at the outset by acknowledging that the detached protector is a functional part of the mind and that objectification is merely a technique to facilitate a better understanding of it. It is also achieved through the ongoing monitoring of the status of the connection.

Another danger of working in this way is the risk that a technique that aims to separate an aspect of the self from the self, can be perceived by the patient as a criticism because of the ego syntonic nature of the problem. This has implications for the therapeutic alliance and the patient's motivation to engage in the work. It highlights further the need for a carefully and collaboratively constructed formulation and a clear explanation of the rationale behind the use of this technique. Strategies for how to facilitate the process of objectification and clinical examples of how the detached protector has been objectified are given below.

Strategies for objectification

Following a clear communication and discussion of the rationale:

1. Get a physical description of the detached protector, for example how it would appear in a cartoon. Include details about height, build, skin colour and other aspects of form.
2. Ask the patient to describe other characteristics, for example tone of voice, gait, posture.
3. Locate the mode, for example where does it reside – beside, behind, in front of the patient?
4. List typical detached protector thoughts, feelings and behaviours. It may not always be possible at this stage to be specific about all aspects of the detached protector and so patients may have to construct a hypothetical list. Alternatively, they can identify the traces or footprints that it leaves, that is those experiences that suggest to patients that the detached protector has been triggered, for example urges to binge or self-harm.

Clinical example

Sophie described her detached protector as an Ice Man, eight foot, thick set and built entirely of ice. He didn't speak but moaned in a monotonous tone drowning out all other experience. He 'lumbered' along, swinging his muscular arms and batting away any distressing thought and feelings. He walked in front of her, clearing her path of experiences. She knew when he was there because she noticed a complete lack of thoughts, as if she were in a trance, felt cold, numb and behaved in a mechanical way, completing tasks automatically as if she had been pre-programmed to do so.

Monitoring

The nature of the detached protector makes this a difficult but essential task. The aim is to bring it into conscious awareness so its function on a daily basis can be observed and better understood. Monitoring is both a means to an end (modification) and an end in itself (monitoring begins the process of modification by raising awareness, the antidote to this mode). As the detached protector exists in an 'awareness-free' vacuum it may be necessary initially to track it by the traces it leaves. It is then helpful to move on to daily monitoring, beginning by asking the patient to rate the intensity of the detached protector across the day (e.g. on a scale of 1 to 10) and then refining this process by using the examples shown in Table 5.2.

Another helpful strategy adapted from mindfulness-based approaches, cultivates a focus in the present moment as a way of reducing the tendency towards mindless automatic behaviour, which increases our vulnerability to problems such as depression and anxiety. It is an exercise which encourages an awareness of the differences between various experiences and an acceptance of them as such. It enables the patient to become aware of the detached protector and observe it in the absence of any pressure to modify it in any way – an ideal environment for understanding and learning more about it.

The best way to clarify what this skill involves is to facilitate the patient's experience of it through practice of the exercise itself.

Table 5.2 Refining the monitoring process

Date	Situation	DP thoughts	DP feelings	DP behaviours	Function
12.03.07	At home	I can't cope with these feelings	Numb, empty	Bingeing and vomiting	To protect me from thinking about the arguments I had with my boyfriend this week

Conveyor belt exercise

I want you to close your eyes and imagine your mind as a conveyor belt. Now I want you to imagine standing beside the conveyor belt. Start the conveyor belt running. Now I want you to imagine that as thoughts pop into your mind or as you become aware of feelings, they appear on the conveyor belt and as they do I want you to watch them roll past you. Do not engage with them, do not jump on to the conveyor belt and follow them; just allow them to continue past you, turning your attention to what is coming next. Maybe you have a thought about this exercise, 'Am I doing this right?' or, 'What is the purpose of this?' or a feeling of anxiety or discomfort.

Now I want you to imagine a box placed at the side of the conveyor belt labelled 'detached protector'. As your thoughts and feelings pass you I want you to remove any of those you suspect are part of your detached protector mode and place them in the box. Remember, the aim is just to sort the detached protector thoughts and feelings and place them into the box, nothing more. There is no need to judge your thoughts and feelings as good or bad; just describe them and place them into the box. If you notice your mind wandering I want you to place the thought or feeling that led you away on to the conveyor belt and continue the exercise, noting that it is perfectly natural for your mind to wander in this way.

This exercise should be continued in this way for approximately five minutes allowing ample time for the patient to become aware of her experience of the detached protector and to remain connected with it long enough to learn more about the way that it functions. Initially the conveyor belt should be introduced and practised in the session when the patient or clinician suspects that the detached protector has been triggered. When the patients feel confident and comfortable with it they should be encouraged to set aside five minutes each day to practise the technique. This encourages them to develop a greater level of awareness on a day-to-day basis and provides a regular opportunity for monitoring of the mode. It is important to remember and to discuss with the patient that although simple, this exercise will be challenging as it requires them to do the opposite of what the detached protector advocates. It may therefore be helpful to provide them with a tape of the above script to guide their practice and monitor their experience of this practice at each session.

Once the patient has become skilled at this technique they should be asked to practise it for a few minutes before they binge or purge (an easily identifiable detached protector behaviour). This is not intended to prevent the behaviour but to allow them to be more connected with their experience of it, which may with time interfere enough with the functioning of the detached protector to enable the patient to re-evaluate their choice to engage in the behaviour.

Construction of a Development Pathway

The patient should now have a good understanding of how and why the detached protector operates on a day-to-day basis. The aim of constructing a developmental pathway is to build upon the idea suggested by the formulation, that the detached protector is the result of an innate part of the self that has become overdeveloped as a result of early experience, combined with the in-built drive in all of us to survive. It involves a detailed review of the patient's life (usually divided into five-year periods to enhance focus on the various stages of development) in order to gather experiences that could have led to and reinforced the development of the detached protector. Once this is complete, a second review is undertaken with the aim of gathering experiences, which suggest that the detached protector is counterproductive. The result is usually a short list of experiences, clustered in early childhood, supporting the need for the detached protector; together with a long list of experiences, usually clustered in later life, suggesting that it is an unhelpful strategy. This data can then be used to consider the possibility that the detached protector was an appropriate and adaptive response to the early environment. However, as this environment has changed and as the patient has a greater ability to make life choices, this mode of interacting with the world is less helpful. This strategy is also a useful challenge to self-critical thoughts about the existence of the detached protector, for example 'Typical! Trust you to pick a coping strategy that is harmful!'.

Negotiation

Up until this point the main aim of the intervention has been to facilitate an awareness and understanding of the detached protector, thus developing the patient's motivation and confidence to modify its influence. The next step is to negotiate with the detached protector to move to one side so that the patient can access the thoughts and feelings that are triggering the maintenance of their eating disorder, thus allowing them to engage in an eating disorder specific treatment. The cognitive behavioural technique of cognitive restructuring can be used for this purpose. This technique has been described in detail elsewhere (e.g. Waller *et al.*, 2007) but in brief is a two-part strategy which enables the patient to evaluate the accuracy of cognitions that are triggering unhelpful emotions and behaviours with a view to modifying them if necessary. Part one involves cognitive challenging to loosen the patient's belief in the cognition. This will give the patient the confidence to engage in part two, behavioural experiments, which will provide the concrete evidence necessary to assess the validity of the cognition. The nature of the detached protector will make accessing thoughts related to it difficult in the initial stages. For this reason, this step of the intervention must follow those outlined above, if it is to be effective.

Counteracting

Mindfulness has been proposed elsewhere (e.g. Linehan, 1993; Waller *et al.*, 2007) as a useful affect regulation tool. It teaches an acute, but particular awareness of emotions that is in-the-moment, non-judgemental and single-minded. These skills enable individuals to make direct contact with their immediate experience while simultaneously achieving some distance from it. This is quite distinct from what happens when the detached protector is triggered and awareness is removed from experience. Mindfulness-based strategies may therefore offer an antidote for the detached protector by enhancing skills at the other end of a continuum of affect regulation. They could usefully be introduced to patients once their motivation and confidence to modify the detached protector has been consolidated (see Kabat-Zinn, 1990; Segal *et al.*, 2002; Waller *et al.*, 2007).

CONCLUSION

The detached protector is an ego syntonic and entrenched coping strategy whose defining feature is an absence of conscious awareness. To identify and modify this coping strategy is very challenging. Initially patients will be difficult to convince of the existence of the detached protector. They will then move through phases of frustration as they struggle to become aware of their experience of it and then become anxious about how they will tolerate their emotions in its absence. Clinicians' feelings are likely to mirror those of their patients. They will start with an initial doubt about the formulation of the detached protector as the obstacle that they are facing in treatment. This will be followed by frustration at the identification stage and then uncertainty about the patient's capacity to proceed without it. It is therefore vital that throughout the work, the patient and clinician use their collaboratively developed formulation as a guide to the intervention and reminder of the rationale behind it.

REFERENCES

Beck, A.T. (1996). Beyond belief: a theory of modes, personality and psychopathology. In P.M. Salkovaskis (ed.), *Frontiers of Cognitive Therapy*. New York: Guilford Press.

Bremmer, J.D., Southwick, S., Brett, E. *et al.* (1992). Dissociation and post-traumatic stress disorder in Vietnam combat veterans. *American Journal of Psychiatry*, **149**.

Coker, S., Vize, C., Wade, T. & Cooper, P. (1993). Patients with bulimia nervosa who fail to engage in cognitive behaviour therapy. *International Journal of Eating Disorders*, **13**, 35–40.

Corstorphine, E. (2006). Cognitive-emotional-behavioural therapy for the eating disorders: working with beliefs about emotions. *European Eating Disorders Review*, **14**,
462–7.

Corstorphine, E., Mountford, V., Tomlinson, S. *et al.* (2006). Distress tolerance in the
eating disorders. *Eating Behaviors*, **8**, 91–7.

Fairburn, C.G., Cooper, Z. & Shafran, R. (2003). Cognitive behaviour therapy for eating
disorders: a 'transdiagnostic' theory and treatment. *Behaviour Research and Therapy*,
41, 509–28.

Fichter, M., Quadfleig, N. & Reif, W. (1994). Course of multi-impulsive bulimia.
Psychological Medicine, **24**, 591–604.

Kabat-Zinn, J. (1990). *Full Catastrophe Living. How to Cope with Stress, Pain and Illness
Using Mindfulness Meditation*. New York: Dell Publishing.

Linehan, M. (1993). *Cognitive-Behavioural Treatment of Borderline Personality Disorders*.
New York: Guilford Press.

Mountford, V. & Waller, G. (2006). Using imagery in cognitive behavioural therapy
for the eating disorders: tackling the restrictive mode. *International Journal of Eating
Disorders*, **39**, 533–43.

Rothschild, B. (1995). Defining shock and trauma in bodypsychotherapy. *Energy and
Character*, **26**.

Segal, Z.V., Williams, J.M.G. & Teadale, J.D. (2002). *Mindfulness-Based Cognitive Therapy
for Depresssion. A New Approach to Preventing Relapse*. New York: Guilford Press.

Spiegal, D., Koopman, C., Cardena, E. & Classen, C. (1996). Dissociative symptoms in
the diagnosis of acute distress disorder. In L. Michelson & W. Ray (eds), *Handbook
of Dissociation*. New York: Plenum.

Waller, G., Kennerley, H. & Ohanian, V. (2007). Schema-focused cognitive behavioral
therapy with eating disorders. In L.P. Riso, P.L. du Toit, D.J. Stein & J.E. Young
(eds), *Cognitive Schemas and Core Beliefs in Psychiatric Disorders: A Scientist-Practitioner
Guide*, (pp. 139–75). New York: American Psychological Association.

Young, J.E., Klosko, J.S. & Weishaar, M.E. (2003), *Schema Therapy: A Practitioner's Guide*.
New York: Guilford Press.

PART IV

OBESITY AND BINGE EATING

CHAPTER 6

PSYCHOLOGICAL GROUP TREATMENT FOR OBESE WOMEN[1]

JULIA BUCKROYD AND SHARON ROTHER
University of Hertfordshire, UK

Despite the prevailing anxiety nationally, and internationally, over levels of obesity, it is clear that there is so far no effective treatment, unless we count the very drastic solution of bariatric surgery. As early as 1991, Garner and Wooley were reporting 'overwhelming evidence that [behavioral and dietary treatments of obesity] are ineffective in producing lasting weight loss' (p. 729). This reality has been obscured because almost everybody can secure short-term weight loss via dietary restriction (Garner & Wooley, 1991). Disappointingly, 'short-term results are frankly misleading indicators of long-term outcome' (p. 737). They reported abundant evidence 'that most individuals will regain most or all of their weight after four or five years' (p. 736).

Nothing has happened in the intervening 15 years or so to change this picture. Recent research suggests that conventional weight loss advice results in weight gain and/or weight cycling (Haslam & James, 2005; Jeffery *et al.*, 2004; Lowe *et al*, 2006; Mark, 2006; Melin *et al.*, 2003; Swinburn & Egger, 2004).

The hope invested in pharmaceutical treatments such as orlistat and sibutramine has not been realised (Adis International, 2006; Collins & Williams, 2001; O'Meara *et al.*, 2004; Yanovski, 2005). Recent reports on the side effects of a newer drug, Acomplia (Rimonabant) from an advisory panel of the United States Food and Drug Administration (FDA), rejected a licence to market the drug in the USA, following research showing that the drug doubled the risk of suicidal thoughts and behaviour and could affect those with no prior history of depression (FDA, 13 June 2007).

Even bariatric surgery has its limitations. Its cost and the need for ongoing monitoring have obvious resource implications. A recent article by Encinosa

---

[1] Some parts of this chapter were previously published in Buckroyd, J. & Rother, S. (2007). *Therapeutic Groups for Obese Women*. Chichester: John Wiley & Sons, Ltd.

Psychological Responses to Eating Disorders and Obesity: Recent and Innovative Work.
Edited by J. Buckroyd and S. Rother. © 2008 John Wiley & Sons, Ltd

(2006) suggests a complication rate of almost 40%. There are also ethical issues related to the more radical and permanent forms of bariatric surgery. All bariatric surgery demands a subsequent pattern of eating that is abnormal.

In December 2006 the National Institute for Health and Clinical Excellence issued guidelines for the treatment and prevention of obesity in the UK. Despite the evidence cited above and the prevailing evidence that available treatments have not impacted on the prevalence of obesity, their guidelines largely repeated old advice to eat less and exercise more.

As many authorities have noted, obesity treatment requires new approaches and rethinking. While the ultimate goal is reduction of calorific intake and an increase in activity (but see Gard & Wright, 2005) it remains an intractable problem for many people to follow this advice. Guidelines are readily available in any popular or health source. Following them is much, much more problematic and for most people apparently, impossible.

Our focus lies in exploring why it is so difficult for people to achieve energy balance. There is a range of answers to this question:

- There is a toxic environment of readily available, inexpensive, calorie dense food in Western societies.
- There is a physical environment that inhibits activity and supports a reduction in effort.
- There is a genetic predisposition to gain weight for some people. This is highly relevant in a society where food is always available.
- There are physiological mechanisms that make permanent weight loss difficult.
- There are psychological mechanisms that inhibit lifestyle change such as a general preference for what is familiar and known.
- There are psychological uses of food that maintain psychic equilibrium for a substantial minority of obese people.

In the rest of this chapter we want to focus on the last of these issues and explore how understanding of the psychological value of overeating for some obese people needs much more attention in the development of treatments and approaches to obesity. We argue first of all that the obese population is not homogeneous and that within it is a group of people, perhaps almost half, whose eating behaviour is emotionally driven.

Recent work by Logue (2004) and Ogden (2003, and this volume) has illustrated the great complexity of eating behaviour for all human beings and has underlined the complex social, cultural and emotional associations attached to food. None of us are eating simply to meet our physiological need. However, literature over the past 15 years has suggested that there is a subgroup of obese people, perhaps as many as 45%, whose eating behaviour is a means of affect management.

Canetti *et al.* (2002) looked at the relationship between emotions and food intake and concluded that negative emotions especially, increase food consumption, among normal weight as well as overweight people, but also concluded that the influence of emotions on eating behaviour is stronger in obese people. They confirmed that obese people eat in response to emotions more than normal weight people. Benjamin and Kamin-Shaaltiel (2004) for instance, related overweight in Israeli women to anger avoidance. We suppose that they imply that food is used to enable the suppression or management of anger.

Steptoe *et al.* (1998) determined that stress leading to increased distress, stimulated alterations in food choice towards greater intake of fat and sugar, in vulnerable individuals. Popkess-Vawter *et al.* (1998) identified power/control, relationships with others and unpleasant feelings as triggers for overeating in overweight women. Epel *et al.* (2001) showed that artificially induced stress promoted 'comfort food intake'. Freeman and Gil (2004) and Schoemaker *et al.* (2002) reported that stress precipitated binge eating. Laitinen *et al.* (2002) showed how stress-driven eaters were at greater risk of obesity. Rosmond (2005) was also interested in the relationship between stress and visceral obesity. He suggested that persistent stress results in the release of excess cortisol which in turn promoted visceral obesity. Gluck *et al.* (2004) came to the same conclusion. Furthermore Heinrichs *et al.* (2003) discovered that social support and oxytocin suppressed cortisol production.

Geliebter and Aversa (2003) reported that overweight individuals overate during negative emotional states and situations. Cartwright *et al.* (2003) reported the same thing for adolescents. Deaver *et al.* (2003) conducted research to explore whether binge eating really helped with affect regulation and concluded that bingeing does indeed produce momentary relief from negative affect. Byrne *et al.* (2003) identified the use of eating to regulate mood or to distract from unpleasant thoughts and moods as one characteristic of obese women who had lost a substantial amount of weight and then regained it. Walfish (2004) found that 40% of a sample of bariatric surgery patients could be identified as 'emotional eaters' and recommended treatment to address this problem to increase the likelihood of long-term maintenance of weight loss.

Some attempt has been made to identify abnormal eating patterns both in the general population and in the obese population. Binge eating has been extensively studied, especially in relation to aversive emotional states (Chua *et al.*, 2004; Deaver *et al.*, 2003; Heatherton & Baumeister, 1991; Kenardy *et al.*, 1996; Telch & Agras, 1996; Vogele & Florin, 1997). Marcus and Wing (1987) found that between 20% and 46% of obese individuals in a weight control programme reported binge eating (see also Yanovski, 2003). More recently Gluck *et al.* (2004) reported that up to 46% of those defined as obese, binge eat and binge eating appears to be more common in females (Freeman & Gil, 2004; Linde *et al.*, 2004). Foreyt and Goodrick (1994) found that weight regain was associated, among other things, with life stress, negative coping style and emotional or binge eating patterns. Agras *et al.* (1997) and Fichter *et al.* (1993) reported that binge eating predicted weight regain.

There is substantial evidence to suggest that those who use food for affect regulation may have significant psychological issues relating to their history. Attachment history has been studied extensively for its relationship to affect regulation. Schore has developed a clear model for the relationship between attachment history, its neurological consequences and the person's capacity to regulate affect. 'Enduring structural changes [as a result of traumatic attachments] lead to the inefficient stress coping mechanisms that lie at the core of . . . post traumatic stress disorders' (Raynes *et al.*, 1989; Schore, 2002, p. 11, see also Schore 2000, 2001, 2003; Zimmerman, 1999). A review of attachment research in eating disorders (Ward *et al.*, 2000) concluded that insecure attachment is common in eating disordered populations. Maunder and Hunter (2001) have extended the scope of the enquiry to evaluate the evidence linking attachment insecurity to illness generally. They cautiously proposed that overeating, leading to obesity, may be a means of managing insecure attachment. Flores (2001) related attachment difficulties to addiction and substance abuse as a means of self-repair. Trombini *et al.* (2003) found that obese children and their mothers had a significant prevalence of insecure attachment style and recommended that treatment of obesity in children needed to include a psychological intervention with the mother. Vila *et al.* (2004) similarly identified disturbance in the families of obese children and recommended family treatment. Ciechanowski *et al.* (2004) found that avoidant attachment patterns were associated with poorer self-management in patients with diabetes – there is an 85% association of Type 2 diabetes and obesity (Eberhardt *et al.*, 2004). Troisi *et al.* (2005) commented that 'persons with eating disorders are expected to have a high frequency of adverse early experiences with their attachment figures and a high prevalence of insecure attachment. . . . The insecure attachment style has been also considered as a risk factor for the development of an eating disorder' (p. 89). Tasca *et al.* (2006) reported that both attachment anxiety and attachment avoidance were related to poorer outcomes in group treatment for binge eating disorder.

Attachment difficulties may well be associated with difficult early experiences (Prior & Glaser, 2006). Felitti (one of the first researchers to explore these themes) observed a 55% dropout rate in a weight loss programme despite the fact that dropouts had been losing weight, not gaining. This observation and subsequent interviews and studies (Felitti, 1991, 1993) indicated that overeating and obesity were often unconscious 'protective solutions to unrecognised problems dating back to childhood' (Felitti, 2003, p. 2).

Felitti's work stimulated an epidemiological study in collaboration with researchers from the Center for Disease Control and Prevention (CDC) in Atlanta, USA: the 'Adverse Childhood Experiences (ACE) Study'. This study sought to examine the relationship between childhood abuse and family dysfunction and many of the leading causes of adult mortality (Felitti *et al.*, 1998).

In relation to obesity, the study found that people who had experienced four or more ACEs had a 1.4 to 1.6-fold increased risk of severe obesity and inactivity (Felitti *et al.*, 1998).

A number of other authors have explored the relationship between earlier adverse life experiences, eating disorders and obesity (Kent *et al.*, 1999; Kopp, 1994, Lissau & Sotrensen, 1994; Williamson *et al.*, 2002; Wonderlich *et al.*, 2001). In a review of the literature of childhood sexual abuse (CSA) and obesity, Gustafson and Sarwer (2004) note that 'studies suggest at least a modest relationship between the two'. A similar result was found in a review by Smolak and Murnen (2002), who found that CSA is associated with an increased likelihood of eating disorder symptoms. A positive correlation between CSA and binge eating has been found (Grilo & Masheb, 2001; Wonderlich *et al.*, 2001).

Mills (1995) found that adults whose obesity dated from childhood had poorer mental health than those who became obese later in life, suggesting early traumatic experience. Power and Parsons (2000) suggested that emotional deprivation in childhood might be related to adult obesity. In studies by Grilo and colleagues, 83% of participants with binge eating disorder (BED) reported some form of childhood maltreatment (Grilo & Masheb, 2001). (BED is a diagnostic description of bingeing combined with a loss of a sense of control which occurs twice a week or more over a period of six months.) A study of bariatric surgery patients found half the females had experienced early sexual abuse (Rowston *et ul.*, 1992) and abuse history was significantly related to overweight/obesity in a sample of female gastrointestinal patients (Jia *et al.*, 2004). In a study of extremely obese bariatric surgery candidates, 69% reported maltreatment (Grilo *et al.*, 2005).

Longitudinal studies over a period of seven years of sexually abused children, revealed higher rates of healthcare utilisation and long-term health problems than comparison groups, and both studies mention comparatively higher rates of overweight and obesity in the abused groups (Frothingham *et al.*, 2000; Sickel *et al.*, 2002). While there are few long-term studies, there is varied literature on the effects of early abuse and neglect upon adult health (Hulme, 2004; Kendall-Tackett, 2002; Leserman, 2005; MacMillan *et al.*, 2001; Roberts, 1996; Stein & Barrett-Connor, 2000; Weiss *et al.*, 1999) and there is some evidence that CSA may negatively influence weight loss in obesity treatment (King *et al.*, 1996). Wiederman *et al.* (1999) discuss how obesity may have an adaptive function for sexually abused women, which lends some support to the findings of Felitti (1993), where participants reported using obesity as a sexually protective device, and overeating to manage emotional distress.

Much of the data quoted above has been gathered by means of questionnaires. However, when obese people have been given the opportunity to talk about their obesity at greater length, the findings have shown very similar results. Qualitative studies have consistently demonstrated the association of poor family functioning and excess use of food. These studies have also shown the importance of the social environment and food use in response to negative affect. Stress, anxiety and loneliness are particularly identified in the data (Bidgood & Buckroyd, 2005; Davis *et al.*, 2005; Goodspeed Grant & Boersma, 2005; Lyons, 1998; Sarlio-Lahteenkorva, 1998; see also Goodspeed Grant, this volume).

In the past 10 years or so evidence has been accumulating which describes the biochemical mechanisms that may be at work in the brain to produce a soothing or sedating effect in response to overeating. Eating particular comfort foods – foods high in fat and carbohydrate – has an effect on the biochemistry of the brain which reduces stress or produces hedonic effects (Colantuoni *et al.*, 2002; Will *et al.*, 2003, 2004). Brooks (2006) and Yanovski (2003) found that the opioid system might be involved in response to ingestion of sweet, high fat foods by women. Dallman *et al.* (2005) demonstrated that eating comfort foods reduces the effects of chronic stress by modifying the biochemical effects. Certain foods, such as fat, sugar and carbohydrates, are known to alter mood states (Brooks, 2006).

Collectively these data suggest that there is a significant subgroup of obese people whose eating is driven by their need for affect regulation, who are likely to binge or have BED and whose history suggests attachment difficulties and traumatic experiences. It seems likely that people whose eating behaviour is determined by these issues and who experience pleasurable biochemical effects as a result of their overeating, will be very unlikely to modify it before other coping mechanisms have been developed. To modify this maintaining factor, the treatment for this subgroup should be psychotherapeutic as a preliminary or an accompaniment to any practical advice.

We have used the research literature to explore whether there are distinctive features in the psychological make-up of the subgroup of obese people that we have identified which might inform treatment. In what follows we address the issues that the literature identifies as specific deficits in the psychological functioning of this subgroup of obese people. These are:

- alexithymia
- poor self-esteem
- lack of support

We consider that addressing these aspects of the lives and history of this particular group of people may enable a focused intervention. This may help them to manage their emotional lives with less reliance on food and thus may lead to maintained weight loss.

There is evidence to suggest that people with eating disorders of all kinds find it difficult to express their feelings in words, a condition known as alexithymia. The relationship between alexithymia, 'a default in the ability to identify and express emotions and a prevalence of externally oriented thinking'

(Pinaquy *et al.*, 2003) and eating disorders (anorexia and bulimia) has already been demonstrated (Cochrane *et al.*, 1993; de Zwaan *et al.*, 1995; Råstam *et al.*, 1997; Schmidt *et al.*, 1993). However, its relationship with obesity has been less researched. Clerici *et al.* (1992) found a high prevalence of alexithymia in obese people. De Chouly De Lenclave *et al.* (2001) found that alexithymia was significantly more frequent in obese patients than in controls but that no significant difference was found between patients with and without binge eating disorder. However, Pinaquy *et al.* (2003) also explored the extent of alexithymia in obese people. They discovered that binge eating disorder was significantly associated with alexithymia. Since BED affects 20–30% of treatment-seeking obese people (Devlin *et al.*, 1992) and is one of the identifying features of about two-thirds of the subgroup of obese people that we have identified, this is an important finding. An inability to express emotions is also strongly associated with emotional eating which, in turn, Pinaquy *et al.* (2003) found to be a significant predictor of BED.

It is known that difficulties in maintaining self-esteem are common in obese people (Franklin *et al.*, 2006; Harvey *et al.*, 2002; Puhl & Brownell, 2003; Tebo, 2005; Wigton & McGaghie, 2001). Improving self-esteem and body-esteem has therefore been seen as a useful component of a psychological approach to obesity (Garner & Wooley, 1991). Lewis *et al.* (1992) found that group therapy directed at improving self-assertion, self-efficacy and self-esteem enabled group members to improve their scores in these areas but also enabled sustained weight loss. Although the group members were not obese, these results are never the less suggestive. Foreyt and Goodrick (1994) agree that improving self-esteem should be a large part of the treatment of obese people. Morrison (1999) confirmed what is clinically well known, that trying to decrease the value placed upon body shape and size as a means of improving women's self-esteem is extremely difficult, but Wardle *et al.* (2001) demonstrated that a reduction in body dissatisfaction was associated with a reduction in binge eating scores for obese women.

In seeking to answer the question of what factors enable maintained weight loss, researchers have identified continuing support as a crucial feature. Qualitative research has identified loneliness and the absence of support as a maintaining feature of overeating (Bidgood & Buckroyd, 2005; Davis *et al.*, 2005; Goodspeed Grant & Boersma, 2005; Lyons, 1998; Sarlio-Lahteenkorva, 1998; see also Goodspeed Grant, this volume). The support from any weight loss programme is useful. Its termination brings support to an end and may explain why weight regain seems to be delayed until the end of that support system following on from a more active intervention (Jeffery *et al.*, 2000; Perri, 2002).

We connect the reported loneliness and lack of support of obese people with the attachment difficulties described above which result, not only in deficits in self-soothing as the literature reported above indicates, but also in a difficulty in finding appropriately supportive relationships. A number of researchers have drawn attention to the need for obese people to develop improved support mechanisms. Steptoe *et al.* (1998) drew attention to the value of social support for people under stress who are otherwise likely to use food to manage it and Hayward *et al.* (2000) emphasised the value of support networks for weight loss. Rabinor (2004) reported use of the group as a helpful support for obese people in group treatment. We believe that the experience of improved support will in turn enable improved self-soothing.

Therapeutic interventions targeted on these aspects of functioning may well prove most useful. We have begun a programme of research to test this hypothesis. We made use of an integrative psychological approach addressing core issues of emotional intelligence, self-nurture and relationship in a 36-week uncontrolled study to explore whether weight loss would result and whether it would be maintained. This study produced maintained weight loss $\geq 5\%$ in six (75%) of completers ($n = 8$) after nine months (Buckroyd *et al.*, 2006). Weight loss was not only maintained but also continued after the end of the intervention in contrast to the reported results of other studies (Jeffery *et al.*, 2000).

We then carried out a further study in which 72 obese women were recruited to a 36-week integrated psychological group intervention carried out over a year. The protocol (Buckroyd & Rother, 2007) focuses on the same core issues of emotional intelligence, self-esteem and relationship, together with material on food choice and increased activity. This intervention is not yet quite complete but we have some initial data. Of 41 completers at end of intervention 22% ($n = 9$) achieved a weight loss of 5% or more of baseline weight. Median weight loss 2.4 kg, maximum loss 15.4 kg, maximum gain 14.4 kg. At six-month follow-up, while telephone support was ongoing, of 26 participants, 46% ($n = 12$) achieved maintained weight loss $\geq 5\%$. Median weight loss 4.7 kg, maximum weight loss 14.7 kg, maximum gain 9.5 kg. As demonstrated by the preliminary study, the current study also shows cumulative and continuing weight loss. Data from participant interviews suggests this approach produces a pattern of initial slow weight loss followed by gradual acceleration as participants applied what they were learning. Full results will be reported in due course.

When we carried out these interventions we were not as clear about the subgroups of obese people as we have since become and consequently, did not screen for the subgroup of obese people that we have since identified as having emotionally driven eating. However it would obviously be more economical in terms of resource use to identify them before offering a psychological intervention. We have developed three ways in which this could be done:

- by identifying those who binge eat
- by identifying those who binge eat, eat emotionally and have high scores on attachment difficulties and trauma
- by offering stepped care

Binge eating seems as though it may be a proxy measure of the other features of the psychological profile of the subgroup we have identified. Other researchers (Keville *et al.* and Seamoore *et al.* in this volume) have come to this conclusion. We are reasonably certain that they have identified the same group of people that we are discussing. This method has the advantage that it is easily administered via a binge eating questionnaire such as 'The assessment of binge eating severity among obese persons' (Gormally *et al.*, 1982).

A second more thorough method is to administer questionnaires which measure all of the indicators that we have identified:

- binge eating
- emotional eating
- poor attachment
- a history of trauma

There are measures for all of these, for example:

- for binge eating (as above, Gormally *et al.*, 1982)
- for emotional eating, The Emotional Eating Scale (Arnow *et al.*, 1995)
- for attachment, The Adult Attachment Interview (George *et al.*, 1996)
- for trauma, Measures in Post-Traumatic Stress Disorder (Turner & Lee, 1998)

The development of stepped-care treatments might also have this function. An initial conventional weight management group would probably identify the small minority of people who can benefit from this approach (20% according to Texeira, 2005). Those who need additional input could be offered a second intervention focusing on lifestyle change, ownership of the treatment and social support. In turn, those who seemed to need further input could be offered a psychotherapeutic treatment designed to address the significant psychological barriers to changes in eating behaviour described above.

As far as a specific therapeutic method is concerned, a number of authors (Cooper, 1995; Fairburn, 1995) have proposed cognitive behavioural therapy (CBT) for binge eating. However the patient group that they describe as benefiting from this treatment does not include the group of women that we have identified. Our belief is that the emotional problems of this group of people may demand greater methodological flexibility than the application of a single modality (Cooper & McLeod, 2007). We are, like many clinicians, aware of the recent research which suggests that the modality of the intervention accounts for very little of the therapeutic effect. There is compelling and pervasive evidence that different modalities have very similar effects (Wampold, 2001). Generic features, especially the relationship with the therapist, the collaboration of the patient and the capacity of therapist and client to agree goals for example, are of far greater significance (Bohart & Tallman, 1999; Castonguay & Buetler, 2006; Downing, 2004; Hollanders, 2003; Tryon & Winograd, 2002). Service user feedback is unanimous on this issue (Cooper,

2005; Lilliengren & Werbart, 2005). Our own experience has been that an integrated treatment plan offers a range of approaches which will be accessed differently by different clients.

Our work, as described above, has developed a particular group intervention for the subgroup of women whose eating seems to be emotionally driven. This intervention is based on our reading of the implications of a history of trauma and poor attachment for psychological functioning. However, it would be perfectly possible to develop alternative treatment interventions based on this same research literature. The currently intractable problem of obesity demands innovative responses. Evidence-based treatments using this literature could take many forms and are urgently needed.

REFERENCES

Adis International Limited. (2006). Pharmacotherapy for the treatment of obesity has only modest benefits and should be used in combination with lifestyle modifications. *Drugs and Therapy Perspectives*, **22**(1), 7–11.

Agras, W.S., Telch, C.F., Arnow, B.A. *et al.* (1997). One year follow-up of cognitive-behavioural therapy for obese individuals with binge eating disorder. *Journal of Consulting and Clinical Psychology*, **65**, 343–7.

Arnow, B., Kenardy, J. & Agras, W.S. (1995). The Emotional Eating Scale: the development of a measure to assess coping with negative affect by eating. *International Journal of Eating Disorders*, **18**(1), 79–90.

Benjamin, O. & Kamin-Shaaltiel, S. (2004). It's not because I'm fat: perceived overweight and anger avoidance in marriage. *Health Care for Women International*, **25**, 853–71.

Bidgood, J. & Buckroyd, J. (2005). An exploration of obese adults experience of attempting to lose weight and to maintain a reduced weight. *Counselling and Psychotherapy Research*, **5**, 221–9.

Bohart, A.C. & Tallman, K. (1999). *How Clients Make Therapy Work: The Process of Active Self-Healing*. Washington, DC: American Psychological Association.

Brooks, A. (2006). Changing food preference as a function of mood. *Journal of Psychology*, **140**(4), 293–306.

Buckroyd, J. & Rother, S. (2007). *Therapeutic Groups for Obese Women: A Group Leader's Handbook*. Chichester: John Wiley & Sons, Ltd.

Buckroyd, J., Rother, S. & Stott, D. (2006). Weight loss as a primary objective of therapeutic groups for obese women: two preliminary studies. *British Journal of Guidance and Counselling*, **34**(2), 245–65.

Byrne, S.M., Cooper, Z. & Fairburn, C.G. (2003). Weight maintenance and relapse in obesity: a qualitative study. *International Journal of Obesity*, **27**, 955–62.

Canetti, L., Bachar, E. & Berry, E.M. (2002). Food and emotion. *Behavioural Processes*, **60**, 1–10.

Cartwright, M., Wardle, J., Steggles, N. *et al.* (2003). Stress and Dietary Practices in Adolescents. *Health Psychology*, **22**(4), 362–9.

Castonguay, L.G. & Buetler, L.E. (2006). Preface. In L.G. Castonguay & L.E. Beutler (eds), *Principles of Therapeutic Change that Work* (p. v). Oxford: Oxford University Press.

Ciechanowski, P., Russo, J., Katon, W. *et al.* (2004). Influence of patient attachment style on self-care and outcomes in diabetes. *Psychosomatic Medicine*, **66**, 720–8.

Chua, J.L., Touyz, S. & Hill, A.J. (2004). Negative mood-induced overeating in obese binge eaters: an experimental study. *International Journal of Obesity and Related Metabolic Disorders*, **28**, 606–10.

Clerici, M., Albonetti, S., Papa, R. *et al.* (1992). Alexithymia and obesity. *Psychotherapy and Psychosomatics*, **57**, 88–93.

Cochrane, C., Brewerton, T., Wilson, D. & Hodges, E. (1993). Alexithymia in the eating disorders. *International Journal of Eating Disorders*, **14**, 219–22.

Colantuoni, C., Rada, P., McCarthy, J. *et al.* (2002). Evidence that intermittent, excessive sugar intake causes endogenous opioid dependence. *Obesity Research*, **10**, 478–88.

Collins, P. & Williams, G. (2001). Drug treatment of obesity: from past failures to future successes? *British Journal of Clinical Pharmacology*, **51**, 13–25.

Cooper, M. (2005). Young people's perceptions of helpful aspects of therapy: a pluralistic model of therapeutic change. Joint Meeting of European and UK Chapters, Society for Psychotherapy Research, Lausanne.

Cooper, M. & McLeod, J. (2007). A pluralistic framework for counselling and psychotherapy: Implications for research. *Counselling and Psychotherapy Research*, 7(3).

Cooper, P.J. (1995). *Bulimia Nervosa and Binge-Eating: A Guide to Recovery*. New York: New York University Press.

Dallman, M.F., Pecoraro, N.C. & la Fleur, S.E. (2005). Chronic stress and comfort foods: self-medication and abdominal obesity. *Brain, Behavior and Immunity*. **19**, 275–80.

Davis, E., Rovi, S. & Johnson, M.S. (2005). Mental health, family function and obesity in African American women. *Journal of the National Medical Association*, **97**, 478–82.

Deaver, C.M., Miltenberger, R.G., Smyth, J. *et al.* (2003). An evaluation of affect and binge eating. *Behaviour Modification*, **27**, 578–99.

De Chouly De Lenclave, M.B., Florequin, C. & Bailly, D. (2001). Obesity, alexithymia, psychopathology and binge eating: a comparative study of 40 obese patients and 32 controls. *Encephale*, **27**, 343–50.

Devlin, M.J., Walsh, B.T., Spitzer, R.L. & Hasin, D. (1992). Is there another binge eating disorder? A review of literature on overeating in the absence of bulimia nervosa. *International Journal of Eating Disorders*, **11**, 333–40.

De Zwaan, M., Bach, M., Mitchell, J.E. *et al.* (1995). Alexithymia, obesity and binge eating disorder. *International Journal of Eating Disorders*, **17**, 135–40.

Downing, J.N. (2004). Psychotherapy practice in a pluralistic world: philosophical and moral dilemmas. *Journal of Psychotherapy Integration*, **14**, 123–48.

Eberhardt, M.S., Ogden, C., Engelgau, M. & Cadwell, B. (2004). Prevalence of overweight and obesity among adults with diagnosed diabetes. *Morbidity and Mortality Weekly Report*, **53**, 1066–8.

Encinosa, W.E. (2006). Healthcare utilization and outcomes after bariatric surgery. *Medical Care*, **44**(8), 706–12.

Epel, E., Lapidus, R., McEwen, B. & Brownell, K. (2001). Stress may add bite to appetite in women: a laboratory study of stress-induced cortisol and eating behaviour. *Psychoneuroendocrinology*, **26**, 37–49.

Fairburn, C. (1995). *Overcoming Binge Eating*. New York: Guilford Press.

Felitti, V.J. (1991). Long-term medical consequences of incest, rape and molestation. *Southern Medical Journal*, **84**, 328–31.

Felitti, V.J. (1993). Childhood sexual abuse, depression and family dysfunction in adult obese patients: a case control study. *Southern Medical Journal*, **86**, 732–6.

Felitti, V.J. (2003). The Origins of Addiction: Evidence from the Adverse Childhood Experiences Study. http://acestudy.org/docs/OriginsofAddiction.pdf [Accessed 3 May 2006]. English version of the article published in Germany as: Felitti, V.J. (2003). Ursprünge des Suchtverhaltens – Evidenzen aus einer Studie zu belastenden Kindheitserfahrungen. *Praxis der Kinderpsychologie und Kinderpsychiatrie*, **52**, 547–59.

Felitti, V.J., Anda, R.F., Nordenberg, D. *et al.* (1998). Relationship of childhood abuse and household dysfunction to many of the leading causes of death in adults. *American Journal of Preventive Medicine*, **14**, 245–58.

Fichter, M.M., Quadflieg, N. & Brandl, B. (1993). Recurrent overeating: an empirical comparison of binge eating disorder, bulimia and obesity. *International Journal of Eating Disorders*, **14**, 1–16.

Flores, P.J. (2001). Addiction as an attachment disorder: implication therapy. *International Journal of Group Psychotherapy*, **51**, 63–81.

Foreyt, J.P. & Goodrick, G.K. (1994). Attributes of successful approaches to weight loss and control. *Applied and Preventive Psychology*, **3**, 209–15.

Franklin, J., Denyer, G., Steinbeck, K.S. *et al.* (2006). Obesity and risk of low self-esteem: a statewide survey of Australian children. *Pediatrics*, **118**, 2481–7.

Freeman, L.M. & Gil, K.M. (2004). Daily stress, coping and dietary restraint in binge eating. *International Journal of Eating Disorders*, **36**, 204–12.

Frothingham, T.E., Hobbs, C.J., Wynne, J.M. *et al.* (2000). Follow up study eight years after diagnosis of sexual abuse. *Archives of Disease in Childhood*, **83**, 132–4.

Gard, M. & Wright, J. (2005). *The Obesity Epidemic: Science, Morality and Ideology*. Abingdon: Routledge.

Garner, D.M. & Wooley, S.C. (1991). Confronting the failure of behavioural and dietary treatments for obesity. *Clinical Psychology Review*, **11**, 729–80.

Geliebter, A. & Aversa, A. (2003). Emotional eating in overweight, normal weight and underweight individuals. *Eating Behaviors*, **3**, 341–7.

George, C., Kaplan, N. & Main, M. (1996). *Adult Attachment Interview*. Department of Psychology, University of California.

Goodspeed Grant, P. & Boersma, H. (2005). Making sense of being fat: a hermeneutic analysis of adults' explanations for obesity. *Counselling and Psychotherapy Research*, **5**, 212–20.

Gormally, J., Black, S., Daston, S. & Rardin, D. (1982). The assessment of binge eating severity among obese persons. *Addictive Behaviours*, **7**, 47–55.

Grilo, C.M. & Masheb, R.M. (2001). Childhood psychological, physical and sexual maltreatment in outpatients with binge eating disorder: frequency and associations with gender, obesity and eating-related psychopathology. *Obesity Research*, **9**, 320–5.

Grilo, C.M., Masheb, R.M., Brody, M. *et al.* (2005). Childhood maltreatment in extremely obese male and female bariatric surgery candidates. *Obesity Research*, **13**, 123–30.

Gluck, M.E., Geliebter, A. & Lorence, M. (2004). Cortisol stress response is positively correlated with central obesity in obese women with binge eating disorder (BED) before and after cognitive-behavioral treatment. *Annals of the New York Academy of Sciences*, **1032**, 202–7.

Gustafson T.B. & Sarwer D.B. (2004). Childhood sexual abuse and obesity. *Obesity Reviews*, **5**, 129–35.

Harvey, E.L., Summerbell, C.D., Kirk, S.F.L., Hill, A.J. (2002). Dieticians' views of overweight and obese people and reported management practices. *Journal of Human Nutrition and Dietetics*, **15**, 331–47.

Haslam, D.W. & James, W.P.T. (2005). Obesity. *Lancet*, **366**, 1197–209.

Hayward, L.M., Nixon, C., Jasper, M.P. *et al.* (2000). The process of restructuring and the treatment of obesity in women. *Health Care for Women International*, **21**, 615–30.

Heatherton, T.F. & Baumeister, R.F. (1991). Binge eating as escape from self-awareness. *Psychological Bulletin*, **110**, 86–108.

Heinrichs, M., Baumgartner, T., Kirschbaum, C. & Ehlert, U. (2003). Social support and oxytocin interact to suppress cortisol and subjective responses to psychosocial stress. *Biological Psychiatry*, **54**, 1389–98.

Hollanders, H. (2003). The eclectic and integrative approach. In R. Woolfe, W. Dryden & S. Strawbridge (eds), *Handbook of Counselling Psychology*. London: Sage.

Hulme, P.A. (2004). Theoretical perspectives on the health problems of adults who experienced childhood sexual abuse. *Issues in Mental Health Nursing*, **25**, 339–61.

Jeffery, R.W., Drewnowski, A., Epstein, L.H. *et al.* (2000). Long-term maintenance of weight loss: current status. *Health Psychology*, **19**(Suppl.), 5–16.

Jeffery, R.W., Kelly, K.M. & Sherwood, N.E. (2004). The weight loss experience: a descriptive analysis. *Annals of Behavior Medicine*, **27**(2), 100–6.

Jia, H., Li, J.Z., Leserman, J. *et al.* (2004). Relationship of abuse history and other risk factors with obesity among female gastrointestinal patients. *Digestive Diseases and Sciences*, **49**, 872–7.

Kenardy, J., Arnow, B. & Agras, W.S. (1996). The aversiveness of specific emotional states associated with binge-eating in obese subjects. *Australia and New Zealand Journal of Psychiatry*, **30**, 839–44.

Kendall-Tackett, K. (2002). The health effects of childhood abuse: four pathways by which abuse can influence health. *Child Abuse and Neglect*, **6**, 715–30.

Kent, A., Waller, G. & Dagnan, D. (1999). A greater role of emotional than physical or sexual abuse in predicting disordered eating attitudes: the role of mediating variables. *International Journal of Eating Disorders*, **25**, 159–67.

King, T.K., Clark, M.M. & Pera, V. (1996). History of sexual abuse and obesity treatment outcome. *Addictive Behaviours*, **21**, 283–90.

Kopp, W. (1994). The incidence of sexual abuse in women with eating disorders. *Psychotherapy, Psychosomatic Medicine and Psychology*, **44**, 159–162.

Laitinen, J., Ek, E. & Sovio, U. (2002). Stress-related eating and drinking behavior and body mass index and predictors of this behavior. *Preventive Medicine*, **34**(1), 29–39.

Leserman, J. (2005). Sexual abuse history: prevalence, health effects, mediators, and psychological treatment. *Psychosomatic Medicine*, **67**, 906–15.

Lewis, V.J., Blair, A.J. & Booth, D.A. (1992). Outcome of group therapy for body-image emotionality and weight-control self-efficacy. *Behavioural Psychotherapy*, **20**, 155–65.

Lilliengren, P. & Werbart, A. (2005). A model of therapeutic action grounded in the patients' view of curative and hindering factors in psychoanalytic psychotherapy. *Psychotherapy: Theory, Research, Practice, Training*, **3**, 324–99.

Linde, J.A., Jeffrey, R.W., Levy, R.L. *et al.* (2004). Binge eating disorder, weight control self-efficacy, and depression in overweight men and women. *International Journal of Obesity and Related Metabolic Disorders*, **28**, 418–25.

Lissau, I. & Sotrensen, T.I.A. (1994). Parental neglect during childhood and increased risk of obesity in young adulthood. *Lancet*, **343**, 324–7.

Logue, A.W. (2004). *The Psychology of Eating and Drinking*. New York: Brunner-Routledge.

Lowe, M.R., Annunziato, R.A., Markowitz, J.T. *et al.* (2006). Multiple types of dieting prospectively predict weight gain during the freshman year of college. *Appetite*, **47**, 83–90.

Lyons, M.A. (1998). The phenomenon of compulsive overeating in a selected group of professional women. *Journal of Advanced Nursing*, **27**, 1158–64.

MacMillan, H.L., Fleming, J.E., Streiner, D.L. *et al.* (2001). Childhood abuse and lifetime psychopathology in a community sample. *American Journal of Psychiatry*, **158**, 1878–83.

Marcus, M.D. & Wing, R.R. (1987). Binge eating among the obese. *Annals of Behavioural Medicine*, **9**, 23–37.

Mark, A.L. (2006). Future: a point of view. *Clinical and Experimental Pharmacology and Physiology*, **33**(9), 857–62.

Maunder, R. & Hunter, J. (2001). Attachment and psychosomatic medicine: developmental contributions to stress and disease. *Psychosomatic Medicine*, **63**, 556–67.

Melin, I., Lappalainen, R., Berglund, L. *et al.* (2003). A programme of behaviour modification and nutrition counselling in the treatment of obesity: a randomised 2-year clinical trial. *International Journal of Obesity*, **27**(9), 1127–35.

Mills, J.K. (1995). A note on interpersonal sensitivity and psychotic symptomatology in obese adult outpatients with a history of childhood obesity. *Journal of Psychology*, **129**, 345–8.

Morrison, A.L. (1999). The effects of alternative group interventions on physical self-esteem in obese women. *Dissertation-Abstracts-International-Section A: Humanities and Social Sciences*, **59**(9A), 3361.

NICE guidelines (2006). Obesity: the prevention, identification, assessment and management of overweight and obesity in adults and children. www.nice.org.uk/guidance/CG43

Ogden, J. (2003). *The Psychology of Eating*. Oxford: Blackwell Publishing.

O'Meara, S.O., Riemsma, R., Shirran, L., Mather, L. & Ter Riet, G. (2004). A systematic review of the clinical effectiveness of orlistat used for the management of obesity. *Obesity Reviews*, **5**, 51.

Perri, M. (2002). Improving maintenance in behavioural treatment. In C.G. Fairburn & K.D. Brownell (eds), *Eating Disorders and Obesity: A Comprehensive Handbook, 2nd edition*. New York: Guilford Press.

Pinaquy, S., Chabrol, H., Simon, C., Louvet, J-P. & Barbe, P. (2003). Emotional eating, alexithymia and binge eating disorder in obese women. *Obesity Research*, **11**, 195–201.

Popkess-Vawter, S., Brandau, C. & Straub, J. (1998). Triggers of overeating and related intervention strategies for women who weight cycle. *Applied Nursing Research*, **11**, 69–76.

Power, C. & Parsons, T. (2000). Nutritional and other influences in childhood as predictors of adult obesity. *Proceedings of the Nutrition Society*, **59**, 267–72.

Prior, V. & Glaser, D. (2006). *Understanding Attachment and Attachment Disorders.* London: Jessica Kingsley.

Puhl, R.M. & Brownell, K.D. (2003). Psychosocial origins of obesity stigma: toward changing a powerful and pervasive bias. *Obesity Reviews,* **4**, 213–27.

Rabinor, J.R. (2004). The therapist's voice. *Eating Disorders,* **12**, 257–61.

Råstam, M., Gillberg, C., Gillberg, I.C. & Johansson, M. (1997). Alexithymia in anorexia nervosa: a controlled study using the 20-item Toronto Alexithymia Scale. *Acta Psychiatrica Scandinavia,* **95**, 385–8.

Raynes, E., Auerbach, C. & Botyanski, N.C. (1989). Level of object representation and psychic structure deficit in obese persons. *Psychological Reports,* **64**, 291–4.

Roberts, S.J. (1996). The sequelae of childhood sexual abuse: a primary care focus for adult female survivors. *Nurse Practitioner,* **21**, 42, 45, 49–52.

Rosmond, R. (2005). Role of stress in the pathogenesis of the metabolic syndrome. *Psychoneuroendocrinology,* **30**, 1–10.

Rowston, W.M., McCluskey, S.E., Gazet, J.C. *et al.* (1992). Eating behaviour, physical symptoms and psychological factors associated with weight reduction following the Scopinaro operation as modified by Gazet. *Obesity Surgery,* **2**, 355–60.

Sarlio-Lahteekorva, S. (1998). Relapse stories in obesity. *European Journal of Public Health,* **8**, 203–9.

Schmidt, U., Jiwany, A. & Treasure, J. (1993). A controlled study of alexithymia in eating disorders. *Comprehensive Psychiatry,* **34**, 54–8.

Schoemaker, C., McKitterick, C.R., McEwen, B.S. & Kreek, M.J. (2002). Bulimia nervosa following psychological and multiple child abuse: support for the self-medication hypothesis in a population based cohort study. *International Journal of Eating Disorders,* **32**, 381–8.

Schore, A.N. (2000). Attachment and the regulation of the right brain. *Attachment and Human Development,* **2**(1), 23–47.

Schore, A.N. (2001). Effects of a secure attachment relationship on right brain development, affect regulation, and infant mental health. *Infant Mental Health Journal,* **22**, 7–66.

Schore, A.N. (2002). Dysregulation of the right brain: a fundamental mechanism of traumatic attachment and the psychopathogenesis of post-traumatic stress disorder. *Australian and New Zealand Journal of Psychiatry,* **36**, 9–30.

Schore, A.N. (2003). *Affect Regulation and the Repair of Self.* New York: W.W. Norton.

Sickel, A.E., Noll, J.G., Moore, P.J. *et al.* (2002). The long-term physical health and healthcare utilization of women who were sexually abused as children. *Journal of Health Psychology,* **7**, 583–97.

Smolak, L. & Murnen, S.K. (2002). A meta-analytic examination of the relationship between child sexual abuse and eating disorders. *International Journal of Eating Disorders,* **31**, 136–50.

Stein, M.B. & Barrett-Connor, E. (2000). Sexual assault and physical health: findings from a population-based study of older adults. *Psychosomatic Medicine,* **62**, 838–43.

Steptoe, A., Wardle, J., Lipsey, Z. *et al.* (1998). The effects of life stress on food choice. In A. Murcott (ed.), *The Nation's Diet: The Social Science of Food Choice.* Harlow: Addison Wesley Longman.

Swinburn, B. & Egger, G. (2004). The runaway weight gain train: too many accelerators, not enough brakes. *British Medical Journal,* **329**(7468), 736–9.

Tasca, G.A., Ritchie, K., Conrad, G. *et al.* (2006). Attachment scales predict outcome in a randomized controlled trial of two group therapies for binge eating disorder: an aptitude by treatment interaction. *Psychotherapy Research*, **16**, 106–21.

Tebo M.G. (2005). A matter of some weight. *ABA Journal*, **91**, 17–18.

Telch, C.F. & Agras, W. S. (1996). Do emotional states influence binge eating in the obese? *International Journal of Eating Disorders*, **20**, 271–9.

Texeira, P.J., Going, S.B., Sardinha, L.B. & Lohman, T.G. (2005). A review of psychosocial pre-treatment predictors of weight control. *Obesity Reviews*, **6**, 43–65.

Troisi, A., Massaroni, P. & Cuzzolaro, M. (2005). Early separation anxiety and adult attachment style in women with eating disorders. *British Journal of Clinical Psychology*, **44**, 89–97.

Trombini, E., Baldaro, B., Bertaccini, R. *et al.* (2003). Maternal attitudes and attachment styles in mothers of obese children. *Perceptual and Motor Skills*, **97**, 613–20.

Tryon, G.S. & Winograd, G. (2002). Goal consensus and collaboration. In J.C. Norcross (ed.), *Psychotherapy Relationships that Work: Therapist Contributions and Responsiveness to Patients* (pp. 109–25). Oxford: Oxford University Press.

Turner, S. & Lee, D. (1998). *Measures in Post Traumatic Stress Disorder: A Practitioner's Guide*. Windsor: NFER-Nelson.

Vila, G., Zinner, E., Dabbas, M. *et al.* (2004). Mental disorders in obese children and adolescents. *Psychosomatic Medicine*, **66**, 387–94.

Vogele, C. & Florin, I. (1997). Psychophysiological responses to food exposure: an experimental study in binge eaters. *International Journal of Eating Disorders*, **21**, 147–57.

Walfish, S. (2004). Self-assessed emotional factors contributing to increased weight gain in pre-surgical bariatric patients. *Obesity Surgery*, **14**, 1402–5.

Wampold, B. (2001). *The Great Psychotherapy Debate: Models, Methods and Findings*. Mahwah, NJ: Erlbaum.

Ward, A., Ramsay, R. & Treasure, J. (2000). Attachment research in eating disorders. *British Journal of Medical Psychology*, **73**, 35–51.

Wardle, J., Waller, J. & Rapoport, L. (2001). Body dissatisfaction and binge eating in obese women: the role of restraint and depression. *Obesity Research*, **9**, 778–87.

Weiss, E.L., Longhurst, J.G. & Mazure C.M. (1999). Childhood sexual abuse as a risk factor for depression in women: psychosocial and neurobiological correlates. *American Journal of Psychiatry*, **156**, 816–28.

Wiederman, M.W., Sansone. R.A. & Sansone L.A. (1999). Obesity among sexually abused women: an adaptive function for some? *Women and Health*, **29**, 89–100.

Wigton, R.S. & McGaghie, W.C. (2001). The effect of obesity on medical students' approach to patients with abdominal pain. *Journal of General Internal Medicine*, **16**, 262–5.

Will, M.J., Franzblau, E.B. & Kelley, A.E. (2003). Nucleus accumbens μ-opioids regulate intake of a high-fat diet via activation of a distributed brain network. *Journal of Neuroscience*, **23**, 2882–8.

Will, M.J., Franzblau, E.B. & Kelley, A.E. (2004). The amygdala is critical for opioid-mediated binge eating of fat. *Neuroreport*, **15**, 1857–60.

Williamson, D.F., Thompson, T.J., Anda, R.F. *et al.* (2002). Body weight and obesity in adults and self-reported abuse in childhood. *International Journal of Obesity*, **26**, 1075–82.

Wonderlich S.A., Crosby R.D., Mitchell, J.E. *et al.* (2001). Eating disturbance and sexual trauma in childhood and adulthood. *International Journal of Eating Disorders*, **30**, 401–12.

Yanovski, S.Z. (2003). Binge eating disorder and obesity in 2003: could treating an eating disorder have a positive effect on the obesity epidemic? *International Journal of Eating Disorders*, **34**, S117–S120.

Yanovski, S.Z. (2005). Pharmacotherapy for obesity – promise and uncertainty. *New England Journal of Medicine*, **353**(20), 2187–9.

Zimmerman, P. (1999). Structure and functions of internal working models of attachment and their role for emotion regulation. *Attachment and Human Development*, **1**, 291–306.

CHAPTER 7

FOOD FOR THE SOUL: SOCIAL AND EMOTIONAL ORIGINS OF COMFORT EATING IN THE MORBIDLY OBESE

PATRICIA GOODSPEED GRANT
State University College at Brockport, USA

INTRODUCTION

The worldwide prevalence, as well as the severity, of obesity is a well-established phenomenon (Freedman *et al.*, 2002; Livingstone, 2000). Extreme obesity is a risk factor for chronic health problems such as type 2 diabetes, high cholesterol, musculoskeletal problems and other health issues (Visscher & Seidell, 2001). There are also emotional and social consequences to extreme obesity. The morbidly obese are subject to ridicule, exclusion and discrimination by peers, healthcare providers and employers, which may have profound implications such as job discrimination and self-esteem problems (Franklin *et al.*, 2006; Harvey *et al.*, 2002; Puhl & Brownell, 2003; Tebo, 2005; Wigton & McGaghie, 2001).

Since biology and culture are inextricably tied together (Liburd, 2003), an understanding of the broader social context in which individuals learn about and experience food and eating is useful for understanding the current obesity phenomenon. Eating is a primal act, and social activities have centred around gathering, preparing and eating food since the beginning of human history. Cultural, social and symbolic meanings are embedded in rituals involving food and eating. Cultural anthropologists have provided some descriptions of these activities, yet this literature is rarely integrated into the existing body of knowledge on obesity and disordered eating. The following literature briefly describes some aspects of the disease model of obesity, as well as some of the literature describing the cultural, social and emotional functions of food. It is grounded in the cultural anthropology of food habits and the psychology of eating.

While attitudes about what is considered ideal human body size are culturally and historically situated (Law & Labre, 2002; Ogden & Thomas, 2003) the

Psychological Responses to Eating Disorders and Obesity: Recent and Innovative Work.
Edited by J. Buckroyd and S. Rother. © 2008 John Wiley & Sons, Ltd

current trend is toward the increasing medicalisation of obesity (Chang & Christakis, 2002; Rguibi & Belahsen, 2006), although there is some criticism of this perspective (Tremblay & Doucet, 2000). Its predominance is reflected in the scientific and medical attention given to the problem and the description of obesity as an epidemic by the World Health Organization (Flegal, 1999; James *et al.*, 2001). Given that the prevalence of obesity continues to rise despite medical interventions, and that relapse after treatment is the norm rather than the exception, there is clearly a missing link between scientific knowledge and individual behaviour. The disease model may not be sufficient to understand all aspects of the problem.

Other approaches have focused on the psychological correlates of obesity. Psychosomatic theories, for example, conceptualise obesity as arising from pathological personality structures. While classic psychosomatic theories assume that obese individuals eat abnormally as a response to emotional distress, current opinions are more apt to view any associated emotional disorders as a result, rather than the cause, of obesity (Allison & Heshka, 1993). From a learning theory perspective, behavioural theories postulate that overeating is a learned behaviour that becomes a way of life. Accordingly, food preferences and eating behaviours are thought to be learned in the family during childhood through modelling and through a system of reinforcements (Krieshok & Karpowitz, 1988). This might occur when children are given food instead of other kinds of attention when they feel stressed (Baldaro *et al.*, 2003) or when food is used to reward certain behaviours.

Interventions that reflect the disease model typically address the educational, behavioural and biological components of overeating. Virtually all interventions include dietary restriction and increased exercise to shift the balance of energy intake and output, with most other modes of intervention functioning to assist the individual to accomplish this objective. Lifestyle changes are addressed by cognitive behavioural therapy, nutritional counselling, behaviour modification, or support groups to maintain motivation. Biological interventions include the use of drugs to suppress the appetite. When these methods fail, the morbidly obese may resort to bariatric surgery, which imposes physical limitations on the quantity of food that can be consumed.

Outcomes of these medical interventions have been disappointing over the long term. Dietary restrictions often have exactly the opposite of the intended effect; that is, they often result in a preoccupation with food (Swinburn & Egger, 2004; Warren & Cooper, 1988) and predict an increase, rather than decrease, in body weight (Herman & Polivy, 1991; Jeffery *et al.*, 2004; Lowe *et al.*, 2006). Nutritional counselling does not necessarily produce changes in eating behaviour (Kalodner & DeLucia, 1990); evidence has not supported behavioural therapy for weight loss (Mark, 2006; Melin *et al.*, 2003). Appetite-suppressant drugs are of questionable benefit (Adis International, 2006; Yanovski, 2005). The medical response to this problem is to propose that any pharmacological intervention should be lifelong (Mark, 2006) since obesity is like any other chronic disease (Agrawal *et al.*, 2000). This solution has so far not led to long-term success.

Nawaz *et al.* (1999) report that physician 'counselling' results in weight-loss attempts for the overweight. Yet even if weight is lost, approximately 95% of individuals will regain it all within five years (Mark, 2006). Further, such advice by physicians, although well-intentioned, may even have negative, rather than positive consequences. Being weighed at the doctor's office is such a shameful, negative experience that many people will avoid medical visits altogether for minor ailments, in order to avoid being weighed. As Jane, one of the research participants who will be introduced later in this chapter, put it:

> When you go to the doctor, they just get mad at you if that scale is up. So even if you are not feeling well, you don't want to call that doctor. Because by God, if you're going in because you have a sinus infection, he's going to put you on that darn scale and he's going to say, 'What are you doing?'

So far, successful interventions for obesity have been elusive. Despite the prolific evidence supporting external and/or environmental causes, obesity interventions continue to place the majority of responsibility upon the individual (Chang & Christakis, 2002). When weight loss does not occur, the obese are often judged as unmotivated, lazy or noncompliant by medical caregivers (Harvey *et al.*, 2002). They are often accused of having no 'willpower' when they cannot restrict their eating. Yet anyone who has ever struggled with obesity knows that controlling excessive eating is not simply a matter of eating less and exercising more. While one could reasonably argue that any health behaviour is, and should be, ultimately under one's control, there are well-known social and cultural components to food choices and eating behaviours that are so powerful that this task becomes much more daunting than medical experts may presume. The drive to eat is powerful and food and eating behaviours are rife with cultural, social and emotional meaning.

Because eating is performed in social interaction with others, meanings attached to food, eating and meals are rooted in subconscious associations (Mirsky, 1981) that result from those interactions (Locher *et al.*, 2005). These interactions may include rites, celebrations and the symbolic meanings associated with culture and social class and are connected with such things as food availability and abundance. People eat more when they are in the presence of others (Clendenen *et al.*, 1994; Redd & de Castro, 1992). Social activities often accompany meals and the physical environment and social factors affect positive experiences of meals (Macht *et al.*, 2005).

In addition to its cultural and social associations, relationships with food are also characterised by powerful emotions (Locher *et al.*, 2005). Certain foods, such as fat, sugar and carbohydrates, are known to alter mood states (Brooks, 2006). Carbohydrates increase tryptophan, which increases serotonin levels, resulting in a better mood. There has been some attempt to identify the particular properties of these foods, as well as the physiological pathways by which individuals gain pleasure from them (Gautier *et al.*, 2000). The sensory properties of chocolate, for example, elevate mood (Macht & Dettmer, 2006). Perhaps the most powerful emotional influence of all, however, is associated with the capacity of food and eating to offer comfort.

'Comfort food' is a phrase used to refer to food choices people make during periods of stress. Wansink *et al.* (2003) examined preferences for comfort foods across gender and age groups. They found that men favoured warm, hearty, meal-related comfort foods (such as steak, casseroles and soup), whereas females preferred snack-related foods such as chocolate and ice-cream. Younger people tended to prefer more snack-related comfort foods compared to those over age 55. Locher and colleagues (2005) investigated the relationship between emotions, memory and food, furthering an understanding of the function of comfort foods. A summary of their findings reveals that a wide range of emotions are associated with food, including anger, anxiety, caring, embarrassment, frustration, guilt, happiness, hate, love, nostalgia, resentment, security and comfort. Some emotions – for example, disgust – are learned through social–emotional interactions with others in food-related activities. Locher asserts that comfort foods have emotional overtones, are associated with childhood and are almost always consumed alone. There is a strong link between memory and the emotional aspects of food. Food choices are associated with these memories, providing comfort by evoking feelings connected to relationships with special others.

Eating as a response to stressful conditions has been well documented (Cartwright *et al.*, 2003; Geliebter & Aversa, 2003; Ng & Jeffery, 2003), particularly for foods that are high in fat and carbohydrates, sugar and chocolate (Laitinen *et al.*, 2002; Ng & Jeffery, 2003). Stress eating occurs in normal weight individuals and there is some debate as to whether the obese actually eat more in response to negative emotions than the non-obese (Allison & Heshka, 1993; Van Strien, 1995). Most of the evidence supports the idea that the obese tend to overeat when experiencing negative emotional states (Geliebter & Aversa, 2003). This issue is complicated, however, and differences in eating patterns between normal and overweight persons are only beginning to emerge. Particularly interesting is that those who practise dietary restriction tend to eat more when stressed than those who do not restrict their eating (Greeno & Wing, 1994). Perhaps dieting itself increases the propensity to eat under stress.

In summary, eating is simultaneously a physiological survival drive, a behaviour, a private emotional experience and a social phenomenon rife with symbolism that is embedded within the culture. The current research was undertaken to broaden knowledge of how social and cultural factors contribute to overeating and how these factors may be incorporated into the literature on weight-loss interventions. The primary goal was to uncover deep, complex, personal and social experiences, which would then be interpreted through an historical and cultural lens in order to contextualise and understand the inner world of the obese client. It does not dismiss the contribution of genetic, lifestyle or any other factors, but seeks to add depth of understanding to the powerful and partially unconscious drive to overeat. This research is primarily concerned with those who are morbidly obese.

METHOD

Methodology speaks to the underlying theory that informs method and procedures (van Manen, 1997). The theoretical basis for this research is hermeneutic phenomenology. Hermeneutics relies upon Ricoeur's (1971) work involving the interpretation of texts. Titelman (1979) transformed Ricoeur's methods into a pragmatic application whereby written phenomenological protocols may be interpreted. Because language is metaphorical, he argued, and because the double meaning of metaphorical language requires the art of deciphering to unfold its many layers of meaning, discourse needs to be interpreted in much the same way that a text needs to be interpreted. The activity of interpretation is analogous to the interpretation of a text (Taylor, 1987; Titelman, 1979). Inquirers are, by necessity, part of the circle of interpretation. Lived experience is never accessed directly, but only through discourse. It is reconstructed from memory and therefore removed from the original experience in place and time, presented in a modified form, with only selected moments captured from the stream of consciousness. This discourse, as told to the researcher, is recorded and transcribed verbatim, rendering the objectified lived experience into a text-analogue which can then be interpreted.

From a phenomenological perspective, experiences in the form of text-analogues are understood as patterns whose internal connections need to be interpreted. It is a dialectical process, where themes are identified, an interpretation written, and then re-read and rewritten. Phenomenological data may have multiple interpretations, which Ricoeur conceptualises as a universal range of address. Like a text, the descriptive protocol may be read by an infinite range of possible readers, who interpret from different personal perspectives and historical situatedness (Titelman, 1979).

The method utilised for this research project was van Manen's (1997) hermeneutic phenomenology. This method seeks the meaning of experience using a descriptive approach to obtain the facts of a given experience to clarify meaning and places this meaning within a socio-historical context (van Manen, 1997). Its focus is on both the emotional tone of interviewees, as well as the wider social, cultural and historical context. It explores sources of emotional eating, as well as some of the insights arrived at by participants during the interview process. The wider social context explores the social and cultural meanings of food and eating, as well as the influence of media on food choices and lifestyles. The research was guided by van Manen's (1997) six research activities, which include:

(1) turning to a phenomenon that interests us
(2) investigating experience as we live it rather than as we conceptualise it
(3) reflecting on the essential themes which characterise the phenomenon
(4) describing the phenomenon through the art of writing and rewriting
(5) maintaining a strong and oriented relation to the phenomenon
(6) balancing the research context by considering the parts and the whole (van Manen, 1997, pp. 30–1).

Eleven participants, two men and nine women aged 30 to 60, were recruited from a weight-loss clinic to participate in a qualitative research interview. Information was gathered by two 90-minute phenomenological interviews. Pursuant to van Manen, transcripts were coded and separated into themes, which were then condensed, distilled and re-analysed through several iterations. Insights were identified through the co-conversations between the researcher and participants in the qualitative interview, where participants typically identified their patterns as the interviews progressed. Material that had been lying just under the surface of consciousness began to emerge through a self-reflexive process, through free association, as participants began to feel more comfortable and trusting. As is typical in qualitative research, the researcher returned to the literature after the initial data analysis to further explicate some of the themes, such as the social and cultural aspects of eating behaviour.

RESULTS

The orienting questions that provided the focus for this research asked individuals to address their family and social relationships. This personal and historical context illuminated the meaning these individuals had ascribed to their eating behaviour. The analysis identified four major themes that incorporate early socialisation experiences in relation to attitudes toward eating meals and preferences for particular foods. All reported themes were derived across multiple interviews. Quotations were chosen because they were typical illustrations of the above themes.

The first major theme, Emotional Hunger, incorporates experiences both from childhood, and in the present. Two sub-themes were identified: Loneliness and Belonging and a Lack of Self-Care, that speak to specific ways in which emotional needs were not met. The second major theme, Mistaking Emotional for Physical Hunger, provides descriptions of times when individuals would turn to food when they were in need of soothing or nurturing. The third theme, Solving the Problem Becomes the Problem, and its sub-theme, Autopilot, describe how eating under stress became a habit that proved extremely difficult to break. The fourth theme, The Missing Element, provides a description of what individuals felt they needed in order to address the emotional components of their problem eating.

Emotional Hunger

Emotional Hunger describes a range of difficulties related to nurturing human relationships. It is analogous to physical hunger in the sense that it was experienced as a longing that arose out of deprivation of a basic human psychological need. Emotional Hunger was connected to as well as preceded by, descriptions of some emotional deficit that arose out of a lack of love, warmth or nurturing that was accompanied by a longing for belonging and social relationships. Several participants described Emotional Hunger in childhood that lingered into adulthood, while others did not experience it until they became adults. Two subsections of this theme represent specific types of Emotional Hunger: Loneliness and Belonging and a Lack of Self-Care.

Loneliness and belonging

Loneliness is a specific type of Emotional Hunger. Eating provided a sense of comfort that substituted for the human connections that participants longed for but did not have. Participants tried to satisfy these emotional needs with food in two specific ways. Sometimes food served to create a connection that was never there; for others, eating recreated a sense of contentment that had been present previously. When Emotional Hunger arose out of conflicted relationships either in childhood or adulthood that were sources of stress, food was used to self-medicate feelings of pain and conflict.

George was a 56-year-old social worker who described a childhood devoid of nurturing:

> It was a very sad time, because I missed out on so much growing up. I didn't have it with peers my age and I didn't have it at home. Didn't have the nurturing, warmth, affection, support, comfort; my parents were incapable of it. I felt alone, hurt, angry.

Angela had also experienced a difficult childhood. She was a 30-year-old, married African American. She had attended a school in an affluent, white suburban district, where she had been taunted and teased. She felt very isolated:

> The kids called me Oreo. [They were] nasty, mean to me. It was hard – messed up, lonely. I was lonely even when I was with people.

Angela's home life was not much happier than her school life. She experienced her father as very controlling. Her parents divorced when she was an adolescent and whatever semblance of a normal family life she had was disrupted. After the divorce, her mother struggled with alcoholism and Angela felt completely alone:

> I found comfort in food. It was my best friend and I slowly gained weight. I didn't have anybody in my life, but I had food.

Angela had used food to comfort the pain of childhood loneliness while, sometimes participants longed for connections that were once important, but no longer existed. Food became a substitute for these missing relationships.

Marion was a single, 50-year-old school teacher who grew up in a large, close-knit family. She had been of normal weight as a child, but as she became an adult, she gradually became obese. She found herself eating ever-larger quantities of her favourite childhood foods after arriving home from a stressful day at school:

> Marion: I wanted the comfort of that popcorn or cookies or tapioca pudding and a lot of it.
>
> Interviewer: What were you seeking comfort from?
>
> Marion: Probably from stress, so that's probably a substitute, boredom, fatigue, stress and all of it.

During the second interview conversation, Marion began to reminisce about her lifetime of overeating:

> That's what was lacking really when I was in Vermont, and when I was in Chicago. I was alone and I was eating alone and longing for the family. There was a lot of that and I found comfort in food. It was my best friend.

Lottie was a 64-year-old black, retired, school teacher who had also grown up in a poor, but generally happy, family. She, too, had turned to the food she had known as a child when she needed comfort. In her case, it was homemade bread and baked goods. She recalled a particular instance when she had moved into a new city. She hadn't yet made any friends, and when her relationship with her significant other had ended, she turned to food:

> I was working with relationships that didn't work out so well. Once the relationship broke – and I don't want to blame that totally – I was feeling a little bit lonely. A little bit frustrated. I think I ate these 80 pounds when I moved here.

Lack of self-care

One gender-related theme that stood out was related to caretaking. Every woman in the study, but none of the men, reported putting others before themselves. Edna, a 60-year-old mother of four who had struggled with her weight most of her adult life, offered the following insight:

> People take too good of care of themselves and they don't care about anybody else. I never wanted to be that kind of a person, so I went too much the other way and didn't take care of myself. I think sometimes that's part of it, you know. So then you say, 'The heck with it! I'm just going to have that candy bar'.

Lottie was also able to articulate how she had learned to put others before herself:

> I think my mother was the ultimate caretaker and I always say – my sister and I talk about [it] – you teach the lessons that you live better than those that you say. You tell your children that they should do this or they should do that. But they're watching you and that's what they pick up.

Tina, a 54-year-old psychiatric nurse, had also spent all of her life taking care of others. She was unmarried and had no children, but she played out her caretaking needs through her vocation:

> Always taking care of others – learned that I could make a difference, at least I thought I could, by keeping the peace and by taking care of things so there was less stress in the family. As his [father's] health declined, I cooked for him for 17 years, every weekend. I think that's part of why I gained so much weight toward the last five years of his life – mainly because I was so sick of it. And so frustrated. Everything that had to be done was a struggle.

Tina was a compulsive eater who used food as a way to practise self-care. During the second interview, she began to realise how taking care of others led her to eat:

> I had no down time. I had no time for myself and I think I was using food more than I had been to take the edge off and medicate myself, reward myself, treat myself. A lot of eating out because it was quick and easy. So that was a recipe for overeating.

It is interesting that both Edna's and Lottie's daughters were also caretakers. They illustrate the power of modelling and unconscious behaviour as agents of learning. They enjoyed cooking, and it seemed natural that food should become a legitimate way for women to take care of themselves. They prided themselves on being good cooks. Several participants indicated that their mothers had been good cooks and their lives were centred around preparing meals for their families.

Mistaking Emotional for Physical Hunger

This theme reports not just the fact of eating for comfort, but also offers detailed descriptions of how the process works. Dorothy was a 60-year-old retiree who began to recognise that she ate for comfort as a result of criticism by her family members, particularly her husband and her mother. Dorothy's mother frequently harped on at her by telling her that she would feel better if she lost weight. Her mother's suggestions did not motivate her to lose weight, but in fact, had the opposite effect; she felt judged and controlled, and ran to food for comfort:

> Picking at you just makes you angry. I just get upset. I've known times when I would run to food if I were upset.

Jane reported eating for similar reasons:

> I think at that time is when I maybe picked – eating was very satisfying. I was in so much pain, you know.

While eating for comfort sometimes operated at the conscious level, it more often occurred subliminally. Sam was a married software engineer with two young sons, one of whom had been diagnosed with Asperger's syndrome. His home environment was quite chaotic. Interestingly, the focus of his son's Asperger's-related obsession was food and a great deal of the family's energy was centred around meeting his son's needs. Sam's wife cooked three separate meals each night: one for each of the children; after they were in bed she would then cook a meal for Sam and herself. Their entire evening was consumed with meal preparation, leaving little time for anything else.

Sam had been given a copy of the focused interview guide approximately one week before the interview. He had used this time to think about what he had wanted to share with the researcher. He identified a nightly pattern of coming home from work, standing in front of the refrigerator and eating as a result of stress:

> Beforehand, I have a level of frustration; I'm tense, and the process of eating either is a release of energy that makes me feel better, or a distraction. Maybe I focus on that, and the kids are – I hear them still, but they're not as loud, because my senses have turned on to something else. I usually know I shouldn't be doing this – I'm consciously aware of it – but at the same time, I still want to eat to comfort the stress or the tension. I'm not really sure what I get out of it. As soon as you're done, you feel very full, or the stress is still there. I'm not sure what the exact feeling is, other than that it is a diversion from the elements that are stressing me. You focus on something else – on food.

Two particularly articulate examples of comfort eating were related by George and Amy. Both ate to provide relief from emotional pain:

> George: Physically the repository for the food, everything emanates from it – the source for energy, source for feelings, in a sense. So rather than stir up the feelings it's easier to put food in there and then I can satiate it now and I can control it with grazing and food. Food was the means to an end – the connection.

Because food allows me to satiate all the other physiological functions and I get some pleasure.

Amy: It feels like you're hooked on it. It is calming. I know it releases endorphins. I know it makes me feel better. I do feel better after I eat. I feel medicated, you know what I mean? I don't know how else to put it. It takes the edge off, I guess.

For both of these people, having both the knowledge and the ability to identify how food functioned for them was not sufficient to keep them from the behaviour. Eating for comfort had become a deeply ingrained habit and difficult to break.

Solving the Problem Becomes the Problem

The participants all recognised that for them emotional eating was, in the short term, a very effective way to dull emotional pain. As with other self-medicating behaviour, the mechanism can work so well that unhealthy patterns become habitual and automatic. Further, the euphoric effect is short-lived and the negative consequences are insidious. Normal eating then became problem eating. Dan was typical in his descriptions of how automatic this process was:

If I need a lot of pleasure I eat a lot of food in a short period of time and it became a pattern.

Amy, too, spoke about how the short-term benefits become a lifelong habit:

Believe me over the years I'm eating for a million reasons. It's just way too many calories. You get stuck on that.

Autopilot

One of the most powerful insights arising from the interviews was that periods of consciousness and intentionality alternated with periods of unconscious eating. Participants assumed that their behaviour was normal. Their behaviour and food choices were so much a part of the landscape that they could not be readily articulated. These themes might not have been identified had they not been explored through dialogue with the researcher. Reminiscing and making connections over the course of two or three interviews allowed this subconscious material to rise to the surface.

Like most of the participants, Lottie had not been aware of why she overate while it happened and it was only in retrospect that she could identify the meaning of her eating. Lottie's insight was particularly interesting because she was one of the least articulate of the participants, although she recalled certain events or feelings as a result of the researcher asking probing questions. Referring to a period of significant weight gain while involved in a stressful relationship, she reminisced:

> I started to comfort myself in a sense with food. I don't know. In hindsight – I didn't know that at the time.

Cultural reproduction is accomplished intergenerationally, in the following instance, through food and cooking preferences (Ahye *et al.*, 2006). Dorothy was a charming retiree who knew little of academic discourse on cultural production. However, her explanations embodied clear evidence for this process:

> If you come from a long line of people who have [been] overweight in the past – I don't know if it's that they eat that way – I don't know if it's the cooks in the family or what it is – they just grow up, everybody cooking the same. Mother cooks like daughter and daughter cooks like mother and it just goes on and on and on.

The Missing Element

All the participants had been involved in many other programmes, but they liked two things in particular about the clinic approach: that it was multidisciplinary and it utilised experts rather than lay helpers. Interestingly, this may be a reflection of how medicine has become the dominant model and therefore becomes the only legitimate trusted authority on obesity. The one thing that participants said was missing, however, was the opportunity to work on psychological issues concurrently with weight loss. Dorothy commented about a commercial programme:

> I wasn't doing the most important piece nor did the programme have any way to facilitate that. You met with someone but they weren't very skilled in terms of being able to look at any of that. To be honest with you, it seemed to be pretty superficial. I don't recall a lot of depth. Maybe just relative to hunger or something.

In summary, participants offered their innermost thoughts and feelings about how they connected food with a deep sense of belonging, either through the memories of comfort foods that reminded them of pleasant childhoods, or through the physiological reward system that brought comfort and pleasure when things in their lives were not going well. They had developed a way to self-medicate through eating that provided comfort in the short term, but ultimately became so ingrained that it became problematic in itself. These patterns became part of a lifestyle that was very resistant to change, even when the behaviour became conscious. Somewhere along the way, normal eating had become problem eating.

Since the participants were co-researchers, they were asked what they would like to share with the medical helpers. This answer stood out:

> Maybe it would open doctors' eyes to the really emotional part of it. Because a lot of times in the medical profession, the humanness things are lost and maybe it could help doctors to see their patients – to make it more personal. Because it is so much more than, 'Stop eating!'. It's so much more than that.

Contrary to the stereotype that the obese have no willpower, the participants were very disciplined, very motivated and were desperate to find some permanent solution to their weight problems. All participants had been dieting most of their adult lives and some had been dieting since childhood. All had been able to lose weight, sometimes as much as 50–80 pounds. Yet after a period of time, each diet resulted in net weight gain rather than permanent loss. When their attention was not fully directed toward maintaining a diet, automatic patterns dominated over new ways of eating that were unfamiliar. Because of their track record of weight cycling, most became so discouraged that they felt defeated before they even began their current weight-loss programme. They knew they could lose the weight, but they also began to believe that there was no point to it all, because they knew the weight would come back.

DISCUSSION

The interviews demonstrated that eating was a social act, where participants created, or recreated, a sense of warmth, belonging and togetherness with significant others. In some cases, eating became a substitute for these missing key relationships. While sheer hunger was a demon to be conquered during periods of restricted food intake, eating had also become a primary way to fulfil emotional and social needs. Restricting food led to frustration and anger. Deprivation occurred on many levels. Participants were feeding emotional as well as physical hunger and dieting deprived them of this coping mechanism, as well as the social aspects of food and eating. Since meals are one source of communal activity, being deprived of this way to connect with others heightened the sense of isolation these individuals felt.

This research has addressed some of the emotional components of eating behaviour related to stress and a need to belong to a social group. Reducing food to its chemical properties of fat, calories and carbohydrates misses the important symbolic functions of food that are rooted in social, emotional and cultural life. These complex, multi-layered levels of experience are intertwined to the extent that omitting any one aspect of such a primal experience as eating will not address the issue of emotional overeating. Eating for comfort for the morbidly obese is not only rooted in these aspects, but also in emotional pain and difficult family and social relationships. Addressing these issues should be an important component of any weight management programme.

The implication of this research is that participants would benefit from a counselling intervention to address their difficulties. There are issues on which it might be useful to focus. The first is the normalisation of the social, emotional and cultural aspects of eating behaviour. The problems to be identified may include stress and the lack of social support. The therapist needs to honour the client's choice of a mode of relief that is less harmful than many other methods of self-medication. It is more helpful to contextualise eating problems than to pathologise them.

The second area of focus is the issue of the emotional function of food for each individual, to help them identify and resolve the emotional pain and hunger that are being nurtured physically. Therapeutic issues, based on this and prior research (Goodspeed Grant & Boersma, 2005) include issues of control, loneliness, stress and conflict, emotional deprivation and lack of self-care. However, these issues are unique and should be assessed for each individual. Counselling interventions, when used in conjunction with a programme of healthy eating, can help clients to recognise the difference between physical and emotional hunger, address emotional issues and identify alternative coping strategies.

The third area of focus is an assessment of the individual's self-concept relative to body image, and self-efficacy. Since morbidly obese people have developed a significant relationship with food as comfort, a new relationship with food is needed. Food needs to be seen as promoting well-being, rather than being an enemy to conquer. In addition, identifying and encouraging healthy social and emotional relationships can help put the relationship with food into a proper perspective.

The primal activity of eating is always embedded in social, cultural and symbolic meaning. Food has psychological associations which are derived from these social interactions. These functions operate at the individual, conscious level as well as at more pervasive, cultural and subconscious levels. The medical model treats the individual as a social isolate and ignores the powerful social functions of food that have always characterised human society. Severe obesity that is addressed solely from either disease or psychological perspectives, without addressing the individual's unique genetic, cultural, social and emotional relationship with eating, is bound to fail.

REFERENCES

Adis International Limited. (2006). Pharmacotherapy for the treatment of obesity has only modest benefits and should be used in combination with lifestyle modifications. *Drugs and Therapy Perspectives*, **22**(1), 7–11.

Agrawal, M., Worzniak, M. & Diamond, L. (2000). Managing obesity like any other chronic condition. *Postgraduate Medicine*, **108**(1), 75–80.

Ahye, B.A., Devine, C.M. & Odoms-Young, A.M. (2006). Values expressed through intergenerational family food and nutrition management systems among African-American women. *Family and Community Health*, **29**(1), 5–16.

Allison D.B. & Heshka, S. (1993). Emotion and eating in obesity? A critical analysis. *International Journal of Eating Disorders*, **13**(3), 289–95.

Baldaro, B., Rossi, N., Caterina, R. *et al.* (2003). Deficit in the discrimination of nonverbal emotions in children with obesity and their mothers. *International Journal of Obesity*, **27**, 191–5.

Brooks, A. (2006). Changing food preference as a function of mood. *Journal of Psychology*, **140**(4), 293–306.

Cartwright, M., Wardle, J., Steggles, N. *et al.* (2003). Stress and dietary practices in adolescents. *Health Psychology*, **22**(4), 362–9.

Chang, V.W. & Christakis, N.A. (2002). Medical modelling of obesity: a transition from action to experience in a 20th-century American medical textbook. *Sociology of Health and Illness*, **24**(2), 151–87.

Clendenen, V.I., Herman C.P. & Polivy, J. (1994). Social facilitation of eating among friends and strangers. *Appetite*, **23**(1), 1–13.

Flegal, K.M. (1999). The obesity epidemic in children and adults: current evidence and research issues. *Medicine and Science in Sports and Exercise*, **31**(11), Supplement 1, S509.

Freedman, D.S., Khan, L.K., Serdula, M.K. *et al.* (2002). Trends and correlates of class 3 obesity in the United States from 1990 through 2000. *Journal of the American Medical Association*, **288**(14), 1758–61.

Franklin, J., Denyer, G., Steinbeck, K.S. *et al.* (2006). Obesity and risk of low self-esteem: a statewide survey of Australian children. *Pediatrics*, **118**(6), 2481–7.

Gautier, J.F., Chen, K., Salbe, A.D. *et al.* (2000). Differential brain responses to satiation in obese and lean men. *Diabetes*, **19**(5), 838–46.

Geliebter, A. & Aversa, A. (2003). Emotional eating in overweight, normal weight, and underweight individuals. *Eating Behaviors*, **3**(4), 341–348.

Goodspeed Grant, P. & Boersma, H. (2005). Making sense of being fat: a qualitative analysis of adults' explanations for obesity. *Counselling and Psychotherapy Research Journal*, **5**(3), 1–9.

Greeno, C.G. & Wing, R.R. (1994). Stress-induced eating. *Psychological Bulletin*, **115**(3), 444–64.

Harvey, E.L., Summerbell, C.D., Kirk, S.F.L. & Hill, A.J. (2002). Dieticians' views of overweight and obese people and reported management practices. *Journal of Human Nutrition and Dietetics*, **15**(5), 331–47.

Herman, P. & Polivy, J. (1991). Fat is a psychological issue. *New Scientist*, **132**(1795), 41–5.

James, P.T., Leach, R., Kalamara, E. & Maryam Shayeghi, M. (2001). Section I: Obesity, the Major Health Issue of the 21st Century. The Worldwide Obesity Epidemic. Obesity Research 9:S228

Jeffery, R.W., Kelly, K.M. & Sherwood, N.E. (2004). The weight loss experience: a descriptive analysis. *Annals of Behavior Medicine*, **27**(2), 100–6.

Kalodner, C.R. & DeLucia, J.L. (1990). Components of an effective weight loss program: theory, research and practice. *Journal of Counseling and Development*, **68**, 427–33.

Krieshok, S.I. & Karpowitz, D.H. (1988). A review of selected literature on obesity and guidelines for treatment. Journal of Counseling & Development, **66**, 326–330.

Law, C. & Labre, M.P. (2002). Cultural standards of attractiveness: A thirty-year look at changes in male images in magazines. Journalism & Mass Communication Quarterly, **79**(3), 697–711.

Laitinen, J., Ek, E. & Sovio, U. (2002). Stress-related eating and drinking behavior and body mass index and predictors of this behavior. *Preventive Medicine*, **34**(1), 29–39.

Liburd, L.C. (2003). Food, identity, and African-American women with Type 2 diabetes: an anthropological perspective. *Diabetes Spectrum*, **16**(3), 160–5.

Livingstone, B. (2000). Epidemiology of childhood obesity in Europe. *European Journal of Pediatrics*, **159**(13), S14.

Locher, J., Yoels, W.C., Maurer, D., & VanElls, J. (2005). Comfort foods: an exploratory journey into the social and emotional significance of food. *Food and Foodways*, **13**, 273–97.

Lowe, M.R., Annunziato, R.A., Markowitz, J.T. *et al.* (2006). Multiple types of dieting prospectively predict weight gain during the freshman year of college. *Appetite*, **47**, 83–90.

Macht, M. & Dettmer, D. (2006) Everyday mood and emotions after eating a chocolate bar or an apple. *Appetite*, **46**, 332–6.

Macht, M., Meininger, J. & Roth, J. (2005). The pleasures of eating: a qualitative analysis. *Journal of Happiness Studies*, **6**(2), 137–60.

Mark, A.L. (2006). Dietary therapy for obesity is a failure and pharmacotherapy is the future: a point of view. *Clinical and Experimental Pharmacology and Physiology*, **33**(9), 857–62.

Melin, I., Lappalainen, R., Berglund, L. *et al.* (2003). A programme of behaviour modification and nutrition counselling in the treatment of obesity: a randomised 2-year clinical trial. *International Journal of Obesity*, **27**(9), 1127–35.

Mirsky, R. (1981). Perspectives in the study of food habits. *Western Folklore*, **40**(1), 125–33.

Nawaz, H., Adams, M.L. & Katz, D.L. (1999) Weight loss counseling by health care providers. *American Journal of Public Health*, **89**(5), 1747–50.

Ng, D.M. & Jeffery, R.W. (2003). Relationships between perceived stress and health behaviors in a sample of working adults. *Health Psychology*, **22**(6), 638–42.

Ogden J. & Thomas, D. (1999). The role of familial values in understanding the impact of social class on weight concern. *International Journal of Eating Disorders*, **25**(3), 273–9.

Puhl, R.M. & Brownell, K.D. (2003). Psychosocial origins of obesity stigma: toward changing a powerful and pervasive bias. *Obesity Reviews*, **4**, 213–27.

Redd, M. & de Castro, J.M. (1992). Social facilitation of eating: effects of social instruction on food intake. *Physiology and Behavior*, **52**(4), 749–54.

Ricoeur, P. (1971). The model of the text: meaningful action considered as a text. *Social Research*, **38**, 529–62.

Rguibi, M. & Belahsen, R. (2006) Body size preferences and sociocultural influences on attitudes towards obesity among Moroccan Sahraoui women. Body Image 3(2006) 395–400.

Swinburn, B. & Egger, G. (2004). The runaway weight gain train: too many accelerators, not enough brakes. *British Medical Journal*, **329**(7468), 736–9.

Taylor, C. (1987). Interpretation and the sciences of man. In P. Rabinow & W.M. Sullivan (eds), *Interpretive Social Science: A Second Look* (pp. 33–81). Berkeley: University of California Press.

Tebo, M.G. (2005). A matter of some weight. *ABA Journal*, **91**(6), 17–18.

Titelman, P. (1979). Some implications of Ricoeur's conception of hermeneutics for phenemonological psychology. In A. Giorgi, R. Knowles & D.I. Smith (eds), *Duquesne studies in phenomenological psychology, Volume III*. Pittsburgh: Duquesne University Press.

Tremblay, A. & Doucet, E. (2000). Obesity: a disease or biological adaptation? *Obesity Reviews*, **1**, 27–35.

van Manen, M. (1997). *Researching Lived Experience*, 2nd edition. London: Althouse Press.

van Strien, T. (1995). In defense of psychosomatic theory: a critical analysis of Allison and Heshka's critical analysis. *International Journal of Eating Disorders*, **17**(3), 299–304.

Visscher, T. & Seidell, J.C. (2001). The public health impact of obesity. *Annual Review of Public Health*, **22**(1), 355–75.

Warren, C. & Cooper, P.J. (1988). Psychological effects of dieting. *British Journal of Clinical Psychology*, **27**(3), 269–70.

Wigton, R.S. & McGaghie, W.C. (2001). The effect of obesity on medical students' approach to patients with abdominal pain. *Journal of General Internal Medicine*, **16**(4), 262–5.

Wansink, B., Cheney, M.M. & Chan, N. (2003). Exploring comfort food preferences across age and gender. *Physiology and Behavior*, **79**, 739–47.

Yanovski, S.Z. (2005). Pharmacotherapy for obesity – promise and uncertainty. *New England Journal of Medicine*, **353**(20), 2187–9.

CHAPTER 8

COGNITIVE BEHAVIOUR GROUP THERAPY FOR OBESITY AND BINGE EATING DISORDER

SASKIA KEVILLE, *University of Hertfordshire, UK*
VERITY BYRNE, *St Ann's Eating Disorder Unit, UK*
MADELEINE TATHAM, *Hertfordshire Community Eating Disorder Service, UK*
and
GERRY McCARRON, *Goldsmiths College, UK*

INTRODUCTION

This chapter outlines a group intervention for obese patients with binge eating disorder (BED) provided by a Specialist Eating Disorder Service based in North London. Due to limited services and a pressure to target patients of a more 'clinically severe' status, the group prioritised those with severe excess weight (mean BMI: 48; range 36–60) so obesity here refers to individuals who are above a body mass index (BMI) of 35.

Obesity is not a psychiatric diagnosis; rather it is a physical condition. Many people who are overweight may not view it as problematic in psychological terms. However, it is now well established that binge eating often occurs within the context of a general tendency to overeat, and it is this pattern that is linked to obesity (Adami *et al.*, 1995). Obesity is a likely consequence, particularly if the individual does not employ weight-modulating compensatory strategies such as self-induced vomiting, excessive exercising or dietary restriction.

Binge eating may be so problematic that a diagnosis of binge eating disorder (BED) is indicated (American Psychiatric Association, 1994). This diagnosis requires the presence of significantly disordered eating patterns and associated emotional distress. There is evidence to suggest that individuals with obesity and BED often have impaired quality of life compared to those with obesity alone (Rieger *et al.*, 2005; de Zwaan *et al.*, 2003), as well as significant levels of psychiatric comorbidity (Anderson *et al.*, 2006; McElroy *et al.*, 2004; Wilfley *et al.*, 2000). This highlights the importance of a treatment that

Psychological Responses to Eating Disorders and Obesity: Recent and Innovative Work.
Edited by J. Buckroyd and S. Rother. © 2008 John Wiley & Sons, Ltd

addresses not only the eating psychopathology but also other psychological and psychiatric problems.

Evidence suggests that deficits in emotional regulation and tolerance and factors such as low self-esteem and low self-efficacy, may act as both triggers to binge eating episodes and as a maintenance factor in BED (Edman *et al.*, 2005; Masheb & Grilo, 2006). There have been similar findings for bulimia nervosa (BN) (Barry *et al.*, 2003; Cooper, 2003; Cooper *et al.*, 2004; Dingemans *et al.*, 2002; Fairburn *et al.*, 2003). Taking these factors into account may prove useful in developing more successful treatments for BED.

To date, most psychological treatments for BED have been based on cognitive behavioural therapy (CBT). CBT is still the most extensively researched treatment for BED with positive results (Devlin *et al.*, 2005; Grilo & Masheb, 2005; National Institute for Clinical Excellence, 2004). However, given the very nature of obesity and its link with binge eating, there may be an essential role for the use of dietetics in its treatment. Research suggests that dietetics can provide a significant role in the treatment of BED and subsequent obesity. Targeting the primary behavioural issue in BED, binge eating, seems pertinent to increasing treatment efficacy (Wonderlich *et al.*, 2003).

Bearing this literature in mind, we would like to present the theoretical rationale for our intervention. It incorporates CBT and specialist dietetics. We begin by discussing the possible functions of binge eating within a framework which understands this behaviour as a means of managing life and/or emotional experiences. Advantages, disadvantages and clinical implications of the strategies commonly utilised to manage difficult experiences are then discussed. Following this, we discuss how our treatment was guided by this conceptualisation and show how it was constructed and adapted to help facilitate change for people within this group. In addition, we present the rationale for electing to offer group treatment as opposed to individual treatment.

COGNITIVE BEHAVIOURAL THEORY

The approach to case conceptualisation used a standard Beckian format adapted to incorporate notions from the Self-Regulatory Executive Function (S-REF) model (Wells, 1997, 2000; Wells & Matthews, 1994). The S-REF model highlights the role of strategic and dynamic self-regulatory processes in emotional disorder, particularly metacognitive and attentional factors. These factors have been proposed to play a role in the development and maintenance of several psychological disorders, for instance, social anxiety, obsessive compulsive disorder, generalised anxiety disorder (Wells, 1997, 2000); depression (Papageorgiou & Wells, 2003); and BN (Cooper, 2003; Cooper *et al.*, 2004). This framework, retaining the top-down influence of schemas proposed by Beck (e.g. Beck, 1976), provides a useful theoretical template to demonstrate the hypothesised mechanisms involved in the maintenance

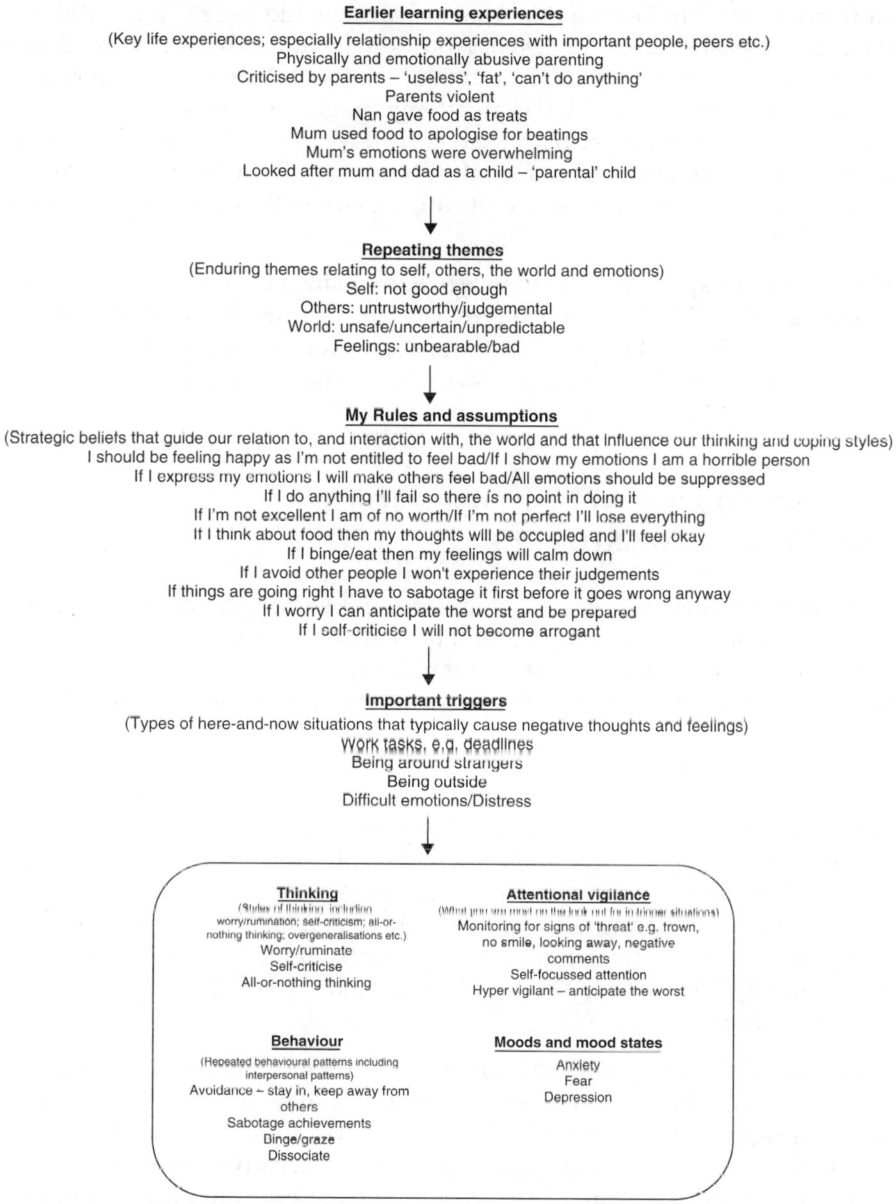

Earlier learning experiences
(Key life experiences; especially relationship experiences with important people, peers etc.)
Physically and emotionally abusive parenting
Criticised by parents – 'useless', 'fat', 'can't do anything'
Parents violent
Nan gave food as treats
Mum used food to apologise for beatings
Mum's emotions were overwhelming
Looked after mum and dad as a child – 'parental' child

↓

Repeating themes
(Enduring themes relating to self, others, the world and emotions)
Self: not good enough
Others: untrustworthy/judgemental
World: unsafe/uncertain/unpredictable
Feelings: unbearable/bad

↓

My Rules and assumptions
(Strategic beliefs that guide our relation to, and interaction with, the world and that influence our thinking and coping styles)
I should be feeling happy as I'm not entitled to feel bad/If I show my emotions I am a horrible person
If I express my emotions I will make others feel bad/All emotions should be suppressed
If I do anything I'll fail so there is no point in doing it
If I'm not excellent I am of no worth/If I'm not perfect I'll lose everything
If I think about food then my thoughts will be occupied and I'll feel okay
If I binge/eat then my feelings will calm down
If I avoid other people I won't experience their judgements
If things are going right I have to sabotage it first before it goes wrong anyway
If I worry I can anticipate the worst and be prepared
If I self-criticise I will not become arrogant

↓

Important triggers
(Types of here-and-now situations that typically cause negative thoughts and feelings)
Work tasks, e.g. deadlines
Being around strangers
Being outside
Difficult emotions/Distress

↓

Thinking
(Styles of thinking including
worry/rumination; self-criticism; all-or-
nothing thinking; overgeneralisations etc.)
Worry/ruminate
Self-criticise
All-or-nothing thinking

Attentional vigilance
(What you are most on the look out for in trigger situations)
Monitoring for signs of 'threat' e.g. frown,
no smile, looking away, negative
comments
Self-focussed attention
Hyper vigilant – anticipate the worst

Behaviour
(Repeated behavioural patterns including
interpersonal patterns)
Avoidance – stay in, keep away from
others
Sabotage achievements
Binge/graze
Dissociate

Moods and mood states
Anxiety
Fear
Depression

Figure 8.1 A means of conceptualising current issues, and their historical context using CBT theory. An example using a formulation developed with group members

of BED (see Figure 8.1). This model also has the advantage of considering comorbid factors and potential interactions, within the sameframework.

This conceptualisation incorporates a functional view of the eating behaviour. Clinical findings support CBT conceptualisations by indicating an interrelationship between the role of emotion and binge eating (Edman et al., 2005; Masheb & Grilo, 2006). Additionally, it has been proposed that binge eating is a response to underlying emotional distress and the restriction of food intake or bingeing is an attempt to gain a sense of mastery over this distress (Heatherton & Baumeister, 1991; McManus & Waller, 1995). Indeed, mastery (in the context of 'control') has often been given a central role in the aetiology and maintenance of eating distress (Cooper, 2003; Fairburn et al., 1999).

The concept of experiential avoidance has also gained popularity as a hypothesised transdiagnostic process (Hayes et al., 2003). Thus the disordered eating behaviour is viewed here as a self-regulatory strategy specifically aimed at the removal or alleviation of emotional/psychological distress.

MANAGEMENT STYLE OF LIFE AND/OR EMOTIONAL EXPERIENCES

These conceptualisations seem to suggest an underlying drive to manage life and/or emotional experience. Several theoretical accounts offer suggestions as to how people manage their emotional experience. Many of these theories are supported by clinical findings, for example, Schema-Focused Theory (Young, 1994); Dialectical Behaviour Therapy (Linehan, 1993); Relational Frame Theory (Hayes et al., 2003); and S-REF (Wells & Matthews, 1994). These theories suggest a number of influences which may inform how people learn to manage their experiences, particularly negative emotional experiences. Many of the theories draw upon developmental models and highlight the role and importance of early learning experience, for example, the influence of emotionally 'invalidating' environments (Linehan, 1993); parental behaviour and parenting style (Mountford et al., in press; Schmidt et al., 1993); the role of traumatic experiences (e.g. sexual, physical and/or emotional abuse) (Kent et al., 1999; Rorty et al., 1994).

Such influences may lead to the formation of underlying core themes about the self, others, the world and emotions. These may develop very early on in life, at a time when individuals have limited autonomy, cognitive ability and/or knowledge base. As a consequence, negative experiences at an early age may result in an increased employment of avoidant-based coping strategies, in an attempt to escape from and/or manage difficult experiences (Hayes et al., 2003). This hypothesis fits with the concept of distress intolerance (Linehan, 1993). Linehan (1993) proposes that growing up in an invalidating environment may result in a decreased ability to manage distress effectively. The habitual use of avoidant strategies could make them more readily available and utilisable as coping mechanisms. The consequence may be restricted access to and/or a decreased ability to use or develop more adaptive coping strategies (Wells & Matthews, 1994).

CLINICAL IMPLICATIONS

Wells (2000) and Hayes *et al.* (2003) suggest that range and flexibility in methods of coping may be important factors in managing internal and external life experiences effectively (e.g. problem recognition and problem solving; processing emotional experiences; acceptance and reducing rumination). Figure 8.2 suggests one means of conceptualising this.

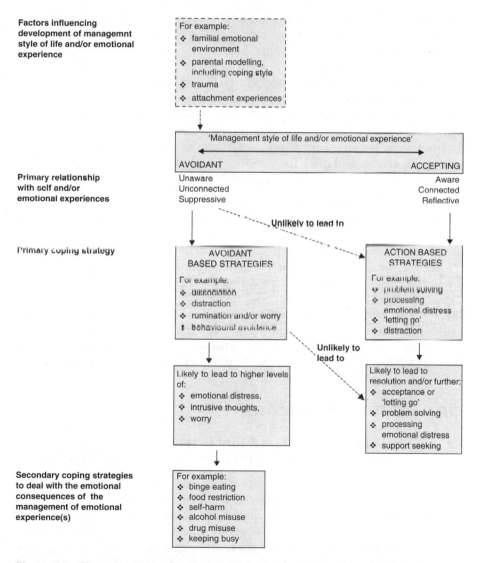

Figure 8.2 Conceptualising the avoidance and acceptance continuum as a means of managing life and emotional experiences; and the coping strategies utilised in response to these

So, for example, individuals employing strategies toward the accepting end of the continuum may be more likely to have a greater repertoire of coping strategies; including adaptive, action-based strategies which in turn, may be more likely to result in positive outcomes when managing life.

On the other hand, individuals employing coping strategies toward the avoidant end of the continuum may be more likely to use suppressive forms of coping. This may include cognitive suppression (e.g. dissociation) or behavioural suppression (e.g. keeping busy or binge eating).

Distraction may fall between the two camps. For example, it may be usefully employed at times when an individual has to focus on achieving or completing tasks in the face of difficult life experiences, such as bereavement. However, if used habitually and extensively, it may also serve a suppressive function, and thus result in an individual having reduced access to a range of adaptive strategies that require awareness and an acknowledgement of one's emotional experience (e.g. reflection, and/or exploration which may then lead to active problem solving and support seeking). Clinical research findings indicate that eating disordered clients tend to have reduced problem-solving capacities, and often use emotion-focused solutions to cope with distress (Janzen et al., 1992; Koff & Sangani, 1996).

Perhaps more significantly, avoidance and suppressive coping may actually serve to exacerbate, amplify and maintain emotional distress and discomfort. It has been shown that the primary use of thought suppression as a coping strategy results in higher levels of depressive and obsessive symptoms (Wegner & Zanakos, 1994). Clearly, this possibility has important implications for the treatment of patients with eating disorders, particularly as a negative emotional state may predict poor treatment outcome (Linde et al., 2004). We would like to suggest that the psychological consequences of employing avoidance and suppressive coping may explain the high prevalence of negative affect in eating disordered populations. If interventions do not target these processes, their continued use may reduce the efficacy of treatment.

THERAPEUTIC INTERVENTIONS

The Utility of Developing Flexibility in the use of Coping Strategies, Particularly Those on the Acceptance-based Continuum

Hayes et al. (2003) have suggested that since distress is part of human experience, a reasonable aim would be to develop a different relationship with experience, for example, developing acceptance and tolerance-based strategies. Similarly, Wells (2000) suggests developing the ability to stand back and think about issues and/or experiences and to utilise appropriate strategies to deal with them. These may include problem solving, 'letting go' and/or avoidance in the face of real threats; rather than utilising reactive and/or avoidance-based strategies 'as if' one were always in a threatening situation. People who are more open to their experiences may be more likely to utilise action-based coping strategies, thereby achieving a more positive, manageable outcome. Conversely, those employing avoidance-based strategies may have a narrower repertoire of coping skills, with minimal access to action-based ones. It is for this reason that we utilised interventions which focused on elaborating and/or developing action-based strategies.

INTERVENTION STRATEGIES FOR OBESITY AND BINGE EATING DISORDER

Informed by the above theoretical framework, our overall aim for the group intervention for clients with obesity and BED was threefold:

- to reduce problematic eating behaviour (i.e. incidents of binge eating)
- to target those areas thought to underlie the function of their problematic eating behaviour
- to address the long-term goal of weight loss

Targets therefore included exploring the clients' awareness of their experiences (such as negative emotional states) and expanding their repertoire of more adaptive, action-based coping strategies. A basic outline of the group programme can be seen in Table 8.1.

AIMS AND OBJECTIVES OF THE GROUP

Our primary goal was to incorporate dietetic and psychological knowledge to address the issue of BED and comorbid obesity. Whilst weight loss is usually a primary goal in the treatment of obesity, it has been suggested that for BED, normalisation of eating habits and weight stabilisation need to occur first (Dingemans et al., 2002). Therefore, our initial focus was to reduce binge eating and enhance the ability to stabilise weight; explore underlying psychological and dietary issues; provide psychological and dietary education; and then facilitate the development of alternative adaptive coping strategies. A realistic expectation of a 10% reduction in body weight was emphasised as a target for long-term weight loss, in order to reap the health improvements shown to be associated with this loss and reduce the risk of re-entering yo-yo dieting and weight increasing cycles. For an evaluation of our treatment please see Keville et al. (submitted).

TREATMENT FORMAT, STRUCTURE AND CONTENT

Individual or Group Treatment?

Although treatments for BED have been provided both individually and within a group format, we believe group therapy may be particularly advantageous. There is a wealth of clinical reports describing negative experiences in social situations for obese people. This suggests an association

Table 8.1 The basic session outline of the group programme and primary intervention target(s)

Session number	Session outline	Intervention target
1	Introductions, hopes and concerns, ground rules, aims and objectives, diary keeping	
2	Feeding: emotional and physical needs. Basic dietary advice – menu planning and portion sizes. Healthy lifestyles	Secondary coping strategies
3	Understanding your problems. Connections between the past and present	Secondary coping strategies
		Relationship with and/or to emotional experience
4	Eating as a coping strategy. Long-term vs. short-term coping	Primary coping strategies
		Secondary coping strategies
5	Listening and responding to needs	Primary coping strategies
6	Alternative coping strategies: problem solving, breaking goals down into manageable steps	Primary coping strategies
7	Alternative coping strategies: learning to stand back, detached mindfulness	Primary coping strategies
		Relationship with and/or to emotional experience
8	Dieting: past experiences, the effects of dieting	Secondary coping strategies
9	The pros and cons of change	Relationship with and/or to emotional experience
10	Anxiety and worry	Experience and exploration of emotional states
11	Depression – hopelessness, helplessness and cognitive distortions	Experience and exploration of emotional states
12	Self-esteem and perfectionism	Experience and exploration of emotional states
13	Anger and assertiveness	Experience and exploration of emotional states
14	Body image, the stigma of obesity, and social anxiety	Experience and exploration of emotional states
15	Dietary advice reviewed. Weight loss following the stabilisation of eating	Secondary coping strategies
16	Alternative coping strategies reviewed	Primary coping strategies
17	Overview: ending and relapse prevention	Experience and exploration of emotional states
		Primary coping strategies
18	Goodbyes	Experience and exploration of emotional states
Follow-up	Three-month follow-up	

with stigma and social ridicule. Indeed, obese individuals are more likely to be socially isolated and have fewer sources of social support (Marcos *et al.*, 2003); and there is a higher frequency of agoraphobia in obesity with BED (Zoccali *et al.*, 2005) and eating disorders (Hinrichsen *et al.*, 2004). Hinrichsen and colleagues subsequently emphasise the additional importance of identifying and addressing social anxiety for those with eating disorders.

This evidence supports the value of group formats in the treatment of obesity and binge eating. Group members have the opportunity to share experiences, face normally avoided contact with others and connect and value qualities within themselves and others. Forming social relationships and connecting with others has been associated with recovery from an eating disorder (Blocks *et al.*, 2004) and maintaining treatment gains (Binford *et al.*, 2005). Furthermore, Webb and Leehan (1996) liken a group to a safe 'family' in which participants can learn, test out and practise new behaviours without fear of retaliation, being ridiculed or criticised.

Group Structure and Outline

Following assessment, suitable clients were invited to join an 18-week pro-gramme and a group follow-up at three months. The duration of each session was an hour and a half and followed a structured, though flexible format of differing topics (see Table 8.1). Discussions were guided by the material and needs presented by group members. For example, at the beginning of each session there was an opportunity for individuals within the group to provide information on how their week had been. Handouts and extra reading were given for a number of these topics and a content summary of each session was typed and given to all group members the following week.

Session Content

To illustrate the content of sessions we have included discussion headings and excerpts from printed handouts used within the group.

SESSIONS 1–5

Whilst sessions 1–5 were predominantly exploratory, they were broadly struc-tured around the following issues:

- group processes
- psycho-education for healthy eating
- preliminary exploration of current coping strategies.

We encouraged flexibility to allow group members the opportunity to raise their own issues, to connect with other group members and to begin to see a more meaningful picture in the struggles they were experiencing.

Group Process

(a) *Setting ground rules*. Introductions and setting ground rules for the group is an ideal way of agreeing boundaries, facilitating group participation and creating a supportive and safe ambience. For example, 'rules' may relate to confidentiality, respectfulness, eating and drinking, commitment to the group, contributing within the group, time keeping and contact outside of the group.

(b) *Hopes and concerns*. This allows group members an opportunity to explore the reasons why they are attending the group, what they hope to achieve and any ambivalence they may have. It also gives facilitators an opportunity to resolve issues that may hinder attendance, for example, resolving practical issues or those relating to a sense of non-entitlement.

Psycho-Education Regarding Healthy Eating

Offering dietary education and advice early on can provide an anchor for developing new eating patterns and challenge current eating issues, particularly through the use of food diaries.

(c) *Normal eating and appropriate portion sizes*. We used the concept of 'normal' eating, based on research funded by the Department of Health (Hunt *et al.*, 1995a,b). This research resulted in the national food guide entitled 'The Balance of Good Health' and specifies five food groups: bread, cereals and potatoes; fruit and vegetables; milk and dairy foods; meat, fish and alternatives; foods containing fat, food containing sugar. It stresses the need to eat a mixture of foods in the right proportions to meet recommended guidelines for a healthy balanced diet. This approach is in contrast to many of the popular exclusionary and/or restricting 'diet' approaches to weight loss and means that people do not have to give up the foods they most enjoy.

The advantage of this approach means that dietary intake can be tailored to individual physiological needs based on age, gender, activity levels and body weight. It also takes into account social and economic factors such as family circumstances, working patterns, income and cooking skills.

(d) *Ameliorating the diet/binge cycle and developing normal eating patterns*. Abraham and Llewellyn-Jones (2001) state the importance of being guided by one's appetite so that 'normally' one is eating regularly throughout the day, for example, three meals plus snacks. We recommended this in an attempt to break the chaotic eating pattern that commonly underpins the cycle of bingeing and restriction, especially as regularly spaced meals (rather than 'feast or famine') is more likely to result in a diet that is varied and balanced (Thomas, 2001).

To reinforce and normalise eating patterns, the completion of food diaries was actively encouraged between each group session (see Appendix 8.1).

Individualised feedback was given based upon medical, psychological and cognitive status and thoughts and reactions to eating.

(e) *Encouraging healthy eating: explaining why diets do not work*. General nutritional education was given throughout the group. This included the role and/or importance of metabolism, food groups and healthy eating. This was a vital component of the intervention, especially given the wide range of available literature promoting novel diets and quick-fix solutions to weight loss that are neither nutritionally safe, nor have any scientific evidence to support them. Other aids to increasing compliance included increasing group members' understanding of:
  – the links between food intake and the efficiency of the metabolic system; and.
  – the absence of an adequate dietary intake resulting in food cravings and subsequent bingeing.

Exploring Coping Strategies

(f) *Why do we eat?* These early exploratory discussions can focus attention on the functions of eating behaviour, and can encourage an emerging awareness of eating as a response to emotional experiences. This awareness was articulated by some group members as follows:
  – It stifles something – emotions, how you're feeling at the time, I'm hiding behind something.
  – Release/relief – it allows myself to let go, to lose control; it's a form of relaxation; relieving stress.
  – To prevent me doing something else like scratching or cutting (the pain makes me calm down) therefore I eat when I'm angry or frustrated.
  – To create other reasons to feel bad – I can focus on how full I feel or how bad I feel rather than focusing on other feelings.

(g) *The consequences of eating*. Following (f) awareness can then be drawn to the disadvantages of bingeing as a coping strategy. Identifying pros and cons is used in motivational interviewing and can help explore ambivalence and enhance motivation to change (Miller & Rollnick, 1991; Schmidt & Treasure, 1997). Examples given by group members included: 'Others not understanding'; 'Negative views of others – fighting social conceptions about being overweight – being told I'm a pig, I have no willpower, I'm lazy or I'm greedy'.

(h) *Coping with difficulties*. Following (f) and (g) coping styles and strategies used to manage life and/or emotional experience can be discussed in terms of their ability to provide:
  – short-term relief but with long-term negative consequences (e.g. binge or graze, self-harm)
  – short-term relief but with long-term negative consequences if done to excess (e.g. over-exercising)

– short-term relief but with minimal long-term negative consequences (e.g. 'having a bath', 'doing something practical like gardening or reading a nice book', 'talking to a friend', or 'resolving problems').

(i) *Exploring the effect of past experiences on current behaviours.* This provided an opportunity to explore earlier life experiences and the relevance these may still have in the present, for example, identifying the habitual 'rules' learned in childhood that are still followed even though the situation and context has changed. At times some group members may recall earlier traumatic experiences and spend time digesting and processing these with the support of others.

SESSIONS 6–14

Overall, sessions 6–14 gave an opportunity to focus on more specific issues. Sessions 6–9 covered advantages and disadvantages of avoidance and suppressive coping strategies and educational information on the development and/or enhancement of alternative coping strategies to manage distress. Later sessions then directly addressed problematic mood states such as depression, anxiety, anger, low self-esteem, body image dissatisfaction and the difficulties of change. Sessions 10–14 directly focused on those underlying issues which might not be addressed if treatment were focused purely on eating behaviour.

Illustrating the Consequences of Suppression

(j) *Managing anxiety and distress.* Psycho-education and normalising the experience of anxiety provided an opportunity for group members to think about the consequences of suppressive coping and the potential of utilising other, more helpful forms of coping (such as problem solving or acceptance). This is illustrated with the following extract from a group session (Figure 8.3).

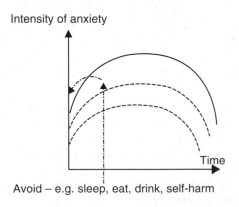

Figure 8.3 The course of anxiety

As anxiety increases (represented by the solid line), if anxiety is allowed to run its course it can result in habituation to it and thus lowered levels of anxiety in future situations (represented by the dotted curve). If suppressive forms of coping are used (represented by the dashed straight arrow) although anxiety may reduce (represented by the dashed curved arrow) habituation may not occur resulting in maintained high levels of anxiety in future situations.

(k) *The White Bear Suppression Test* (Wegner *et al.*, 1987). This provided an opportunity to use an experimental paradigm to illustrate the potential effects of suppression on thoughts and feelings. It involves asking group members to think about what they will be doing in the evening, and whilst doing so, to *not* think of a white bear. They are then left silently for a few minutes in order to complete the exercise. Following this, they are asked what they experienced (generally a bear is in their plans or thoughts). Their reflections are used to illustrate the negative consequences of suppression. From this, the futility of attempting to suppress experiences that have already been experienced can be illustrated.

Alternative Coping Strategies

(l) *Learning to stand back and detached mindfulness* (Wells, 2000). The inclusion of psycho-education and mindfulness techniques can promote the idea of flexibility in managing life and/or emotional experience. We also introduced the concept of 'object' and 'meta' mode. Within 'object' mode we are reacting 'as if' we are in a state of threat and within 'meta' mode, we are aware of threats *and* we are also thinking about them and actively problem solving them and/or thinking of alternatives. Discussion therefore provides the opportunity to present a range of strategies for developing these 'meta mode' skills and the flexibility to utilise them. For example, using detached mindfulness (attentional training advocated by Wells, 2000); analogies are used to help people distance themselves from the content of their worries, or planned worry periods are introduced (for providing a contained period to focus episodes of worrying).

(m) *Problem solving*. Effective problem solving usually involves a range of differing abilities and skills. It became apparent during our groups that some group members had no awareness of these steps, whilst others used them in some contexts but not others (e.g. at work, but not within their personal lives). Reviewing the steps of problem solving appeared to be helpful for all group members (e.g. identifying and defining the problem; generating solutions and picking one to carry out; identifying the steps needed to carry out the solution; implementing the solution and evaluating the outcome). It also provided an opportunity to explore those factors that may hinder the ability to solve problems, for example, 'fear of failure' or 'fear of success', or 'not knowing what to do'.

(n) *Compassion, acceptance and living life according to one's values.* Discussions utilising concepts such as 'the compassionate mind' (Gilbert, 2002) and 'valued living' (Hayes *et al.*, 2003) can be useful, particularly for counterbalancing issues such as low self-esteem and negative body image (see point (q)).

Mood States and Emotions

(o) We believe that psycho-education relating to the issue of emotions and emotional experiences was a vital component of the intervention, particularly given that many clients routinely employed the use of avoidant coping strategies in response to negative emotional states. This component provided basic information relating to identifying emotions. This is particularly pertinent given that increasing awareness of internal emotional experiences can be difficult for those who habitually suppress experiences. Greenberg and Paivio's (1997) conceptualisation of primary emotions (immediate and here-and-now); secondary emotions (emotions about our emotions); instrumental emotions (using an emotion to influence a situation and/or person) were used to help identify and label emotions.

(p) *Depression, anxiety and worry, anger and assertiveness.* These discussions provided a further opportunity for group members to explore underlying issues in binge eating and whether there may be more helpful ways of managing them. They help to place emotional experiences within a context, thereby normalising them, and emphasise the importance of emotions in signifying that a real issue may exist which may need to be resolved.

Exploring Other Issues

(q) *Stigma, body image and social anxiety.* This issue may be central to the dilemmas faced by those with obesity. Its inclusion provided an opportunity to explore the issue of esteem and how to connect with more positive images of oneself. Addressing this once group members have developed positive relationships with each other can provide more objective and positive evidence to counterbalance self-critical tendencies. It can also give group members a forum within which to share and validate past, current and future struggles.

SESSIONS 16–18

As a means of preventing relapse, sessions 16–18 provided an opportunity to review all the previously discussed issues. They also provided an opportunity to discuss the emotional experience of the group ending and possible losses and gains associated with it.

Relapse Prevention and Ending Therapy

(r) *Alternative coping strategies reviewed and recovering from relapses.* Addressing these issues can be crucial for a group that has an ending point. This is particularly true within the National Health Service (NHS) where treatment tends to have a finite time span. Furthermore, as the use of suppression and avoidance has often been group members' habitual coping style, it is possible that some may struggle to maintain an awareness of the material provided. Sensitive reinforcement and habituation of group members to the use of alternative coping strategies may therefore be beneficial.

(s) *What keeps us eating or prevents us from changing?* By discussing this issue one can return to all the underlying motivators to binge eating and bring them, once again, to awareness. Making them explicit in this way, can give group members a greater say in whether to change or maintain change. This discussion can elicit a wide range of issues, for example, the tendency to put oneself down in the belief that it will stop others from doing so; the habitual desire to suppress experiences; the difficulty with intimacy and the need to maintain excessive weight to avoid it.

(t) *Endings and goodbyes.* Ending the group can be a difficult time for group members, particularly for those who are only just beginning to connect with their experience. Members may also struggle with the idea of losing the regular support that the group provides and may have to confront feelings of rejection and abandonment. Directly addressing and validating these feelings can be therapeutic, even if these issues remain unresolved because the group still has to end.

CONCLUSION

As a specialist eating disorder service, we often see individuals with a broad spectrum of complex, long-standing issues and high BMIs. Generally they have not responded to previous treatments or weight-reducing diets. In our experience group members also have a wide range of non-eating related issues which may underpin eating distress and/or maintain current difficulties. Accordingly, in order to reduce the risk of treatment 'failure' we advocate the use of psychological theory and dietetic knowledge to guide clinical practice. Furthermore we believe that it is important to:

- explore and work on underlying issues
- facilitate a reduction in the use of habitual patterns of managing life that may be unhelpful in the long term
- facilitate the development of a broader range of practical skills to manage life experiences
- allocate time and space within sessions to process difficult past experiences
- provide a group format as a means for sharing experiences and connecting with others

We have discussed the theoretical issues underpinning our group intervention, as we believe it is important to present a rationale for treatment in order to increase our knowledge base and improve intervention strategies and outcomes. Perhaps this may be achieved through the following means:

- developing psychological models for BED based on theory and experimental research;
- developing treatment strategies based on these models;
- broadening the focus of treatment to underlying issues;
- utilising dietetics and psychology;
- and thinking long term to help break lifelong habits and maintain change rather than focusing on short-term fixes.

This latter point is equally relevant to service users and providers, reflecting a need for longer time frames for treatment.

REFERENCES

Abraham, S. & Llewellyn-Jones, D. (2001). *Eating Disorders: The Facts*, 5th edition. Oxford: Oxford University Press.

Adami, G., Gandolfo, P., Bauer, B. & Scopinaro, N. (1995). Binge eating in massively obese patients undergoing bariatric surgery. *International Journal of Eating Disorders*, **17**(1), 45–50.

Anderson, K., Rieger, E. & Caterson, I. (2006). A comparison of maladaptive schemata in treatment-seeking obese adults and normal weight-control subjects. *Journal of Psychosomatic Research*, **60**(3), 245–52.

American Psychiatric Association (1994). *Diagnostic and Statistical Manual of Mental Disorders*, 4th edition, Washington, DC: American Psychiatric Association.

Barry, D.C., Grilo, C.M. & Masheb, R.M. (2003). Comparison of patients with bulimia nervosa, obese patients with binge eating disorder, and non-obese patients with binge eating disorder. *Journal of Nervous and Mental Disease*, **191**(9), 589–94.

Beck, A.T. (1976). *Cognitive Therapy and Emotional Disorders*. New York: International Universities Press.

Binford, R.B., Mussell, M.P., Crosby, R.D. *et al.* (2005). Coping strategies in bulimia nervosa treatment: impact on outcome in group cognitive behavioural therapy. *Journal of Consulting and Clinical Psychology*, **73**(6), 1089–96.

Blocks, H., van Furth, E.F., Callewaert, I. & Hoek, H.W. (2004). Coping strategies and recovery in patients with a severe eating disorder. *Eating Disorders*, **12**, 157–69.

Cooper, M. (2003). *The Psychology of Bulimia Nervosa. A Cognitive Perspective*. Oxford: Oxford University Press.

Cooper, M., Wells, A. & Todd, G. (2004). A cognitive model of bulimia nervosa. *British Journal of Clinical Psychology*, **43**, 1–16.

de Zwaan, M., Mitchell, J.E., Howell, L.M. *et al.* (2003). Characteristics of morbidly obese patients before gastric bypass surgery. *Comprehensive Psychiatry*, **44**(5), 428–34.

Devlin, M.J., Goldfein, J.A., Petkova, E. *et al.* (2005). Cognitive behavioral therapy and fluoxetine as adjuncts to group behavioral therapy for binge eating disorder. *Obesity Research*, **13**(6), 1077–88.

Dingemans, A.E., Bruna, M.J. & van Furth, E.F. (2002). Binge eating disorder: a review. *International Journal of Obesity*, **26**(3), 299–307.

Edman, J.L., Yates, A., Aruguete, M.S. & deBord, K.A. (2005). Negative emotion and disordered eating among obese college students. *Eating Behaviors*, **6**(4), 308–17.

Fairburn, C.G., Cooper, Z. & Shafran, R. (2003). Cognitive behaviour therapy for eating disorders: a "transdiagnostic" theory and treatment. *Behaviour, Research and Therapy*, **41**(5), 509–28.

Fairburn, C.G., Shafran, R. & Cooper, Z. (1999). A cognitive behavioural theory of anorexia nervosa. *Behaviour, Research and Therapy*, **37**(1), 1–13.

Gilbert, P. (2002). Body shame: A biopsychosocial conceptualisation and overview with treatment implications. In P. Gilbert & J. Miles (2002). *Body Shame. Conceptualisation, Research and Treatment*. Hove: Brunner-Routledge.

Greenberg, L.S & Paivio, S.C. (1997). *Working with Emotions in Psychotherapy*. New York: Guilford Press.

Grilo, C.M. & Masheb, R.M. (2005). A randomized controlled comparison of guided self help cognitive behavioral therapy and behavioral weight loss for binge eating disorder. *Behaviour, Research and Therapy*, **43**(11), 1509–25.

Hayes, S.C., Strosahl, K.D. & Wilson, K.G. (2003). *Acceptance and Commitment Therapy. An Experiential Approach to Behaviour Change*. New York: Guilford Press.

Heatherton, T.F. & Baumeister, R.F. (1991). Binge-eating as an escape from awareness. *Psychological Bulletin*, **110**, 86–108.

Hinrichsen, H., Waller, G. & van Gerko, K. (2004). Social anxiety and agoraphobia in the eating disorders: associations with eating attitudes and behaviours. *Eating Behaviours*, **5**(4), 285–90.

Hunt, P., Rayner, M. & Gatenby, S.J. (1995a). A national food guide for the UK? Background and development. *Journal of Human Nutrition and Dietetics*, **8**, 323–34.

Hunt, P., Rayner, M. & Gatenby, S.J. (1995b). The format for the National Food Guide: performance and preference studies. *Journal of Human Nutrition and Dietetics*, **8**, 335–53.

Janzen, B.L., Kelly, I.W. & Saklofske, D.H. (1992). Bulimic symptomatology and coping in a non-clinical sample. *Perceptual and Motor Skills*, **75**, 395–9.

Kent, A., Waller, G. & Dagnan, D. (1999). A greater role of emotional than physical or sexual abuse in predicting disordered eating attitudes: the role of mediating variables. *International Journal of Eating Disorders*, **25**, 159–67.

Keville, S., Byrne, V., Wellsted, D. & McCarron, G. (submitted). Cognitive behaviour group therapy for obese binge eating disorder: evaluating outcome.

Koff, E. & Sangani, P. (1996). Effects of coping style and negative body image on eating disturbance. *International Journal of Eating Disorders*, **22**, 51–6.

Linde, J.A., Jeffrey, R.W., Levy, R.L. *et al.* (2004). Binge eating disorder, weight control self efficacy, and depression in overweight men and women. *International Journal of Obesity*, **28**(3), 418–25.

Linehan, M.M. (1993). *Cognitive Behavioural Treatment of Borderline Personality Disorder*. New York: Guilford Press.

Marcos, Y.Q., Cantero, M.C.T. & Sebastian, M.J.Q. (2003). Assessment of social support in eating disorders patients: a review study. *International Journal of Clinical and Health Psychology*, **3**(2), 313–33.

Masheb, R.M., & Grilo, C.M. (2006). Emotional overeating and its associations with eating disordered psychopathology among overweight patients with binge eating disorder. *International Journal of Eating Disorders*, **39**(2), 141–6.

McElroy, S.L., Kotwal, R., Malhotra, S. *et al.* (2004). Are mood disorders and obesity related? A review for the mental health professional. *Journal of Clinical Psychiatry*, **65**(5), 634–651.

McManus, F. & Waller, G. (1995). A functional analysis of binge-eating. *Clinical Psychology Review*, **8**, 845–63.

Miller, W.R. & Rollnick, S. (1991). *Motivational Interviewing: Preparing People to Change Addictive Behaviour*. New York: Guilford Press.

Mountford, V., Corstorphine, E., Tomlinson, S. & Waller, G. (in press). Development of a measure to assess invalidating childhood environments in the eating disorders. *Eating Behaviours*.

National Institute for Clinical Excellence (2004). Eating disorders. Core interventions in the treatment and management of anorexia nervosa, bulimia nervosa and related eating disorders. www.nice.org.uk.

Papageorgiou, C., & Wells, A. (2003). *Depressive Rumination: Nature, Theory & Treatment*. Chichester: John Wiley & Sons Ltd.

Rieger, E., Wilfley, D.E., Stein, R.I. *et al.* (2005). A comparison of quality of life in obese individuals with and without binge eating disorder. *International Journal of Eating Disorders*, **37**(3), 234–340.

Rorty, M., Yarger, J. & Rossotto, E. (1994). Childhood sexual, physical and psychological abuse in bulimia nervosa. *American Journal of Psychiatry*, **151**, 1122–6.

Schmidt, J., Slone, G., Tiller, J. & Treasure, J. (1993). Childhood adversity and adult defence style in eating disorder patients – a controlled study. *British Journal of Medical Psychology*, **66**, 353–62.

Schmidt, U. & Treasure, J. (1997). *The Clinician's Guide to Getting Better Bit(e) by Bit(e)*. Hove: Psychology Press.

Thomas, B. (2001). *Manual of Dietetic Practice*, 3rd edition. Oxford: Blackwell Science.

Wells, A. (1997). *Cognitive Therapy of Anxiety Disorders: A Practice Manual and Conceptual Guide*. Chichester: John Wiley & Sons Ltd.

Wells, A. (2000). *Emotional Disorders and Metacognition*. Chichester: John Wiley & Sons Ltd.

Wells, A. & Matthews, G. (1994). *Attention and Emotion*. Hove: Psychology Press.

Webb, L.P. & Leehan, J. (1996). *Group Treatment for Adult Survivors of Abuse: A Manual for Practitioners*. Thousand Oaks, CA: Sage.

Wegner, D., Schneider, D.J., Carter, S.R. & White, T.L. (1987). Paradoxical effects of thought suppression. *Journal of Personality and Social Psychology*, **53**(1), 5–13.

Wegner, D. & Zanakos, S.I. (1994). Chronic thought suppression. *Journal of Personality*, **62**, 615–40.

Wilfley, D.E., Schwartz, M.B., Spurrell, B. & Fairburn, C.G. (2000). Using the Eating Disorders Examination to identify the specific psychopathology of BED. *International Journal of Eating Disorders*, **27**, 259–69.

Wonderlich, S.A., de Zwaan, M., Mitchell, J.E. *et al.* (2003). Psychological and dietary treatments of binge eating disorder: conceptual implications. *International Journal of Eating Disorders*, **34**, S58–S73.

Young, J. (1994). *Cognitive Therapy for Personality Disorders: A Schema-focussed Approach*, 2nd edition. Sarasota, FL: Professional Resource Press.

Zoccali, R., Bruno, A., Muscatello, M.R.A. *et al.* (2005). Panic-agoraphobic spectrum in obese binge eaters. *Eating and Weight Disorders*, **9**(4), 264–8.

Appendix 8.1 An example of a dietary intake diary for BED

Name:

Day/Date:

Time	Situation	Food eaten	Binge (B) Meal (M)	Associated thoughts and feelings	Coping strategy	Alternative coping strategy
	(a) What was going on immediately before you began eating? (b) What was your emotional state (e.g. happy, sad, frustrated, angry)?	Describe the food and quantities of what you ate	Would you class this as a binge or a meal/snack?	(a) What kind of thoughts and/or images were going through your mind, if any? (b) What was your emotional state (e.g. happy, comforted, sad, frustrated, guilty, embarrassed, nothing)?	(a) Did you do anything else to cope with your eating e.g. vomit, laxatives, kept busy, stopped thinking? (b) How would you describe the way you coped with this (e.g. avoidance, problem solving, seeking support, thinking the issue through, feeling the feelings)?	If this was a binge or negative eating experience was there anything else you could have done?

CHAPTER 9

A FEMINIST, PSYCHOTHERAPEUTIC APPROACH TO WORKING WITH WOMEN WHO EAT COMPULSIVELY[1]

COLLEEN HEENAN, *Bolton Institute, UK*

In this chapter I present material from a feminist psychodynamic therapy group for women with a variety of eating problems. I focus on how inter-weaving both discursive and unconscious approaches to understanding the gendered function of weight can facilitate change. As a feminist psychody-namic therapist I work with the concept that the body is an interface between the conscious and unconscious mind within both an internal and a social world. I use this framework to enable clients to understand the connections between socially constructed frameworks of femininity, emotions and bodily sensations, rather than to act on them through some form of bodily abuse. This approach is based on my adaptation of Susie Orbach's (1978) *Fat is a Feminist Issue* therapeutic model for working with compulsive eaters. While arguing that a feminist psychoanalytic framework is crucial in this type of work, I suggest that it is essential to combine this with cognitive and be-havioural therapeutic interventions in order to provide a structure in which food, eating and body size come to be seen as meaningful.

The group of women I want to focus on are 'compulsive eaters' (Orbach, 1978). These women feel 'out of control around food' but unless they have put on enough weight to cause themselves, or others concerned, to suggest a weight-reducing diet, they have no visibly identifiable bodily 'problem'. This is because eating more than is physically necessary, or eating 'unhealthy' or unnecessary food is 'normal' in the relative affluence of British society today. Indeed, what defines obesity or 'normal weight' has changed over the years and no doubt will change again. (While the current 'moral panic' over

---

[1] An earlier version of this article was published as 'A feminist psychotherapeutic approach to working with women who eat compulsively', in *Counselling and Psychotherapy Research*, 5(3) 238–45, September 2005. Reproduced with permission of Taylor and Francis.

Psychological Responses to Eating Disorders and Obesity: Recent and Innovative Work.
Edited by J. Buckroyd and S. Rother. © 2008 John Wiley & Sons, Ltd

obesity and 'excessive' eating appears to be relatively new, Bruch noted a similar 'panic' in 1957 in the USA.) Moreover, the link between the amount of food consumed and body size and shape is itself contentious, in turn making terminology and 'diagnosis' difficult. Some compulsive eaters are not obese and some obese people do not eat compulsively.

To contextualise further, the label 'eating disorder' is also contentious as it suggests there is something called 'normal eating' which may well be socially, culturally, class and gender specific. However, as a psychotherapist, when a woman tells me she feels out of control around food, my concern is to understand her distress, albeit within a psycho-social context. The term 'eating disorder' is useful for compulsive eaters and obese women as it offers a means for these women to access psychological help. In addition, it offers a framework for comprehending what women often experience as individual madness, greed or failure.

When Susie Orbach's *Fat is a Feminist Issue* was published in 1978, the book cover promised women they could 'lose weight permanently'. However, inside it presented an exciting and challenging hypothesis that women might *want* to be fat. It was exciting because it offered a psychoanalytic account of what Orbach defined as 'compulsive eating' and it was challenging because it also offered a feminist critique of why thinness might not be very inviting. Like many feminist authors since, Orbach proposed that eating disorders are a physical expression of the contradictions women experience in attempting to meet their emotional needs, symbolised through food and body image.

Orbach's thesis was that understanding women's relationships with their bodies and with food requires a twofold perspective. First, it must be feminist, incorporating an awareness of the social conditions for current forms of femininity; second, the perspective must be psychodynamic, comprehending how social processes influence women's mental and emotional processes. This framework explores the way women engage in an internal as well as external negotiation of their contradictory social status. Discourses of femininity require women to place their own needs second or to deny them altogether; at the same time, women's social status depends on their ability to nurture others, including others' sexual fantasies, through having specific body sizes and shapes. Women may come to feel they are 'starved for affection' through emotional overspending and undernourishment. However, when the dominant gendered identity is constructed around this notion of vicarious care giving, dissatisfaction can feel unwarranted and confusing.

Like Orbach (1982, 1985) feminist psychoanalysts Bloom, and her co-authors from the Women's Therapy Institute in New York (1994), draw on British object relations theory (Greenberg & Mitchell, 1983) in order to demonstrate how food's material and symbolic connection with the infant's primary caretaker makes it a key 'transitional object' in development and one that continues to play a significant role throughout life. From a psychoanalytic perspective, the feeding process involves not just physical consumption but also the unconscious 'introjection' of the relationship between infant and caretaker. Infants incorporate into their subjective, interior world, specific emotional qualities of the interpersonal feeding relationship. The infant's psychic life is 'peopled' with unconscious representations of aspects of others, or 'objects', which are then further acted upon internally.

Winnicott (see Greenberg & Mitchell,1983) suggests that a key element of the psychological developmental process of separation and individuation involves the infant projecting feelings about itself and others on to 'transitional objects' (teddy bears, blankets and food, for instance). The infant's creative capacity to imbue these objects with emotional and symbolic meaning enables them to be used to manage feelings, impulses and desires. In addition, with the development of a sense of its own separateness, the infant begins to experience the emotional pleasure of sensing that a separate other takes part in assuaging needs. Autonomy can be further effected through the infant's expression of a wish for, or a rejection of, a specific food; these actions represent attempts to establish a sense of self distinct from others, as well as a more finely tuned expression of desire. Food can easily become a transitional object that not only resonates with early feeding and relational experiences but also is available for other projections.

Bloom et al. suggest that consumer culture can be considered a form of '"maternal" matrix to which individuals consciously and unconsciously attach' (1994, p xiii). Active participation in, and attachment to consumer culture, resonates with individuals' developing psychological structures, such that public culture functions as 'another facilitating environment for intrapsychic life and for people to feel interpersonally connected' (Gutwill, 1994a, p. 18). Consumerism is able to bridge the gap between the public and the private through the ways in which dominant cultural symbols are embodied in consumer objects that actively encourage attachment through possession (Cushman, 1995). The role of the primary caretaker is then that of the 'female culture mother' (Bloom & Kogel, 1994, p. 49), who directly and indirectly imparts the knowledge required to enact subjectivity; directly in the feeding process through the use of manufactured baby foods and indirectly through the use of television as 'babysitters' (Gutwill, 1994a). While immediate caretakers are busy elsewhere, consumer culture actively steps in to function as a cultural parent.

This 'subject-seeking' nature of consumerism is such that its cultural symbols seem to 'know' not just what the consumer wants, but what she or he needs. Mass culture is actively introjected and generates attachments through the culturally symbolic and gender-specific meanings attached to these transitional objects; for instance, food and clothes. Adolescent attachment to culture comes through the personal reproduction of culturally determined 'ways of being'. This functions as an adolescent 'rite of passage' through which 'looking good' is equated with 'being right'. Looking 'good' means having clothes with the 'right' label. For girls, looking good and being right are equated with having the right body size and shape (Bloom *et al.*, 1994). However, the further paradox of consumerism is that, while encouraging consumption, it also promotes regulation, particularly in relation to the body. This constructs a perpetual dilemma: how does one take up a place in this culture whilst simultaneously exercising moral and physical restraint?

Bloom *et al.* maintain that the diet industry represents one of the most gendered and tenacious ways in which consumerism 'seeks out' women. It is tenacious because it both tantalises and seduces through the symbolic happiness that the diet represents. At the same time, should the consumer not respond, there is the threat of isolation, rejection and punishment. Of course, dieting is 'a business that thrives on failure' (Gutwill, 1994b, p. 32), despite failure being deemed to be the fault of the woman rather than the diet. This dynamic pathologises individual women while simultaneously providing a means to redemption – through another diet.

Eichenbaum and Orbach (1982) have proposed that the ongoing social construction and reconstruction of 'choices' about body size and shape feed into and exacerbate women's underlying sense of body insecurity that derives from the gendered mandate to 'transform the self'. From a psychoanalytic perspective, part of consolidating gender identity involves an early stage in which children seem to want to display and use their bodies, as if to have their sense of bodily self not just confirmed but admired. However, rather than this being a specific developmental phase for females, 'a little girl's mandate to appear (rather than to act or be) and to focus on her appearance, is confirmed as intrinsic to her being and equal to being an adequate female' (Bloom & Kogel, 1994, p. 49). Moreover, 'to some degree, for all women, the critical work of separation, differentiation and integrating sexuality are displaced on to a struggle to manage one's appetite for food and to transform one's body' (Bloom & Kogel, 1994, p. 53). (Like many feminists and psychotherapists, Bloom and Kogel make a number of universalistic claims about 'all women', something which has been challenged by authors such as Thompson (1994), Trepagnier (1994) and Nasser, Katzman and Gordon (2001).)

Thus, the psychodynamics of gendered subjectivity for contemporary western women fit in with the consuming and regulatory dynamics of consumerism both publicly and privately. Women 'work on themselves', fantasising about how they would look if they lost weight or exercised more. The conflicts that arise through participating in rather than resisting the 'disciplines of femininity', can be managed by employing the psychological defence mechanism of 'identifying with the aggressor'.

The insidious and tenacious nature of dieting mirrors Fairbairn's (1952) view of the individual's internal world, in which blaming the self functions as a way of managing disappointment with the environment. Fairbairn believed that people only internalise 'bad' objects; that is, those linked with unhappy feelings. This results in an internal sense of persecution, experienced as an 'internal saboteur'. He suggests that this occurs as a result of the infant's attempts to retain a sense of omnipotent control of the mother because of its dependency on her. Internalising only the 'bad' and experiencing this as part of the self, enables the infant to retain some kind of attachment to the real mother in the face of environmental disappointment. Fairbairn's 'moral defence' is twofold: first the infant blames herself and not the other, then the infant attempts to transform herself into whatever her persecutory superego demands. The strength of this defence mechanism is that it maintains hope that future satisfaction will be achieved through transforming the self; at the same time it preserves self and other from disturbing feelings about the relationship (Greenberg & Mitchell, 1983).

For many women it is common to seek out the symbolic happiness that the diet represents. At the same time, there is an underlying threat of punishment should one fail to diet. Gutwill (1994a, p. 31) describes the resulting internal conversation as: 'Go on – try the diet. If...if only...I were good enough, giving enough, sexy, pleasing, or thin enough....If only I could stay on this diet, I could be acceptable and lovable....But the truth is that I am not good enough; I am selfish, fat, stupid for wanting and needing, ugly and weak. I deserve all I get. It's my own fault'.

Mothers are increasingly subject to intense pressure to curb their daughters' physical and psychological appetites (Eichenbaum & Orbach, 1982). The continual curbing of women's needs and body size, alongside the encouragement to attend to others, can lead women to construct numerous internal 'false' boundaries, which keep shameful, uncomfortable, forbidden aspects of the self separate from each other. This psychological splitting can extend to constructing a false boundary between emotions and bodily experiences, such as hunger, or even between different parts of the body (Dana, 1987; Orbach, 1985). Orbach (1978) suggested that women may feel anxious and frightened when their emotional needs are stirred up, unsure not only what the feelings are but additionally anxious because they are not supposed to have either an emotional or a physical appetite.

The rapid and simultaneous translation of need into 'hunger' and 'greed' can be understood when it is located within the gendered prescriptions of a 'subject-seeking' culture that is built on the paradox of gratification rather than satisfaction. This 'false feed' (Bloom & Kogel, 1994, p. 42) alienates the consumer from his or her need; for instance, the video 'Looking in the Fridge for Feelings' (1980) illustrates how, unsure of what she feels or wants, a woman opens the refrigerator door and looks inside, hoping that an item of food might offer her a hint as to what her mood means so that she can connect to it. Eating may gratify the need for some sense of soothing through taking in particular foods that symbolise comfort, or through further dissociation from feelings. Indeed, food is also a 'subject-seeking' consumer object and the food industry is able to negotiate a variety of moral positions for itself by promoting 'healthy' food as the 'best option', whilst 'recognising' that it is not possible to maintain constant restraint.

The following statements from an eating disorder therapy group demonstrate the multiplicity of meanings that women project on to food and eating. Lindsay (names have been changed to protect confidentiality) says, 'It's as if the biscuit tin's shouting, "What about me?"' For Pam, 'It's like a statement, isn't it?'. Maureen feels, 'It's a defiance again, isn't it?' While Pam next suggests, 'But it's also a comfort though, isn't it?' She adds, 'It's kind of lots of things. I think that's what food is really. You know, it takes the place of whatever'. Lila says, 'I think it's something you're trying to achieve. I'm just, I'm saying I can do this'. But then she adds, 'I don't think I see it as a treat. I see it as like a punishment'. While these statements arise within a particular therapeutic context, they mirror some of the tensions implicit in a culture which markets food while simultaneously disparaging consumption.

I have been working with compulsive eaters since the 1980s in a variety of therapeutic capacities, from facilitating self-help groups to individual psychodynamic psychotherapy. I have adapted practical fantasy work and other exercises from Orbach's (1978, 1982) self-help approach, trying them out within a variety of group models. These ranged from 12-week groups for women with a range of eating problems, with a fairly psycho-educational rather than psychodynamic aim, to one-year groups specifically for compulsive eaters. Orbach's *Fat is a Feminist Issue* model includes tasks such as the following:

1. Getting women to fantasise about becoming fatter and thinner in social situations and exploring how they felt in these differently sized bodies, particularly noting issues around their sexuality, own and others' authority and the quality and tone of interactions. This exercise aims to help explore the hopeful, frightening and often contradictory fantasies women may have about the power of their bodies now and in the future.
2. Asking women to spend time in front of full-length mirrors, preferably in the nude. What parts of their bodies do or don't they notice? What thoughts or feelings do they have about these? What sorts of bodies do they feel they need as women? This exercise aims to help women 'own' their bodies as they are now, rather than in fantasy, to locate the gendered projections made about parts of bodies, for example 'fat bums' as unacceptable parts of themselves. This exercise usually highlights the way in which women's bodies are so central to identity and so easily used to condemn.
3. Following a guided fantasy in which women are taken back to childhood eating situations such as family meals. The focus is on the dynamics of the situation:
   - who gets fed first?
   - who gets the largest portion?
   - where is mother?

In addition, old 'messages' about eating and body size/shape are articulated and explored for their contemporary salience.

Although I started off facilitating self-help groups with a fairly structured format - for example working in pairs, carrying out fantasy exercises, setting homework - I moved to a more psychodynamic framework which was more unstructured and interpretive, with the group leader taking more of a back seat. Group tasks were reduced and the focus was much more on unconscious individual and group processes. The most recent model I implemented was a one-year feminist psychodynamic therapy group for women with a range of eating problems (six 'compulsive eaters', one 'bulimic', one 'anorexic'). Although members were set 'homework' in between sessions, which was taken up in the group, this was not a central focus. I did not intervene in clients' patterns of eating or their body size; instead I encouraged them to explore their feelings and fantasies about bodily, emotional and relational change. I offered individual and group psychodynamic interpretations to explore feelings and behaviour around food in order to reveal unconscious contradictions central to the women's physical and emotional needs.

One of the main functions of the feminist psychoanalytic psychotherapist is to articulate these psycho-social discourses. Working with the concept that the body is an interface between the conscious and unconscious mind, within both an inner and an outer world, the therapist interprets the connections between feelings and bodily sensations. By distinguishing the client's 'own' self from her 'public' self, she re-presents this 'self' to the client, in order to enable her to re-negotiate this socially constructed framework. For instance, in the group, Maureen describes how she is struggling to reframe her perception of herself, constituted by a discourse of acceptable body size: 'When people say to me, "You do, you do look nice. You've lost weight", *it was like food to me* and I decided this week that I'm not going to, not, not enjoy it but it's not going to be the be-all and end-all. You know if somebody says to me that I, I look slim, which somebody did yesterday and I thought, "Yes that's very nice", but it, it sort of used to go *to the core of me'* [my emphasis].

This quotation contains a wealth of relevant information, not just about the multiplicity of metaphors about food and feeding, but also how they are embedded in gendered experiences of the body. Maureen is complimented about the acceptability of her female body. The phrases 'You do look nice, You've lost weight', focus attention on her body being smaller, more pleasing to the eye. They indicate the public nature of women's bodies, both demanding and eliciting a self-consciousness constructed around body-consciousness. They are 'like food'; that is, they feed her gendered appetite for approval for this body/self. She is unused to separating self from body, used to experiencing compliments as going 'to the core of me', although they relate to her outer appearance. While she distinguishes different selves, an outer layer and an inner core, she also sees the 'core' as more representative of her 'real' self.

While the topic of eating disorders is located within and between mind and body, at the same time it clearly arises out of gendered discourses of normality and abnormality. Prior to defining herself as having an eating disorder, Helen experienced herself in this way: '*I was quite a health freak*, healthy, slim, no problems at all. I mean a nice size 10. Um, conscious, *always conscious about how I looked* but I ate sensibly as I remember it. But it now it's like there's no control whatsoever' [my emphasis]. For Helen, being a 'health freak' was normal for her as a woman, just as it was normal for her to be 'always conscious about how I looked'.

Feminist therapy encourages women to understand their hidden needs and wishes, to connect up but differentiate between emotional and physical needs, and consequently to articulate and act on them. At times, bodies feel uncontrollable or uncontainable, seemingly having a life of their own. As Helen expressed it, 'Now it's like there's no control whatsoever'. Physical hunger can also arouse strong emotion. Maureen describes her experience of this clearly, 'Sometimes I'm actually frightened of being hungry and I don't know why. If I'm out somewhere and I'm getting hungry, quite hungry and I'm a long way from home, it, I actually feel fear and I have no idea why. I'm frightened of being hungry and I, I don't know what that relates to at all'. I interpret Maureen's fear of hunger as reflecting her dread of her emotional needs. Reminding her of her needs contradicts the self-denial she associates with being a wife and mother. She enacts this in relation to eating: 'Say at a mealtime and there's been sort of, perhaps some leftovers and a fresh lot of food. Over the years I've found myself, "Oh, that'll do for me". You know, I'll have the leftovers. It's good enough for me'. However, she is also expressing her distress in being reminded she has a body that requires feeding. Her appetite arouses too many contradictory feelings for her as a woman.

Sometimes bodies and minds feel completely merged. Lila describes this when she says, 'I find that I'm stronger when I don't eat at all, when I'm anorexic or whatever. And when I'm compulsive eating, that's when I totally give up everything and I don't care about anything because there's no other mix. There's no boundaries. You just eat and eat and eat and eat. There's no stopping you and that's when I become really unsociable and I hate everybody and I hate myself and that's when I shut myself away because I'm so disgusted. But there's no boundaries to stop [me] and that's when I become weak, really weak'. Some of Lila's discomfort relates again to shame and fear about appetite. Not eating means she is 'stronger'. Eating compulsively means she is 'weak, really weak'. She is angry; angry with others, angry with herself, angry with containing her appetite and then exhausted with the struggle. This quotation again highlights the problematic and symbolic nature of women's appetites which when unbounded, feel out of control.

Feminist psychoanalytic theorists such as Orbach, Lawrence and Bloom *et al.* have offered numerous insights into the psychosocial aspects of eating disorders which have been particularly helpful in understanding compulsive eating and obesity – eating problems which have been under-researched from a psychodynamic perspective. However, it remains a considerable and constant challenge to enable women to construct satisfying relationships with their bodies. My experience is that interpreting these gendered issues within a psychodynamic and feminist framework is not enough to enhance self and bodily esteem, or to render eating less 'compulsive'. There is a need to integrate this approach with cognitive behavioural interventions, which some of the above sample 'tasks' do achieve. For instance, extending the 'social situation' fantasy to everyday experiences such as imagining oneself getting bigger or smaller, doing mundane tasks like washing dishes or gardening, encourages women to make ongoing connection between cognition, behaviour and emotion. This can be incorporated into imagining what would happen if one didn't binge, eat excessively, or eat when not hungry. While one might well ask, 'What is feminist about this?', I suggest that what underpins these tasks is the need to facilitate women's right and capacity to 'have a voice'; that is, to use words to express feelings through the accepted currency of language, not eating and body size. In addition, experimenting with behavioural changes in fantasy may help some women to think about how to manage potentially dangerous situations, such as the husband who may well be violent if his wife doesn't prepare the evening meal.

I believe that the above ideas, generated from my own and other feminist therapists' work, are central to understanding the onset and maintenance of women's distress about their bodies and eating. Through clinical extracts, I have demonstrated how this distress may be articulated in ways that are clearly gendered and culturally specific. In addition, I have given some examples of the practical application of feminist psychodynamic and cognitive behavioural models of eating disorder work. While I see a need to revise these models continually, I conclude that any approach to understanding and 'treating' obesity and compulsive eating needs a gendered framework.

REFERENCES

Bloom, C., & Kogel, L. (1994). Tracing development: the feeding experience and the body. In C. Bloom, A. Gitter, S. Gutwill, L. Kogel & L. Zaphiropoulos, *Eating Problems: A Feminist Psychoanalytic Treatment Model*. New York: Basic Books.

Bloom, C., Gitter, A., Gutwill, S. *et al.* (1994). *Eating Problems: A Feminist Psychoanalytic Treatment Model*. New York: Basic Books.

Bruch, H. (1957). *The Importance of Obesity*. New York: W.W. Norton.

Cushman, P. (1995). Constructing the Self, Constructing America: A Cultural History of Psychotherapy. Reading, MA: Addinson-Wesley.

Dana, M. & Lawrence, M. (1988). *Women's Secret Disorder: A New Understanding of Bulimia*. London: Grafton Books.

Eichenbaum, L. & Orbach, S. (1982). *Outside In, Inside Out*. Harmondsworth: Penguin.

Fairbairn, W.R.D. (1952). *Psychoanalytic Studies of the Personality*. London: Routledge.

Greenberg, J.R. & Mitchell, S.A. (1983). *Object Relations in Psychoanalytic Theory*. Cambridge, MA: Harvard University Press.

Gutwill, L. (1994a). Women's eating problems: social context and the internalization of culture. In C. Bloom, A. Gitter, S. Gutwill, *et al. Eating Problems: A Feminist Psychoanalytic Treatment Model.* New York: Basic Books.

Gutwill, L. (1994b). The diet: personal experience, social condition, and industrial empire. In C. Bloom, A. Gitter, S. Gutwill, *et al. Eating Problems: A Feminist Psychoanalytic Treatment Model.* New York: Basic Books.

Lawrence, M. (1984). *The Anorexic Experience.* London: Women's Press.

Lawrence, M. (ed.) (1987). *Fed Up and Hungry: Women, Oppression and Food.* London: Women's Press.

'Looking in the Fridge for Feelings' (1980) Clare Calder-Marshall (Director). National Film School. Distributed in the UK by Concord Video & Film Council Ltd.

Nasser, M., Katzman, M. & Gordon, R. (eds) (2001). *Eating Disorders and Cultures in Transition.* Hove: Brunner-Routledge.

Orbach, S. (1978). *Fat is a Feminist Issue.* London: Paddington Press.

Orbach, S. (1982). *Fat is a Feminist Issue . . . II.* London: Hamlyn.

Orbach, S. (1985). Accepting the symptom: a feminist psychoanalytic treatment of anorexia nervosa. In D.M. Garner & P.E. Garfinkel (eds), *Handbook of Psychotherapy for Anorexia Nervosa and Bulimia.* New York: Guilford Press.

Thompson, B. (1994). *A Hunger So Wide and So Deep: American Women Speak Out On Eating Problems.* Minneapolis: University of Minnesota Press.

Trepagnier, B. (1994). The politics of black and white bodies. *Feminism and Psychology, Special Issue on Shifting Identities. Shifting Racisms,* **4**(1), 199–205.

CHAPTER 10

CHANGES IN EATING BEHAVIOUR FOLLOWING GROUP THERAPY FOR WOMEN WHO BINGE EAT: A PILOT STUDY

DEBORAH SEAMOORE, *Community Mental Health Team, UK*
JULIA BUCKROYD AND DAVID STOTT, *University of Hertfordshire, UK*

INTRODUCTION

Past research has demonstrated that as many as 40% of obese individuals with a body mass index (BMI) of 31–42 'reported serious binge eating problems' (Marcus, 1995, p. 441). It has also been found that there is a higher incidence of binge eating among women (Kinzl *et al.*, 1999; Lynch *et al.*, 2000; Spitzer *et al.*, 1992).

Individuals who engage in frequent periods of sustained overeating with loss of control, without compensatory behaviour, such as induced vomiting and excessive exercise, may be described as binge eaters. Stunkard (1959) first described binge eating as a distinct eating pattern in some obese individuals. Binge eating disorder is included in the *Diagnostic and Statistical Manual of the American Psychiatric Association IV* (1994) research criteria sets. It is associated with poor prognosis for weight control, distress and psychological difficulties (Baker & Brownell, 1999).

Compulsive eating is a similar phenomenon, defined by Romano and Quinn (1995). Overeating may occur within defined periods such as meal times or throughout the day and is not generally a response to hunger. Preliminary data highlight differences in the psychological health of compulsive overeaters compared with individuals who regularly binge eat (Spitzer *et al.*, 1993).

The pattern of binge eating or compulsive eating is frequently followed by attempted dieting or fasting to control this behaviour and subsequent weight gain (Alexander-Mott & Lumsden, 1994; Williamson, 1990). Dietary restraint

Psychological Responses to Eating Disorders and Obesity: Recent and Innovative Work.
Edited by J. Buckroyd and S. Rother. © 2008 John Wiley & Sons, Ltd

appears to increase hunger and craving and bingeing often occurs when control can no longer be maintained or the diet is broken (Dolan & Ford, 1991; Polivy & Herman, 1993).

Little literature addresses the psychological aspects of compulsive eating, binge eating and resulting obesity in some individuals. Recently, there has been an increase of literature in these fields (e.g. Streigel-Moore & Franko, 2003; Williamson & Martin, 1999; Yanovski, 2003a), but much research is still needed with regard to effective interventions and the factors that create and maintain overeating behaviour.

It is possible that overeating may be connected to the area of interpersonal relationships, with food being used as a substitute and as a means of affect regulation (Deaver et al., 2003; Stunkard et al., 2004; Telch et al., 1998). There is also much anecdotal evidence that more extreme overeating may be a compensatory activity (Chernin, 1985; Orbach, 1978; Roth, 1992). If so, very few resources exist to address this problem.

An approach that integrates awareness of the determining and maintaining factors for overeating and provides the opportunity to be in relationship with others with similar difficulties, such as a group, may offer an important therapeutic opportunity.

Research demonstrating the efficacy of group therapy goes back over a decade, and was originally the chosen approach for this study because of the anticipated benefits of group cohesion and interpersonal learning (Yalom, 1985), which may be important therapeutic factors in working with this population (Eldredge et al., 1998; Hayaki & Brownell, 1996; Moreno et al., 1995; Wanlass et al., 2005).

LITERATURE REVIEW

Studies researching the effectiveness of group therapy interventions for binge eating and obesity demonstrated largely positive results (Ciano et al., 2002; Tanco et al., 1998; Wilfley et al., 2002). Most literature has been descriptive of group treatments and outcome; those for women who compulsively eat (Ball & Norman, 1996; Hudson et al., 1999; Orbach, 1978) have anecdotally reported group interventions as beneficial. In some literature, support and relationships offered by group interventions for obesity and binge eating are mentioned as significant (Hayaki & Brownell, 1996; Romano & Quinn, 1995).

Findings from literature regarding obesity and eating disorder symptomatology reported internalisation of negative affect (Eldredge et al., 1998) and the use of food as an alternative to feeling (Popkess-Vawter et al., 1998; Zaitsoff et al., 2002).

Previous research identified two effective psychological treatments for binge eating: cognitive behavioural therapy (CBT) and interpersonal therapy (Wilfley & Cohen, 1997; Wilson & Fairburn, 1998). Research on group cognitive behavioural treatment has also been undertaken. A study by Peterson *et al.* (1998) researched three CBT group treatment conditions: therapist-led, partial self-help and self-help with a wait list control group. All three conditions showed a decrease in binge eating and significantly greater improvement compared with the wait list condition. Findings from this study suggest that CBT for binge eating could be effective in a structured self-help group format.

Reiss (2002) discussed an integrative model of group therapy for bulimia, which appeared to achieve symptom reduction by addressing factors that affect eating behaviour and interpersonal relationships. Much of the literature supports the hypothesis that a group approach which addresses the educational, psychological and behavioural components of overeating may be beneficial.

It appears that little research has been undertaken on the effectiveness of group therapy with obese women who binge eat and compulsively eat, and few specific treatments have been developed for this population. Lyons (1998) recommended the institution of 'other treatment modalities' for obesity and binge eating in a study.

At the same time, there has been much commentary on the failure of dietary and behavioural models as effective interventions in this field. In contrast, few studies that integrate dietary, behavioural and psychological interventions appear to have been undertaken. Shaw *et al.* (2002, p. 4) comment, 'There are still major gaps in our understanding of the roles of diet, exercise and psychological therapies in weight reduction'.

The health strategy set out in the government White Paper 'Saving Lives: Our Healthier Nation' (Department of Health, 1999a) includes mental health and obesity-related coronary heart disease in national targets. Development of group interventions that aim to address both interconnected issues seems highly relevant and in line with current policy.

STUDY AIMS

As this is an undeveloped area of enquiry, the study aimed to evaluate whether a group intervention, which used an integrative treatment, could improve eating pathology and address possible interpersonal and intrapsychic factors in binge and compulsive eating in adult women. This chapter reports changes in eating behaviour following the intervention.

METHODOLOGY

Study Design

This study was a before and after uncontrolled pilot study, where participants attended a once-weekly group for 24 sessions over a period of six months.

Eating behaviour, subjective well-being, problems and symptoms, function-ing and risk were measured before and after the group intervention using the Binge Eating Scale (BES) (Gormally *et al.*, 1982) and the Clinical Outcomes in Routine Evaluation (CORE) measure (Evans *et al.*, 2002). Before and after interviews with participants were recorded, transcribed and analysed the-matically (Boyatzis, 1998). All measures were repeated six months after the group intervention for follow-up.

Ethics

A local National Health Service ethics committee gave ethical approval for this study. In the initial protocol, participants were to be recruited exclusively from primary care, but there were a number of problems with this method and few participants were found due to the time constraints of general practitioners. Two amendments were required to the original protocol, utilising practice nurses in primary care, inclusion of other recruitment sources and widening the geographical area considerably. Ethical approval was granted for both amendments.

As participants were random volunteers, a potential ethical dilemma was the possibility that participants could be related and this would not be evident until the group convened. Other dilemmas were the possibility of a high dropout rate, the health status of extremely obese participants who may have required urgent medical attention, and undisclosed mental health problems or extreme distress becoming evident during the process of the group. None of these dilemmas presented during the study.

Participants

Eight to 12 female participants were sought for the group; nine participants between the ages of 24 to 56 years were recruited from primary and secondary care sources across the North and East Hertfordshire region. All participants were of white British ethnicity, and from a wide spectrum of professional and educational backgrounds. The two youngest participants were single, three were married and four divorced. Five of the women were mothers before the age of 20 and five of the participants had been raped in adolescence; the personal histories of all the women were a highly significant aspect of their eating problems. The scope of this chapter does not allow for elaboration of these issues.

In primary care, six general practices assisted with recruitment. Advertise-ments were placed in public areas, directing participants to practice nurses who held information about the study and contact details.

The researcher established contact with two departments of nutrition and dietetics, a primary care counselling service, a department of psychology and local mental health services. Following liaison with managers, departmental staff passed on information packs to potential participants.

Participants initiated contact via a telephone messaging service. At a preliminary meeting to discuss the study, participants were encouraged to ask questions and were given information to read. Each participant had one week to consider joining the study; the participants were then invited to attend an interview with a research assistant prior to the group intervention where the researcher obtained written consent for participation in the study and baseline measurements were taken.

Criteria

Criteria for participants required that they were obese female adults (aged 18–60 years) experiencing subjective distress related to binge eating and/or compulsive eating.

Interviews/Outcome Measures

For this pilot study, primary measures were CORE and the BES. Secondary measures were a qualitative thematic analysis of interviews (Boyatzis, 1998). Interviews and primary outcome measures were collected at 0-, 26- and 52-week intervals at a National Health Service Trust community premises where the group was also conducted.

A research assistant interviewed participants on three occasions: pre-group (week 0) post-group (week 26) and for six-month follow-up (week 52). At each interval, the researcher weighed each participant and monitored completion of inventories.

The pre-group interview elicited the participant's personal history, with particular focus on eating behaviour, weight history, body image and self-concept past and present. Post-group interviews focused on collecting information about the group process, and how participants experienced the group. They were also questioned about awareness of changes, body image, self-concept, eating behaviour and relationship to food. Follow-up interviews also elicited information about maintenance, improvement or reversal of changes. All interviews were recorded with audio equipment for transcription purposes.

Primary Outcome Measures

The CORE outcome measure is the 34-item client self-report component of the CORE system, used extensively across the National Health Service. Data from CORE have not been reported in this chapter, as it measures different domains to eating behaviour. The BES is a 16-item self-report measure that assesses the extent of binge eating problems. The scale appraises both the behavioural manifestations of binge eating as well as feelings/cognitions that cue or follow a binge.

The BES has good test–retest reliability, and discriminates between participants with bulimia nervosa and normal controls (Wilson, 1993). It has been used extensively to select and characterise patient samples in studies of obese binge eaters (Marcus *et al.*, 1988), and has been shown to discriminate between individuals who have no, moderate or severe binge eating problems. Several studies have shown that an instrument such as the BES can be used to measure overall treatment effects (Garner *et al.*, 1993).

Intervention

Nine participants attended a once-weekly group conducted by the researcher, in the evening, for 24 sessions over a six-month period. Participants were all within the obese to morbidly obese range according to calculations of BMI (mean BMI 43). Each 90-minute session took the form of a semi-structured group, where themes relevant to group members were introduced, together with relevant experiential activities.

The group was taken through various stages, drawing upon a range of therapeutic models. The first stage involved exploration of weight history and personal history; the next stage was psycho-educational in nature, exploring nutrition, activity, the relationship between dieting and binge eating, obesity and health risk factors.

Subsequent stages were based on a cognitive behavioural approach using personal journals, food diaries and various items of literature, which were followed by exercises using projective techniques such as writing and drawing, visualisation and role play.

In addition to focusing on cognitions, food and behaviour, body image, confidence, relationships (within and outside the group), family influences, emotion, socio-cultural influences, self-agency and self-image were explored in depth.

The concept of the group was greatly influenced by Orbach (1998, 2002), who has written extensively about working in groups with women who eat compulsively. The work of Fairburn (1995) informed the cognitive behavioural approaches adopted in the group.

Group sessions were not mechanically recorded as this may have affected process. Instead, the researcher who conducted the group made extensive notes following each session.

Data Analysis

A thematic analysis of qualitative data was conducted by a systematic search of interview transcripts. Themes were identified pertaining to changes in eating behaviour and developed inductively from the data; groups of defined categories emerging from this theme were developed from similar statements by participants. A compare and contrast process was then utilised 'to extract observable differences between or among the samples' (Boyatzis, 1998). The inductive process has much in common with Grounded Theory (Strauss & Corbin, 1998) in that emerging information is 'grounded' in the data, but a difference is that themes may also be generated deductively from theory and prior research.

RESULTS ANALYSIS/FINDINGS

Post-group (week 26) interviews and primary measures demonstrated various levels of changes in eating behaviour and reduced binge eating in all participants, measured by the BES. In contrast, two participants reported no positive change to eating behaviour in interviews, but reported changes in other domains as a result of the group intervention.

Interviews and primary measures at follow-up (week 52) demonstrated maintenance of changes in eating behaviour in five of the nine participants. Four had made considerable improvement which they reported significantly affected emotional well-being, self-esteem, confidence and relationships.

Changes in binge eating from baseline to six-month follow-up are demonstrated in Figure 10.1.

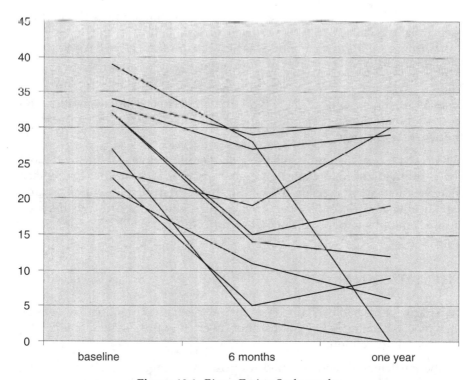

Figure 10.1 Binge Eating Scale results

Table 10.1 Binge Eating Scale scores for all participants ($n = 9$): summary statistics

Summary statistics	Baseline (week 0)	Six months (week 26)	One year (week 52)
Mean	29.4	16.8	15.1
Standard deviation	6.0	9.7	12.6
Median	32	15	12

Table 10.2 Change in Binge Eating Scale scores for all participants ($n = 9$): summary

Summary statistics	Baseline (week 0) to six months (week 26)	Six months (week 26) to one year (week 52)	Baseline (week 0) to one year (week 52)
Mean	−12.7	−1.7	−14.3
Standard deviation	6.9	10.9	13.5
Median	−11	2	−14
Sign[1]	0.008	0.953	0.021

Note: [1]Wilcoxon signed ranks test.

BINGE EATING SCALE SCORE: SUMMARY FINDINGS

Results indicate a fall in BES scores for eight participants. Tables 10.1 and 10.2 reveal that the fall in BES scores averaged over 12 and that the difference in scores from baseline to six months was highly significant ($P = 0.008$ Wilcoxon signed rank test).

There is evidence from six months to one year that this fall from the mean of 29.4 to16.8 is sustained. There is an overall decline in the mean BES score from six months to one year, but some of this fall is due to a major decline in the score for one participant.

What can be noted is that while there is overall relative stability in the BES scores, individuals follow quite divergent paths, evident from the successive increase in standard deviation. The difference from baseline to one year is statistically significant ($P = 0.021$ Wilcoxon signed ranks test). Differences from six months to one year are not significant ($P = 0.953$ Wilcoxon signed ranks test).

THEMATIC ANALYSIS

Two participants had been unable to maintain changes identified at week 26; they reported eating behaviour had not reverted to the extent of that prior to the group intervention.

Of the participants who reported no positive change at week 26, one had been referred for surgical intervention (gastric banding) due to further weight increase (BMI 68.7) and resulting physical problems. Neither participant had been able to change eating behaviour within the timescale of this study, but changes in other domains such as awareness, relationships and assertiveness had been maintained.

The central theme 'Changes in Eating Behaviour' was sought and explicated from qualitative data (Boyatzis, 1998). Four subcategories which were reported as the constituents of changes in this area emerged:

- changes in dichotomous thinking;
- changes in awareness of eating behaviour;
- changes in nutritional choices; and
- emotional and cognitive detachment from food.

Two subcategories were identified for the constituents of reversal/no change:

- inability to change; and
- reversal of previous changes.

Changes in Dichotomous Thinking

During the group intervention, participants described guilt and ambivalence about their relationship with food. All participants wanted to lose weight and had attempted this in the past by dieting and other methods. As a result of this, most of the women had an 'all-or-nothing' attitude in relation to their eating behaviour and a schema of 'good and bad foods' which seemed to set up a cycle of attempted restriction and overeating.

Following the intervention, many participants stated that changes in dichotomous thinking had been important in helping them to break the cycle of dieting, overeating and guilt. Examples of statements by participants describe how overcoming a 'diet mentality' reduced overeating:

> Before, you'd eat a bar of chocolate and that would stuff you up for the next three months because you're feeling guilty. That doesn't happen any more. It's such a relief. If I want a packet of crisps I'll have a packet of crisps and then you don't want to eat all those things in between, punishing yourself.

> I keep saying, 'I'm not on a diet, and if I want some chocolate, I'm going to have it' and it doesn't bother me. I don't think about it either; it's like you miss out that whole thought process. I have it. I don't feel guilty about it. I don't even acknowledge it; I just have it and it's fine. I just move on and I eat whatever I want – but by doing that it's not holding me anymore.

> I eat when I am hungry and I eat the things that I want instead of the things I think I should have – and then eat what I want afterwards anyway.

Changes in Awareness of Eating Behaviour

All of the participants reported changes in awareness of eating behaviour following the group; prior to the group many were unaware of precipitants to binge eating. Examples of insights were binge eating when lonely, when powerful emotions were present or at times of stress where food acted as a pacifier or sometimes as a form of self-harm. Some identified that the attendant self-recrimination diverted the focus of distress; feelings of fullness were equated with safety and sedation. Being overweight was equated with invisibility as a woman, particularly sexually. For some, awareness had been a significant catalyst of changes, but others had been unable to utilise this to effect changes to binge eating. During the group and afterwards, participants identified several underlying factors; these were emotional, unconscious, environmental and behavioural. The following comments reflect some of these themes:

> The things that had changed by the end of the group was my awareness was better and taking it from a completely different angle. There are definitely ways that I think about it now that I never thought about before in relation to food, and seeing it much more emotionally and psychologically linked.

> I like the fact that I can think, 'I don't really like this; what am I eating this for if I don't like it?' I've never had that before!

> I think more than anything really, was being aware that it was comfort eating, that I was eating to cover the pain that I felt and being aware of that.

> I know that I eat with boredom, I definitely know that – and when I am upset – definitely.

Changes in Nutritional Choices

Eight of the nine participants stated that they had made changes to nutritional choices. The changes varied from major dietary alterations to gradual exchange of high-fat and sugar items for low-fat and sugar-free alternatives.

Foods high in sugar, salt and fat would characteristically be the choice when eating compulsively or binge eating and most participants did not eat a healthy diet. Many of the women described emotional and health benefits as a result of changes in diet. Changes in nutritional choices are depicted in the following statements:

> It's true, 'You Are What You Eat'. All these different foods make you feel better. If you are eating better foods your body feel better and things like that.

> I've started to kind of yearn for really ordinary fresh food. I just get complete satisfaction out of eating this food that I've prepared with my own hands that hasn't got a single additive in it of any kind.

> I'm eating much more healthily than I have been for a long time.

> I still comfort eat quite a lot, I've been doing that for 50 odd years; it's very difficult to break. I continue to try and to change the things that I'm eating. I will comfort eat with fruit if I can, or a seed bar or something along those lines.

Emotional and Cognitive Detachment from Food

All the participants acknowledged the prominence of food in their lives. In the post-group data, varying degrees of emotional and cognitive detachment from food were reported which appears to be an important variable in modifying eating behaviour. Those participants whose statements indicated greater detachment made most changes and had reduced weight. Examples of statements follow:

> I never thought about food this way or why I ate. I feel quite whole, a lot more confident in myself because I'm not living around food.

> It's not where I've lost the weight; it's where I put into practice where I don't think of anything now in relationship to food. I've got something else to think about and I'm sort of awake now, rather than this black cloud of eating and being down, bloated, moody and things like that.

> But it was almost fine letting it go perhaps – psychologically – it just followed through and I've been eating really well and making better choices, but I just don't seem to have that huge emotional attachment.

> I'm so much more – I wouldn't even say in control of it because it is almost the opposite – I just don't need it any more. I don't have that need.

> I think there's been a kind of a shift to recognising what food is really for in a way – that it's to fuel and nourish the body – that's why it's got to be simple, ordinary. And all the rest of it is a lot of excess and silliness.

> I had this thing that because it's breakfast I needed to eat, and I really have taken on board this 'If I'm not hungry then I don't need to eat'.

Inability to Change Eating Behaviour

Of the two participants who made no change to eating behaviour, one articulated clear reasons for this, namely, fear of change as overeating was masking and containing painful emotions, something she was not aware of prior to the group. The other gave reasons that were connected to life events. She had recently divorced her husband after many years of unhappiness and went to live with a new partner in another part of the country. As a result she lost her job, her family were separated and it took her a great deal of courage, as for years she had been unassertive and dominated. Paradoxically she was happier, but her eating escalated after the group ended to a point where her health was compromised. This participant has elected to have a gastric banding procedure in the future. Comments by these two participants included the following:

> It's given me a bit of hope to think that there are some good things there that I can do. But you know, it's actually taking up and putting into place the things that she said. It's getting started with them and sort of persevering at them. That's where I have my major difficulties, but the hope is there that if I can start them that I will have a positive outcome at the end of it.

> We were given huge opportunities to change it and some powerful things that we were given about potential to change, but I didn't allow it to.

> I've identified why I can't. The things that I don't do to help me change. I won't admit I have any problems because on the outside I don't think I do. I obviously

do, but I can't face up to my feelings about things. I tend to push them down because I'm frightened they will be too painful for me.

I still sit there and think 'I shouldn't have eaten that' but again I carry on.

Reversal of Previous Changes

Two participants reported reversal in eating behaviour at six-month follow-up interviews. Both reported adverse life events and resulting emotional difficulties as the reasons for this. One participant had separated from her long-term partner and the other was going through a difficult dispute with her employers that she felt could jeopardise her professionally.

Sometimes, I don't worry about food. In between times I didn't have a problem. My main problem has been where the stress has piled on. The last three weeks has just been just sheer comfort eating, but I recognise that's what it is.

Unfortunately I feel I've reverted back to my old behaviour since my fiancé and I split up, so it's been a bit of a rough time coping with that and it's brought down my depression. I feel less able to make myself adhere to the changes that I previously made.

I think the group has given me the confidence to actually – I don't think I've gone as far down as I could have done. I think before the group if I'd been going through the split I think I would have put on ridiculous amounts of weight – just ate constantly, whereas now I am consciously trying not to go that far.

I'm more aware of the fact that I use food for comfort and I know when I'm doing it. I'm more conscious of it than I was before the group. Before I would do it without thinking and reach for the nearest chocolate bar or whatever, and now I actually realise when I'm doing it. I just don't necessarily stop myself.

DISCUSSION

All the women who elected to join the study completed the group intervention and willingly participated in the data collection. Many of the participants felt a great deal of despair and shame and were emotionally isolated. The data revealed that the universal environment of the group was extremely important and may have positively influenced outcome, which is comparable with findings of Romano and Quinn (1995), Hayaki and Brownell (1996) and Tantillo and Sanftner (2003). Wing and Jeffrey (1999) also found that social support produced better outcome for weight loss and maintenance in a randomised controlled trial.

Participants were obese (BMI > 34.8) to morbidly obese (BMI > 40.3); those who reverted or made no positive change were morbidly obese. All of these four women used food to manage affect; one in particular articulated her fear of change in case she 'would not be able to cope'. This is consistent with the escape theory of Heatherton and Baumeister (1991). Wallis and Hetherington (2004) also propose enhanced intake relates to escape from self-awareness.

Two participants had been unable to maintain previous improvements; both had experienced significant life events in the time period between interviews and identified stress, anxiety, change and isolation as factors. This is congruent with the findings of Lyons (1998), Vanderlinden et al. (2001) and Pendleton et al. (2001). It is also possible that these participants could not maintain changes once the intervention ended.

Four participants felt eating behaviour and life satisfaction had substantially improved following the group and reported higher levels of confidence, emotional well-being and improved relationships. Although three had lost considerable amounts of weight, they did not attribute positive changes to weight loss, but to 'letting go' of the underlying issues that held them in a cycle of overeating and compensatory behaviour. These reports support the emotional and restrained eating patterns that Lindeman and Stark (2001) described.

Seven of the nine participants mentioned that changes in dichotomous thinking had been a factor in modifying eating behaviour. In a recent study, Byrne et al. (2004, p. 1353) found that a key predictor of weight regain in obesity is a general dichotomous thinking style. This may be a significant finding as it indicates 'that the modification of this all-or-nothing thinking style might enhance weight maintenance' and is a possible direction of future research.

All the women who participated in this study had increased awareness of eating behaviour, but this variable had a mixed outcome. Increased awareness alone does not appear to generate changes in eating behaviour, although some participants stated how important awareness had been, particularly of emotional eating.

Many of the participants were preoccupied by food. Emotional and cognitive detachment from food was strongly reported by those participants who had stopped binge eating or eating compulsively.

During the intervention, the participants described favoured foods when binge eating, which tended to be calorie-dense processed foods, high in fat, salt and sugar. Recent research (Colantuoni et al., 2002; Will et al., 2003, 2004; Yanovski, 2003b) seems to point to possible neurological factors in the maintenance of overeating on typical binge foods.

While the data demonstrate that participants overate for largely emotional reasons, many of them reported craving the pleasure (hedonic response) of bingeing on foods like chocolate. Many participants managed to make nutritional changes, which were more biased towards healthy eating. It is possible that these changes contributed to reduction in binge eating which would support the behavioural neuroscience research findings.

While findings appear to support previous research in some areas, limitations of this pilot study have been the small scale. While eliciting very rich data, findings have insufficient power to be generalisable. Follow-up of participants was restricted to six months, so the long-term efficacy of the intervention on eating behaviour cannot be measured.

CONCLUSION

Data from this study raise some interesting questions and results. It offers support for further studies utilising an integrative group intervention for binge eating and compulsive eating in obesity, as opposed to diet and behaviour alone, because of indications that addressing various psychological issues is of central importance. It is possibly significant that changes in dichotomous thinking, detachment from food, exploring personal issues and the group environment were reported factors in changing eating behaviour.

Replication of this study on a larger scale with controls would be a natural progression providing greater statistical power; a group of longer duration could also be the subject of further research.

Examinations of the variables in change and no change participants and the complex relationships between psychological, interpersonal, behavioural and neurological aspects of overeating all warrant further investigation.

There may be scope for the development of various group interventions for different levels of severity of binge eating and compulsive eating in obesity; this also raises issues with regard to assessment and motivation for change. Following further research, it may be possible to develop a group protocol for health professionals, such as nurses, working with obese clients who binge or compulsively eat. This would be in accordance with the National Service Frameworks for mental health (Department of Health, 1999b) and for coronary heart disease (Department of Health, 2000). Services specifically designated for women with eating disorders would also be in accordance with recommendations in the consultation document 'Women's Mental Health: Into the Mainstream' (Department of Health, 2002).

Nurses from the fields of general medicine and psychiatry may often encounter individuals who are obese. The shame and subjective distress which often accompanies this kind of eating behaviour, as well as sufferers' assumptions about health professionals' perceptions, may result in limited or nondisclosure of difficulties. While maintaining sensitivity and empathy, thorough assessment of eating behaviour may disclose significant problems with binge eating or compulsive eating which may warrant referral to specialist services.

ACKNOWLEDGEMENTS

To Lorna Marchant, who conducted all interviews and was a great source of support. To Professor Chris Hawley and Dr Tim Gale from Hertfordshire Partnership Trust Research and Development, who gave invaluable assistance and support with this study. I am indebted to all the women participants in the group, who were so courageous and open, and generous with their commitment.

REFERENCES

Alexander-Mott, L. & Lumsden, D.B. (1994). Obesity. In L. Alexander-Mott & D.B. Lumsden (eds), *Understanding Eating Disorders* (pp. 219–87). Washington, DC: Taylor & Francis.

American Psychiatric Association (1994). *Diagnostic and Statistical Manual of Mental Disorders*, 4th edition. Washington, DC: American Psychiatric Association.

Baker, C.W. & Brownell, K.D. (1999). Binge eating disorder: identification and management. *Nutrition in Clinical Care*, 2, 344–53.

Ball, J. & Norman, A. (1996). 'Without the group I'd still be eating half the co-op' An example of groupwork with women who use food. *Groupwork*, 9, 48–61.

Boyatzis, R.E. (1998). Transforming Qualitative Information. London: Sage.

Byrne, S.M., Cooper, Z. & Fairburn, C.G. (2004). Psychological predictors of weight regain in obesity. *Behaviour Research and Therapy*, 42, 1341–56.

Chernin, K. (1985). *The Hungry Self*. New York: Times Books.

Ciano, R., Rocco, P.L., Angarano, A. *et al.* (2002). Group-analytic and psychoeducational therapies for binge-eating disorder: an exploratory study of efficacy and persistence of effects. *Psychotherapy Research*, 12, 231–9.

Colantuoni, C., Rada, P., McCarthy, J. *et al.* (2002). Evidence that intermittent, excessive sugar intake causes endogenous opioid dependence. *Obesity Research*, 10, 478–88.

Deaver, C.M., Miltenberger, R.G., Smyth, J. *et al.* (2003). An evaluation of affect and binge eating. *Behaviour Modification*, 27, 578–99.

Department of Health (1999a). *Saving Lives: Our Healthier Nation* Stationery Office, London. Available at: http://www.archive.official-documents.co.uk/document/cm43/4386/4386.htm (accessed 12 January 2006).

Department of Health (1999b). *A National Service Framework for Mental Health*, Department of Health, London. Available at: http://www.dh.gov.uk/assetRoot/04/01/45/02/04014502.pdf (accessed 12 January 2006).

Department of Health (2000) *National Service Framework for Coronary Heart Disease*. Department of Health, London Available at: http://www.dh.gov.uk/assetRoot/04/05/75/26/04057526.pdf (accessed 12 January 2006).

Department of Health (2002). *Women's Mental Health: Into the Mainstream*. London: Department of Health.

Dolan, B. & Ford, K. (1991). Binge-eating and dietary restraint: a cross-cultural analysis. *International Journal of Eating Disorders*, 10, 345–53.

Eldredge, K.L., Locke, K.D. & Horowitz, L.M. (1998). Patterns of interpersonal problems associated with binge eating disorder. *International Journal of Eating Disorders*, 23, 383–9.

Evans, C., Connell, J., Barkham, M. *et al.* (2002). Towards a standardised brief outcome measure: psychometric properties of the COREOM. *British Journal of Psychiatry*, 180, 51–60.

Fairburn, C.G. (1995). *Overcoming Binge Eating*. New York: Guilford Press.

Garner, D.M., Rockert, W., Davis, R. *et al.* (1993). Comparison between cognitive-behavioural and supportive-expressive therapy for bulimia nervosa. *American Journal of Psychiatry*, 150, 37–46.

Gormally, J., Black, S., Daston, S. & Rardin, D. (1982). The assessment of binge eating severity among obese persons. *Addictive Behaviours*, 7, 47–55.

Hayaki, J. & Brownell, K.D. (1996). Behaviour change in practice: group approaches. *International Journal of Obesity and Related Metabolic Disorders: Journal of the International Association for the Study of Obesity*, **20**, S27–S30.

Heatherton, T.F. & Baumeister, R.F. (1991). Binge eating as escape from self-awareness. *Psychological Bulletin*, **110**, 86–108.

Hudson, I., Ritchie, S., Brennan, C. & Sutton-Smith, D. (1999). Consuming passions: groups for women with eating problems. *Group Analysis*, **32**, 578–83.

Kinzl, J.F., Traweger, C., Trefalt, E. *et al.* (1999). Binge eating disorder in females: a population-based investigation. *International Journal of Eating Disorders*, **25**, 287–92.

Lindeman, M. & Stark, K. (2001). Emotional eating and eating disorder psychopathology. *Eating Disorders*, **9**, 251–9.

Lynch, W.C., Everingham, A., Dubitzky, J. *et al.* (2000). Does binge eating play a role in the self-regulation of moods? *Integrated Physiological and Behavioural Science*, **35**, 298–313.

Lyons, M.A. (1998). The phenomenon of compulsive overeating in a selected group of professional women. *Journal of Advanced Nursing*, **27**, 1158–64.

Marcus, M.D. (1995). Binge eating and obesity. In K.D. Brownell & C.G. Fairburn (eds), *Eating Disorders and Obesity: A Comprehensive Handbook* (pp. 441–4). New York: Guildford Press.

Marcus, M.D., Wing, R.R. & Hopkins, J. (1988). Obese binge eaters: affect, cognitions and response to behavioural weight control. *Journal of Consulting and Clinical Psychology*, **56**, 433–9.

Moreno, J.K., Fuhriman, A. & Hileman, E. (1995). Significant events in a psychodynamic psychotherapy group for eating disorders. *Group*, **19**, 56–62.

Orbach, S. (1978). *Fat is a Feminist Issue*. Feltham, Middlesex: Hamlyn.

Orbach, S. (1998). *Fat is a Feminist Issue and its Sequel*. London: Arrow Books.

Orbach, S. (2002). *On Eating*. London: Penguin Books.

Pendleton, V.R., Willems, E., Swank, P. *et al.* (2001). Negative stress and the outcome of treatment for binge eating. *Eating Disorders*, **9**, 351–60.

Peterson, C.B., Mitchell, J.E. & Engbloom, S. (1998). Group cognitive behavioural treatment of binge eating disorder: a comparison of therapist-led versus self-help formats. *International Journal of Eating Disorders*, **24**, 125–36.

Polivy, J. & Herman, C.P. (1993). Etiology of binge eating: psychological mechanisms. In C.G. Fairburn & G.T. Wilson (eds), *Binge Eating: Nature, Assessment and Treatment* (pp. 173–205). New York: Guildford Press.

Popkess-Vawter, S., Brandau, C. & Straub, J. (1998). Triggers of overeating and applied intervention strategies for women who weight cycle. *Applied Nursing Research*, **11**, 69–76.

Reiss, H. (2002). Integrative time limited group therapy for bulimia nervosa. *International Journal of Group Psychotherapy*, **52**, 1–26.

Romano, S.J. & Quinn, L. (1995). Binge eating disorder: description and proposed treatment. *European Eating Disorders Review*, **3**, 67–79.

Roth, G. (1992). *When Food is Love*. New York: Plume.

Shaw, K., Kennardy, J., O'Rourke, P. & Delmar, C. (2002). Psychological interventions for obesity. The Cochrane Database of Systematic Reviews, issue 4. Available at: http://gateway2.ovid.com/ovidweb.cgi (accessed 27 December 2002).

Spitzer, R.L., Devlin, M.J., Walsh, B.T. *et al.* (1992). Binge eating disorder: a multisite field trial of the diagnostic criteria. *International Journal of Eating Disorders*, **11**, 191–203.

Spitzer, R.L., Yanovski, S., Wadden, T. *et al.* (1993). Binge eating disorder: its further validation in a multisite study. *International Journal of Eating Disorders*, **13**, 137–53.

Strauss, A. & Corbin, J. (1998). *Basics of Qualitative Research: Techniques and Procedures for Developing Grounded Theory*, 2nd edition. London: Sage.

Streigel-Moore, R.H. & Franko, D.L. (2003). Epidemiology of binge eating disorder. *International Journal of Eating Disorders*, **34**(S1), S19–S29.

Stunkard, A.J. (1959). Eating patterns and obesity. *Psychiatric Quarterly*, **33**, 284–92.

Stunkard, A.J., Faith, M.S. & Allison, K.C. (2004). Depression and obesity: a complex relationship. *Psychiatric Times*, **21**, issue 11, October. Available at: http://www.psychiatrictimes.com/p041081.html (accessed 2 April 2005).

Tanco, S., Linden, W. & Earle, T. (1998). Well being and morbid obesity in women: a controlled therapy evaluation. *International Journal of Eating Disorders*, **23**, 325–39.

Tantillo, M. & Sanftner, J. (2003). The relationship between perceived mutuality and bulimic symptoms, depression and therapeutic change in group. *Eating Behaviours*, **3**, 349–64.

Telch, C.F., Pratt, E.M. & Niego, S.H. (1998). Obese women with binge eating disorder define the term binge. *International Journal of Eating Disorders*, **24**, 313–17.

Vanderlinden, J., Grave, R.D., Vandereycken, W. & Noorduin, C. (2001). Which factors do provoke binge-eating? An exploratory study in female students. *Eating Behaviours*, **2**, 79–83.

Wallis, D.J. & Hetherington, M.M. (2004). Stress and eating: the effects of ego-threat and cognitive demand on food intake in restrained and emotional eaters. *Appetite*, **43**, 39–46.

Wanlass, J., Moreno, J.K. & Thomson, H.M. (2005). Group therapy for eating disorders: a retrospective case study. *Journal for Specialists in Group Work*, **30**, 47–66.

Wilfley, D.E. & Cohen, L.R. (1997). Psychological treatment of bulimia nervosa and binge eating disorder. *Psychopharmacological Bulletin*, **33**, 437–54.

Wilfley, D.E., Welch, R.R., Stein, R.I. *et al.* (2002). A randomized comparison of group cognitive behavioural therapy and group interpersonal psychotherapy for the treatment of overweight individuals with binge eating disorder. *Archives of General Psychiatry*, **59**, 713–21.

Will, M.J., Franzblau, E.B. & Kelley, A.E. (2003). Nucleus accumbens muopioids regulate intake of a high-fat diet via activation of a distributed brain network. *Journal of Neuroscience*, **23**, 2882–8.

Will, M.J., Franzblau, E.B. & Kelley, A.E. (2004). The amygdala is critical for opioid-mediated binge eating of fat. *Neuroreport*, **15**, 1857–60.

Williamson, D.A. (1990). *Assessment of Eating Disorders: Obesity, Anorexia, and Bulimia Nervosa*. New York: Pergamon Press.

Williamson, D.A. & Martin, C.K. (1999). Binge eating disorder: a review of the literature after publication of DSM-IV. *Eating and Weight Disorders*, **4**, 103–14.

Wilson, G.T. (1993). Assessment of binge eating. In C.G. Fairburn & G.T. Wilson (eds), *Binge Eating: Nature, Treatment and Assessment* (pp. 227–49). New York: Guilford Press.

Wilson, G.T. & Fairburn, C.G. (1998). Treatment of eating disorders. In P.E. Nathan & J.M.A. Gorman (eds), *Guide to Treatments That Work* (pp. 501–3). New York: Oxford University Press.

Wing, R.R. & Jeffrey, R.W. (1999). Benefits of recruiting participants with friends and increasing social support for weight loss and maintenance. *Consulting and Clinical Psychology*, **67**, 132–8.

Yalom, I.D. (1985). *Theory and Practice of Group Psychotherapy*, 3rd edition. New York: Basic Books.

Yanovski, S.Z. (2003a). Binge eating disorder and obesity in 2003: could treating an eating disorder have a positive effect on the obesity epidemic? *International Journal of Eating Disorders*, **34** (S1), S117–S120.

Yanovski, S.Z. (2003b). Sugar and fat: cravings and aversions. *Journal of Nutrition*, **133**, 835S–837S.

Zaitsoff, S.L., Geller, J. & Srikameswaran, S. (2002). Silencing the self and suppressed anger: relationship to eating disorder symptoms in adolescent females. *European Eating Disorders Review*, **8**, 51–60.

INDEX

Psychological Responses to Eating Disorders and Obesity: Recent and Innovative Work.
Edited by J. Buckroyd and S. Rother. © 2008 John Wiley & Sons, Ltd